AF574848

Also by Garry Hogg:

The Shell Book of Exploring Britain
Market Towns of England
The Best of England
Museums of England
Facets of the English Scene
Priories and Abbeys of England
Customs and Traditions of England
Odd Aspects of England
Great Houses of England
Castles of England
The English Country Inn
Pageantry in Britain

The Shell Guide to Viewpoints of England

Garry Hogg

Osprey/Philip

for
PHILIP
Fons et Origo

Published in 1975 by
Osprey Publishing Limited
137 Southampton Street, Reading, Berkshire
Member company of the George Philip Group

ISBN 0 85045 032 2

While sponsoring this book, Shell Marketing Limited would point out that the author is expressing his own opinions

Designed by Adrienne Kapadia
Filmset and Printed by BAS Printers Limited, Wallop, Hampshire

Preface

'To the making of books [about England] there is no end.' In this book, however, a new approach has been adopted. Essentially it is a map book with a 75,000 word text and some 150 photographs. The specially-drawn maps, fifteen in all, have been distributed southwards from Cumbria and Northumbria by way of Yorkshire, the Pennines, Salop, the Cotswolds, Wiltshire and the Chilterns to the South Downs and thence westwards through Dorset, Somerset and Exmoor to Dartmoor.

Each map is drawn to the standard motorist's scale of 5 miles to 1 inch, offering an area of approximately 900 square miles around a central Viewpoint. From most of these Viewpoints a fair proportion of the circle can be surveyed, should the motorist choose to start his exploration from that spot. Many of them can be reached by car: Wrynose Pass and Blakey Ridge for example; others require a final few hundred yards on foot over undulating turf: Ditchling Beacon, Glastonbury Tor and the Wrekin. Only Rogan's Seat calls for any sustained effort on turf.

All the circles lie within an easy half-day's drive from several large conurbations, thus inviting the week-end motorist to explore what lies virtually on his doorstep: the Viewpoint of Mam Tor in the Derbyshire Pennines, for example, has the vast complexes of Manchester and Stockport, Sheffield and Rotherham, Chesterfield, Derby, and Nottingham, either on or close to the perimeter of the circle drawn at a radius of 17½ miles. Where possible, the circles have avoided large towns, since it is assumed the motorist goes in search of open country and all that this has to offer.

Each circular map is divided into eight equal segments. Tracing them clockwise round the circle, beginning at the northernmost, the outstanding places of interest within each are indicated by a symbol and a figure on the map, keyed to a table of symbols, so that they can be readily identified.

They include places of outstanding interest ranging from great houses, castles, museums, and historic and prehistoric sites open to the public, to medieval bridges, memorable churches, Iron Age forts, Bronze Age stone circles, Roman remains, natural features such as the 'forces' of Yorkshire and the tors of Dartmoor, the clapper-bridges and packhorse bridges in Derbyshire and Somerset, Cheddar Gorge, and so on. All are referred to in detail in the text, and many are illustrated by photographs. There are in addition very many other places of interest mentioned in the accompanying text; the number of them is indicated by a glance at the index.

As to the stately homes, castles and major sites open to the public, only a general reference to their opening dates appears in the text. The visitor who wishes to avoid disappointment is advised to obtain the ABC Historical publication *Historical Houses, Castles and Gardens Open to the Public* (30p) which covers the British Isles and is revised annually. Obtainable at any bookshop, it is quite invaluable, giving exact times and dates of opening, price (if any) of entry, easiest route for the visitor not having his own transport, and a note as to whether or not refreshments are available. Ampler information is of course ordinarily available in booklet form on site, particularly at the stately homes and the larger Roman or other sites being excavated.

Three other most useful sources of information may be added to the essential one already mentioned. These are: The British Tourist Authority at 64 St James's Street, London SW1 (tel. 01-629-9191) and also at 239 Old Marylebone Road, London NW1 (tel. 01-262-0141); The English Tourist Board at 4 Grosvenor Gardens, London SW1 (tel. 01-730-3400); and The National Trust at 42 Queen Anne's Gate, London SW1 (tel. 01-930-0211).

It is the author's sincere hope that readers of this, his second comprehensive book on the country, will find, in the areas covered by these fifteen maps, much more than the items to which he has drawn specific attention. After a lifetime of exploration he still finds something new and of beauty and interest at every other turn. Small as England is, it is infinitely rich in its variety.

Groombridge G.H.

Contents

Photographs

WRYNOSE PASS

HOUSESTEADS

BROADWAY TOWER

SILBURY HILL

IVINGHOE BEACON

DARTMOOR

Photographs not otherwise acknowledged are by the author

The Screes, Wast Water

Wrynose Pass

It is no exaggeration to state categorically that more books have been written about the Lake District than about all the other individual regions of England put together. About 700 square miles in all, this is the largest single area officially designated as of 'Outstanding Natural Beauty'; even on a small-scale map of five miles to an inch, the familiar letters 'NT' seem to jostle one another for room: the National Trust – the largest single land-owner in the country (apart from the Forestry Commission) – has, thanks to Canon Rawnsley, sometime Rector of Crosthwaite and co-founder of this admirable organisation, set its mark here, there, and everywhere in English Lakeland.

There was only one problem in finding a viewpoint here. Unlike, say, Glastonbury Tor, The Wrekin, Broadway Tower, or Ditchling Beacon, which are 'naturals', and isolated, here is a genuine *embarras de choix*. There are in this closely circumscribed region nearly 200 mountain-tops, peaks, pikes, summits, and fell-ridges surpassing the 2,000-foot mark. Scafell Pike, at 3,210 feet the highest peak in England, tops the lot. But Skiddaw, at 3,053 feet, runs it close; Saddleback (2,847 feet), Great Rigg (2,513 feet), Pike o' Stickle (2,323 feet), and Pike o' Blisco (2,304 feet) are not so far behind; with Grisedale (1,929 feet) and Black Sail (1,800 feet) very close to the 2,000-foot mark. The names ring splendidly on the ear: Bracken-thwaite Fell, Sergeant Man, Red Pike and Helvellyn, Glaramara and the Old Man of Coniston, and the rest. There are some twenty mountain passes that top the 1,000-foot mark, and their names, too, evoke magic: Sty Head, Kirkstone and Hard Knott, Whinlatter,

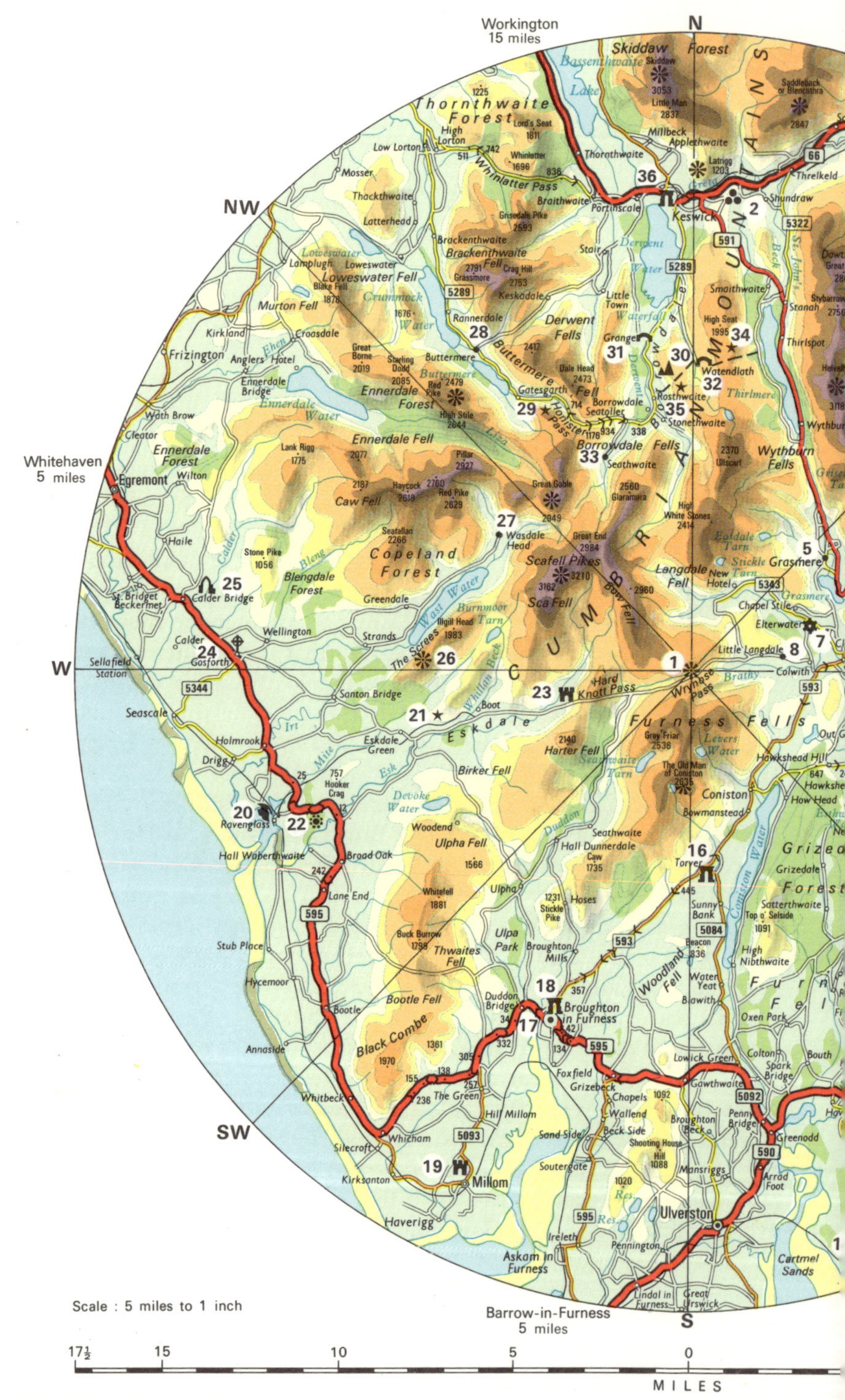

Scale : 5 miles to 1 inch

17½ 15 10 5 0

MILES

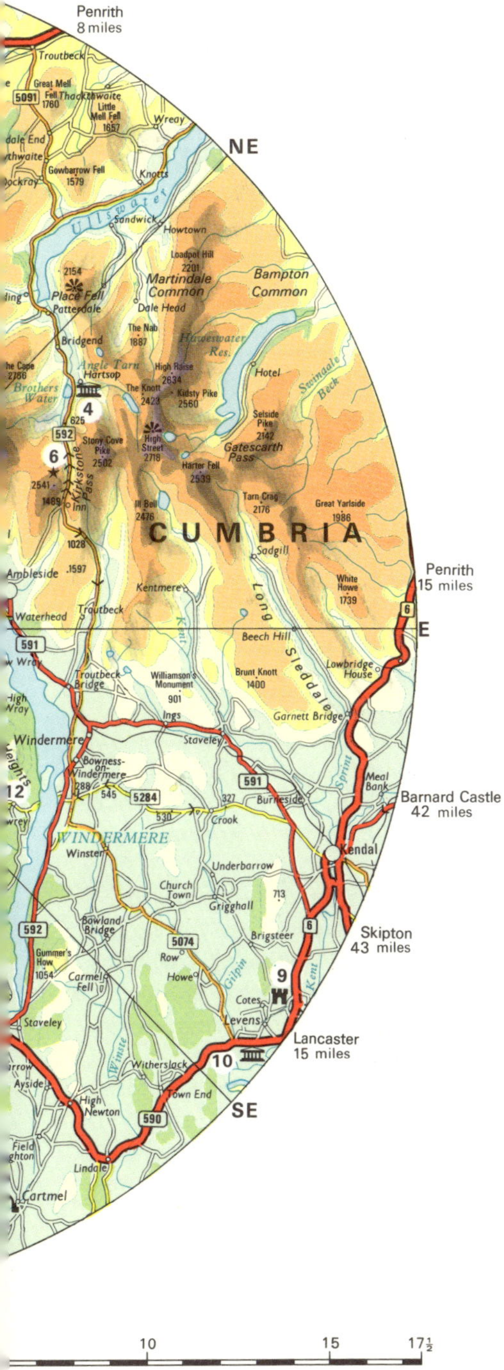

Wrynose Pass

1 ❋ Wrynose Pass
2 ♣ Castlerigg Stone Circle
3 ☗ White Horse Inn
4 🏛 Hartsop Hall
5 • Grasmere
6 ★ Kirkstone Pass
7 ✡ Elterwater
8 • Little Langdale
9 ♜ Sizergh Castle
10 🏛 Levens Hall
11 ♆ Hawkshead
12 ☗ Near Sawrey
13 ⋂ Cartmel
14 ❂ Holker Hall
15 ❂ Graythwaite Hall
16 Π Torver
17 • Broughton-in-Furness
18 Π Broughton Tower
19 ♜ Millom Castle
20 ⚓ Ravenglass
21 ★ Ravenglass and Eskdale Railway
22 ❂ Muncaster Castle
23 ♜ Hardknott Castle
24 ✝ Gosforth
25 ⋂ Calder Abbey
26 ❋ The Screes, Wast Water
27 • Wasdale Head
28 • Buttermere
29 ★ Honister Pass
30 ▲ The Bowder Stone
31 ⌒ Grange-in-Borrowdale
32 ⌒ Watendlath - farm and bridge
33 • Seathwaite
34 ★ Track E. to Thirlmere
35 ★ Track W. to Rosthwaite
36 Π Keswick

Wrynose, and their peers. The peaks are for the climbers and the sturdiest fell walkers; the passes (or many of them at any rate) for the keen motorist and the less athletic walker.

The viewpoint selected, among so many strong claimants, is Wrynose, at 1,270 feet. For two good reasons: it is about as central to the area as any and, perhaps more important, it carries the famous Three Shire Stone within yards of its crest. The Three Shire Stone stands shoulder high: a thick, flat-sided slab with, on its rear side, the inscription 'W.F. 1816' and, on the side facing the road, the solitary word 'Lancashire', reading from the bottom upwards. The stone has suddenly become history; for on 1 April 1974 the counties of Cumberland, Westmorland, and Lakeland Lancashire were, willy-nilly, merged into one all-embracing authority, Cumbria. It is ironic that the one county name involved that is inscribed on it has now ceased, so far as Lakeland is concerned, to have any meaning. The inhabitants of former Cumberland and Westmorland, as well as those of north Lancashire, feel and will doubtless continue to feel bitter about this.

Because there are so many, and so much greater, heights near Wrynose Pass, it cannot be stated (as it can of Silbury Hill or Ivinghoe Beacon, for example, each of which dominates low-lying country) that from it you can see far and wide in all directions. There is, indeed, a superb view eastwards down the Brathay valley towards Little Langdale and the head of Windermere; westwards down towards Cockley Beck and on to the huge shoulder of Hard Knott; northwards to the Langdale Pikes; southwards to the Tilberthwaite Fells and thence to Coniston Water. But then, in the Lake District, 'every prospect pleases' – and never was there a greater topographical understatement!

So now, from the general to the particular: the map has been divided into eight segments, and we make our way, as will be the mode of practice throughout this book, from due north clockwise round to our starting-point, taking each of the segments in order.

Some two miles or so to the east of Keswick, close to a minor road, lies Castlerigg Stone Circle. Dating from the Bronze Age, it consists of a ring of nearly forty megaliths, with a diameter of a hundred feet or so. Though it may appear to be a circle, in fact, unusually, it is oval in shape, and contains within its perimeter an oblong of perhaps a dozen more stones. It is reminiscent of Oxfordshire's Rollright Stones, but infinitely more spectacularly sited. From the

The Three Shire Stone on Wrynose Pass

high plateau on which the stones were erected, thousands of years ago, you can obtain, virtually without effort, a superb view over this north-eastern segment of the Lake District, notably when looking south and west.

If you are on the look-out for a typical out-of-the-way and little-known Lakeland inn, either for a drink or for an overnight stop, then only a few miles farther along the Penrith road there is the White Horse, worth a visit if only for its remarkable exhibits in plaited straw and its ancient Bible which, according to the Deeds of the place, must never be permitted to cross the threshold. This small, snug inn crouches beneath the towering mass of Saddleback or, to give it its more romantic name, Blencathra, 2,847 feet high.

Due south you have, if it is lakes rather than mountains that lure you on, the choice between Ullswater and the smaller Thirlmere, four miles in length, very narrow, and completely ringed by a major and a minor (and much more attractive) road. Between them soars Helvellyn (3,118 feet), whose well-named Striding Edge forms one of the most popular 'high walks' – one which demands a good head for heights and also a whistle in the pocket for use in case of a characteristically sudden onset of swirling mist.

South-by-east, in the second segment, is diminutive Brothers Water, formerly Broadwater, but now named after two brothers who had the misfortune to be drowned in it. On the opposite side of the road that descends from Kirkstone Pass, with its famous inn right on the summit (another glorious view westwards and northwards from here), is Hartsop Hall, a sixteenth-century ancestral home that, as so often happens, is now just a Lakeland farm. It has one special peculiarity not easy to match elsewhere in the whole country: a bridle-way passes directly through an extension to the original building, added to it in the eighteenth century; this right-of-way is still punctiliously exercised at set intervals 'to maintain the right for the would-be user'.

Haweswater is now, alas, a vast reservoir, the subject of inter-county controversy, and so perhaps best ignored, in this second segment of the circle; Shap Abbey, too, must be ignored if we are to adhere strictly to our established perimeter, for it lies a long stone's-throw beyond it. So, then, to the best-known of all Lakeland villages, five miles west of Kirkstone Pass and its inn: Grasmere, on the edge of the lakelet that shares its name. Here Wordsworth, most notable of the so-called Lakeland School of poets, lived at Dove Cottage for nine years. You may visit the cottage and soak yourself in its undoubted atmosphere if that is your bent, and then go on barely a mile to Rydal Water, which is almost as closely associated with the poet as Grasmere itself. He spent the last thirty-seven years of his long life there at Rydal Mount, and died there shortly after his eightieth birthday, in 1850.

A few miles to the south the road divides. The left-hand fork will take you eastwards to the road that carries you over Kirkstone Pass northwards to Troutbeck. You may be puzzled, for there is a Troutbeck at the southern foot of the pass; but the name is not uncommon in the Lake District, and the Troutbeck of the much-

Kirkstone Pass Inn

sung huntsman, John Peel, is to be found far to the north, beyond Ullswater, near the junction of the A5091 and the main Keswick–Penrith road (A66) beside which Castlerigg is to be found, and the White Horse sheltering beneath the vast shoulder of Blencathra.

The right-hand fork, however, leads you eastwards along the Brathay to Skelwith Bridge, whence you may make for lovely Elterwater, with its Britannia (formerly Hare and Hounds) Inn immediately overlooking a stretch of water that is visited every year by a flotilla of whooper swans at the falling of the first snow, who linger on there until Easter. Alternatively you may make for the hamlet of Little (or Great) Langdale, at the foot of Wrynose itself.

Windermere, largest by far of all the lakes, stretches across the whole of the third segment of the circle and part of the fourth. Seven or eight miles to the east of its southern tip, on the extreme periphery, are Sizergh Castle, the cherished home of the Strickland family for no less than seven hundred years, incorporating a fourteenth-century pele tower; and Levens Hall, an Elizabethan mansion with some of the finest examples of topiary work in the whole country. Both Sizergh and Levens are open to the public, generally from spring until autumn, but visitors to the Lake District, as to other regions containing houses open to view, will of course be wise to ascertain in advance, and from some up-to-date source, the dates and hours of opening. These vary up and down the country; there are individual dates 'out of season' when they may be specially opened, and individual dates 'in the season' when for one reason or another they may be temporarily closed.

In this third segment, but very much nearer the centre of the circle, are two much smaller houses that should not be missed. One of these is at Hawkshead, near the head of Esthwaite Water. Here is the old grammar school, built as long ago as 1585, at which young William Wordsworth was a pupil. It is now a small museum, of primarily local interest, and you can see the desk on which he carved his name when he was sent there, at the age of eight, from his birthplace at Cockermouth, two or three miles outside the north-western segment of the circle; that house is hideous, but is still the object of veneration by lovers of his work, even though it is not in the same league as Dove Cottage, Grasmere, or Rydal Mount.

At the southern end of this same small lake is another house, a place of pilgrimage for thousands who have been brought up on the gentle, whimsical activities of Jemima Puddleduck, Tabitha Twitchet, Pickles, and Mr Todd – among other Lilliputian immortals. Yes, here in the hamlet of Near Sawrey lived Beatrix Potter; she would probably be surprised if she were to see the exhibitions of her work that have recently been part of the cultural scene!

On the periphery of the fourth segment, overlooking Morecambe Bay, is the picturesque village of Cartmel, with a market cross dominated by the gatehouse of the fourteenth-century priory which, for a century and a half after the Dissolution of the Monasteries, served as the local grammar school. A couple of miles away is sixteenth-century Holker Hall at Cark-in-Cartmel, with its gardens and deer park, open to the public from Easter until October. And now a choice of minor roads will lead you northwards by way of Newby Bridge to the Furness Fells and, beyond these, to the magnificent gardens of Graythwaite Hall, separated from Coniston Water by Satterthwaite and Grizedale Forest.

Langdale village

Still in this fourth segment, on the opposite side of Coniston Water, you will find in the tiny hamlet of Torver an inn with a name, and an origin, more commonly found in South Devon than in Cumbria: Church House Inn. It stands close to St Luke's Church. Neither building looks, or indeed is, old: the church was rebuilt in the nineteenth century, but on a site known to have held a church at least as long ago as 1538, and quite possibly two centuries earlier than that. The original inn was probably built either when the church was first built, or when it was rebuilt in the early sixteenth century. The men who built the church would have been accommodated here – as was the case with the many South Devon church inns. Over what is now the main bar is what is known to the locals as 'The Long Room'. Records show that for many years this served as 'Court House and Hanging Room' – terms which are grimly self-explanatory; here sheep-stealers were sentenced to death, and their sentences may even have been carried out beneath this roof. The present landlord is curiously uninterested in the past history of the building.

From Torver south-eastwards you can follow the track of the now-disused railway that once linked the quarries and copper mines of Coniston with Broughton-in-Furness (in the fifth segment) and, by way of the Duddon Channel, with the open sea ten miles distant. If you happen to be in Broughton-in-Furness – a good place, incidentally, for exploring the Duddon Valley, about which Wordsworth wrote a number of poems – on the right date in August you will be able to hear the annual Proclamation of the Charter in the market square – one of the few such ceremonies that have been maintained from medieval times until today.

It will perhaps be some small compensation for the fact that you cannot, as even some up-to-date road maps indicate, any longer visit historic Broughton Tower. Though the original tower, and the dungeons, survive, they are now all encompassed within a more modern building that is in fact, ironically enough, a school for children in poor health. Near by is Millom Castle. Do not, however, expect too much here; as at Harlsey, in the eastern part of North Yorkshire, what was once a medieval castle is now but a farm, and you have to look with some care to locate what remains of the fourteenth- and fifteenth-century stonework.

Ravenglass, nipped tightly in the Esk Estuary (sixth segment), was a Roman port of some significance two thousand years ago, give or take a century or two. From it a road ran right over Hard Knott to Penrith, nearly forty mountainous miles distant. The ruins, known as Walls Castle, or Clanoventa, are among the best preserved in the North-West, and reminiscent in a small way of those at Housesteads on Hadrian's Wall far to the north-east.

It is here, in Eskdale, between Ravenglass and Boot – a hamlet much more charming than its blunt name would suggest – that the well-loved Ravenglass and Eskdale miniature railway runs its seven-mile length, a fifteen-inch-gauge track that lies snugly in this beautiful open valley. Affectionately known as 'Owd Ratty' after its designer and builder, one Ratcliffe, it is a feature not to be missed, especially if you are exploring this part of the Lake District with children. At its southern end it passes close to Muncaster Castle. The edifice that confronts you today was built in the eighteenth century, but there was a pele tower here in the late twelfth century, and the Penningtons, lords of Ravenglass Manor, enlarged this and built for themselves a fortified manor house somewhat reminiscent of that at Elsdon, in Northumberland, in the early fourteenth century. Their descendants live there to this day, and the grounds and bird garden are open to the public from Easter until early autumn.

Eastwards of Boot, Eskdale steepens dramatically and you come soon to the initial slope of Hard Knott. As you climb it, you will see on your left, commanding the pass, the remains of a walled Roman camp, Hardknott Castle. Established alongside this important through-route to Penrith and the Roman Wall beyond Carlisle, it is strongly reminiscent of the larger and better-known *Ad Fines* Roman camp site on the southern slopes of the Cheviots. The best view of it is a distant one, from the actual summit of the pass, before you begin the tortuous one-in-three descent eastwards down to Cockley Beck, and thence up Wrynose Pass to the Three Shire Stone. Its low, dark walls run squarely across a slope of the fells, broken through here and there but obviously, even from a distance, dating from many, many centuries before the boundary walls that criss-cross so many of these fells, as they do the Pennines from Derbyshire northwards to Hadrian's Wall. The site almost certainly contained a fort to begin with, constructed to the orders of Agricola in the first century AD. It is known to have been garrisoned at least until the early second century when Hadrian's Wall was being built between Solway and Wallsend-on-Tyne; in its later period, however, it was no longer required as a garrison base, and came to serve as a mere halting-place on the arduous route inland from the Irish Sea.

Only two segments remain to be explored before we find ourselves back at our starting-point. In the seventh segment we have, on the extreme fringe of this Area of Outstanding Natural Beauty, the village of Gosforth. No great beauty here, it must be admitted; but the churchyard of St Mary's is well worth a visit because it contains a vivid reminder that, a thousand years ago, this part of England was overrun by the Norsemen. In that churchyard there is a very striking fifteen-foot cross shaft. It is remarkable because it tells a double story. Elaborately carved up the full length of one side is a scene depicting the Norseman's devil-god Loki, his wife Sigun, and other figures from the sagas, who may include Baldur and the enemy who slew him (or it could be Odin himself); on the other side – and here is the strange thing – is a representation of Christ crucified. Why a double story? Because here Norse mythology, deeply rooted in the hearts of the men who came up these estuaries and tackled these

Buttermere, from the south-east end

gaunt passes, is intermixed with the Christian ethic that was beginning to be implanted here by the monks who had come over from Ireland in their tiny boats.

Experts put the date of this unique cross shaft at about 1000 AD. No one, of course, can say who it was who here so subtly turned paganism into Christianity. It could not have been the monks from the Cistercian abbey at Calder, a few miles to the north, for this was not established until the middle of the twelfth century. Today only parts of the nave, the aisles, and the cloisters remain to be seen, standing isolated just above Calder Bridge beside the river from which the abbey took its name.

It is inland from Gosforth and Calder that drama recommences: the unbelievable Screes of Wast Water. Though by no means the largest of the lakes, Wast Water is by far the deepest. It lies long and narrow, beneath the grim summit of Illgill Head, which rises to just short of the 2,000-foot mark. Down its steep slope, only just at the recognised angle-of-rest, there pours (particularly at the southern end of the lake) an enormous skirt of rubble and stone, immobilised by time yet suggesting imminent motion. This constitutes the famous Screes, indicated even on small-scale maps, one of the most spectacular sights in the whole of the Lake District, strangely menacing even in bright sunlight, more than alarming in shadow. Even viewed from the twisting road on the west side of the lake that terminates at Wasdale Head, the Screes present a forbidding aspect; but for the fact that they are grey, you might imagine them to be an arrested lava flow.

It is hardly surprising that this small road alongside Wast Water comes to an explicit, definitive end at Wasdale Head. For now you are beset by Lakeland's highest summits. Two miles to the south-east as the buzzard soars is the mighty summit of Scafell Pike, 3,210 feet high; two miles by the same flight to the north-east is Great Gable (2,949 feet); two miles again, but due north this time, is Pillar (2,927 feet); two miles north-west is Red Pike (2,629 feet). Sty Head Pass will take you (if you have stout boots and a stout heart) beneath the eastern face of Great Gable and, if you carry on, eventually to the very source of the River Derwent; Black Sail Pass, no less demanding, will lead you between Kirk Fell and Pillar and at last down to the south-eastern end of Buttermere. But these are passes that should not be undertaken lightly; they are for the practised fell walker only.

Looking west from the summit of Honister Pass

River Derwent, in Borrowdale

Great Gable is located in our final segment – the one, incidentally, (and for those who prefer the less exacting of the region's challenges), that contains the largest number of lakes. Near the periphery is little Loweswater, joined by a small beck to Crummock Water, which in turn is virtually joined to Buttermere. From the eastern end of this lake the road climbs steeply and tortuously up and over Honister Pass, and thence down into Borrowdale and the valley of the Derwent, which flows northwards into Derwentwater, at the head of which lies Keswick, so that the little town likes to call itself Keswick-on-Derwentwater.

The valley is set about by high fells, notably on its western side. Just short of Grange, with its beautiful slate-stone bridge, you will find, a few hundred yards along a track that climbs undulating away on the opposite side of the road, the famous Bowder Stone. No need for the 'Stone' in its appellation, for this is a boulder indeed. A rough rounded cube with sides approximately fifty feet square, it is estimated to weigh some 2,000 tons. It fell – no one can say just when – from the great cliff above and, strangely, miraculously, remained poised on one corner instead of on one flat side. Like any logan or 'rocking' stone (though this one is immovable) it stands in perfect equilibrium upon a quite improbably small area; two long-armed people, with joined hands, lying on the ground below, can encircle this!

Beyond, Grange-in-Borrowdale is approached by one of Lakeland's most graceful old bridges, of Cumbrian slate, wider by a good deal than the one at Watendlath, still too narrow for more than one vehicle at a time; it marks the northern limit of the most beautiful part of this undramatic, peaceful dale; only a mile or so farther on the water that flows beneath it enters the lake.

Almost at that very point, a sharply-turned track doubles back and climbs steeply from the road, making purposefully for what must, with Seathwaite, surely be the smallest, remotest hamlet in all Lakeland: Watendlath. Three miles of narrow, twisting track, negotiable by car if you are prepared for complicated manoeuvring at the occasional passing-point, brings you to a tiny cluster of stone-built cottages, a farmstead overlooking a packhorse bridge, and the jewel of Watendlath Tarn just beyond. Here, without overmuch difficulty, you will have succeeded in arriving at world's end. You can go no farther by car; but a footpath, or bridle-way, leads almost due east over the fells and so to Thirlmere, just two miles

The Bowder Stone, in Borrowdale

Watendlath

distant in an almost straight line, and one that is not unduly exacting. Another runs more steeply, especially in the last half mile or so, down to Rosthwaite, in Borrowdale. Back on the Borrowdale road once more, however, and you are bound for Keswick itself; the Derwent, meanwhile, flows on beyond Keswick and into Bassenthwaite Lake, the greater part of which lies within the periphery of this last segment of our circle.

It is a far cry from the isolation and the drama of Wrynose and the Three Shire Stone to the relative sophistication of erstwhile Cumberland's county town. Though it has literary associations that include not only Wordsworth and his sister Dorothy, and their friends Coleridge and Southey, but writers as disparate as Charles Lamb, Shelley, Sir Walter Scott, Alfred, Lord Tennyson, John Ruskin, and the late Hugh Walpole – who set his *Rogue Herries* novels in the Lake District – you yourself may remember it best, however often you have found yourself there, for its quaint Moot Hall on that island site in the main street, with its wrought-iron-railed approach steps, its whitened stone quoins, the graceful little turret topped by a weather-vane and, most of all, its unusual single-handed clock. But then who, after all, needs to know the *exact* time in Lakeland?

The Moot Hall, Keswick

Housesteads

Even the most perfunctory glance at a map, drawn to any scale, large or small, will show that a circle based on or near Housesteads contains the emptiest and, superficially at any rate, most featureless area in all England, not forgetting Dartmoor or Bodmin Moor. One major highway, linking Newcastle upon Tyne with the Lowlands of Scotland, skims through the outer curved edge of two of its north-eastern segments; a lesser road running north-westwards from Durham crosses three of its segments, to join the first-mentioned beyond Otterburn at Elishaw, right on the perimeter; one major road, from Newcastle to Carlisle, spans the circle, bisecting it almost exactly from east to west; a smaller road roughly parallels this a few miles to the north of it for part of the way; three or four minor roads wander across the moorland in the southern half, aimlessly, it would seem, but gathering significance as they make for Teesdale and North Yorkshire. Otherwise – nothing.

Nothing? But that is to have overlooked a feature of major importance: the Roman Wall, built at the direction of the Emperor Hadrian in the early decades of the second century AD to mark the northernmost limit of the vast Empire of Rome, to serve as a line of demarcation and, when necessary, a manned barrier against the Picts and Scots who roamed the huge emptiness of the moors that extend northwards from the Wall to the Cheviots and beyond.

It was designed to run unbroken from Wallsend (hence the name of the relatively modern suburb) to Bowness-on-Solway, an overall distance of more than seventy miles across England at its narrowest point. In fact, though its construction occupied some ten years

Old Tollhouse, Warden, near Hexham

N
S
W
NW
SW
Jedburgh 23 miles
Carlisle 8 miles
NORTHUMBERLAND
CUMBRIA
Wark Forest
Kielder Forest
Bakethin
Plashetts
Emblehope
Earl's Seat 1303
Blackburn Common
Padon Hill 1240
Elishaw
Dargues
Highgreen Manor
Blackmoor Skirt 1193
Troughend Common
Comb
Gatehouse
Mounces
North Tyne
Falstone
Shilburn Haugh
Stannersburn
Donkleywood
Greenhaugh
Lanehead
Charlton
Low Cranecleugh
Hott
Birks
Bower
Hesleyside
Dunterley
Bellingham
Chirdon Burn
Bewcastle Fells
Sighty Crag 1701
Black Knowe 1615
White Lyne
Whitelyne Common
The Flatt
Paddaburn Moor
Churnsike Lodge
1024
Blackpool Gate
Blacka Burn
Round Top 1065
Whygate
Warks Burn
Stonehaugh
Wark
Bewcastle
Shopford
Butterburn
Spadeadam Forest
Lyneholmeford
Winter Shields
1026
1089
Haughton Common
North Greenhill
Spadeadam
Greenlee Lough
Broomlee Lough
Grindon
Whiteside
Thirlwall Common
Edges Green
Kirkcambeck
Moscow
Farglow
Grindon Hill
Settlingstones
Lees Hill
West Hall
Gilsland Spa
Greengate Well
Nickie's Hill
Park Nook
Kiln Hill
Hadrian's Wall
1230
King Water
Burthinghurst
Triermain
Longbyre
Gilsland
Greenhead
Twice Brewed
Chesterwood
Banks
Wall Bowers
Upper Denton
Thorngrafton
Haltwhistle
Melkridge
Henshaw
Redburn
Bardon Mill
Bellingham
Ridley
South Tyne
Haydon Bridge
Plenmeller
Willimontswick
Low Row
Brampton
Denton Fell
Plenmeller Common
Allen
Langley
Rowfoot
Milton
Stublick
Hallbankgate
Tindale
Midgeholme
Lambley
Farlam
Tindale Tarn
Halton Lea Gate
Stonehouse
Whitfield
Bearbridge
Catton
Talkin
Tindale Fells
Forest Head
1541
Cold Fell 2041
Glendue Fell
Snope Common
Whitfield Moor
1723
Allendale Town
Knarsdale
Ouston
Ninebanks
Studdon
King's Forest of Geltsdale
Gelt
1582
West Dun Hill 1893
Slaggyford
Chareheads
Geltsdale Middle
Barhough
1719
Limestone Brae
892
Ayle
1940
Hard Rigg 1793
Grey Nag 2154
Carr Shield
1876
Tom Smith's Stone 2071
Raise
Alston
Nenthall
2013
The Dodd
Coalcleugh
Gilderdale Forest
Bayles
Leadgate
Nenthead
Flinty Fell 2013
Nag's Head 2207
1513
1357
Ashgillside
A69
A689
B6318
B6320
B6295
B6303
A686
B6294
B6277
1
4
5
18
19
20
21
22
23
24
25
26
27
28
29
30
31
32
33
34
35
36
Scale : 5 miles to 1 inch
17½
15
10
5
0
MILES

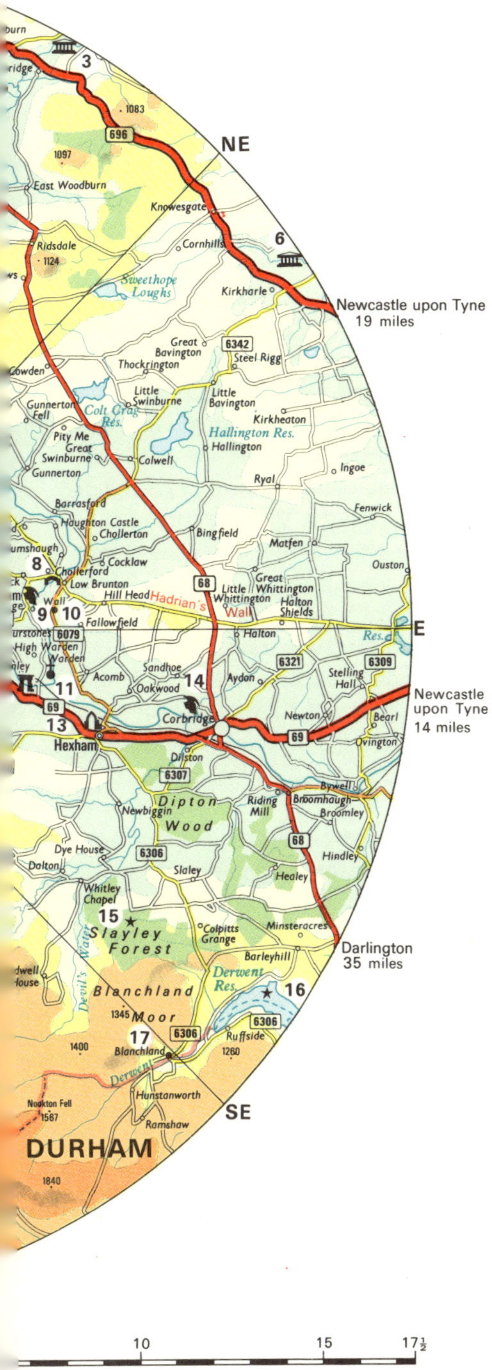

Housesteads

1 Housesteads
2 Otterburn
3 Elsdon
4 Bellingham Church
5 Wark
6 Wallington Hall
7 Simonburn Church
8 Chollerford
9 Chesters or Cilirnum
10 Wall
11 Warden Church
12 Tyne Tollhouse
13 Hexham Priory Church
14 Corstopitum/Corbridge
15 Slayley Forest
16 Derwent Reservoir
17 Blanchland
18 Allendale Town
19 East Allen Dale
20 West Allen Dale
21 Alston
22 Nenthead
23 Gilderdale Forest
24 Snope Common
25 Pennine Way
26 Plenmeller Common
27 Haltwhistle
28 Thirlwall Castle
29 Naworth Castle
30 Lanercost Priory
31 Lanercost Bridge
32 Bewcastle Church
33 Whitelyne Common
34 Wark Forest
35 Falstone
36 Kielder Forest

or more, it was never fully completed from end to end. But what was built was superbly sited, along the undulating, serpentining line of the Great Whin Sill, a basaltic outcrop that marches spectacularly east–west and is to be seen at its most dramatic in the immediate region of Housesteads. Beneath it to the north, shadowed for much of the day by the sheer height of the Whin Sill, lie Crag Lough, Greenlee Lough, Broomlee Lough, and a cluster of smaller, unnamed, forbidding waters; and also the interminable acres of marshy, inhospitable land that characterise this space between the Whin Sill and the upper reaches of the North Tyne, interspersed with moorlands that rise on occasion to more than 1,000 feet.

Even though so much of Hadrian's Wall has now vanished – cannibalised for its fine quarried and hewn stone, as may be seen almost at a glance in the walls of farms and other buildings in the vicinity – there remain stretches of it substantial enough to offer some of the finest walking in all England. Moreover, the Roman road that was built for the purpose of transport and supply has been properly maintained, and you may approach the Wall by way of side roads and tracks, none of them more than a few hundred yards in length and almost all of them, naturally owing to the lie of the land, on the southern side. As good an approach as any is from a point midway between the Twice Brewed and Grindon Hill.

The height of the Wall above sea level varies, and in fact there are one or two points just to the east of Housesteads that are higher than this famous Roman 'fortified city' by perhaps a couple of hundred feet – Sewing Staels (or Shields), for example; and also Hotbank Crags to the west. But Housesteads (the Romans' Borcovicus), now National Trust property, is so much the finest of all the Roman sites along the Wall that it is the obvious choice for our viewpoint.

It is some five acres in extent, and is believed to have housed no fewer than 5,000 legionaries, together with unnumbered camp-followers and others. The whole site has been skilfully excavated, the buildings named, and details emphasised. Here you can see the foundations of the men's barracks, the commandant's and other officers' quarters, the storehouses and bath-houses and granaries and lavatories and a host of other lesser, but nonetheless interesting, features. Among these are the water troughs, the massive stone edges of which have been scalloped as a result of generations of sword-sharpening by the men of the garrison prior to or after their forays against the marauding Picts and Scots, or mere defensive actions. On the south side there is clear evidence of how and where the camp-followers lived: the remains of some sort of hostelry, of shops and – a macabre feature – the so-called Murder House in which, in the course of excavating, two skeletons were unearthed, of a woman and a man, the latter with a dagger still embedded between his ribs.

It is tempting to devote the whole of this section to the multifarious features of Hadrian's Wall: to write of the Mithraic temple and the hoard of coins found near Procolitia, a few miles to the east; of the museum at Corbridge, the Romans' Corstopitum, further to the east still; of the bridge works at Chollerford; the camps at Gilsland, Birdoswald, and elsewhere to the west; the Roman milestone (the only one still *in situ* so far discovered) near Bardon Mill to the south; the enormous *vicus*, or civilian township, Vindolanda, now being systematically excavated and likely to engage the time and expertise of archaeologists and their many voluntary assistants for perhaps two decades to come. And – but all this and much more has been written up elsewhere, and there are guide-books galore in the book-shops and on the sites themselves, with which every Wall-walker should equip himself. We, meanwhile, will proceed to the most northerly point on the circle's perimeter and begin to explore it, segment by segment, clockwise from Otterburn.

This is a quiet enough little place today; but in a field on its north-west outskirts, close alongside the road that crosses the Scottish Border at Carter Bar, there is a beautifully-proportioned tapered stone on a plinth, commemorating the famous Battle of Otterburn in 1388, when the Scots, under the Earl of Douglas, fought the North Country men, led by Sir Henry Percy, in the dark of the night. The doughty Douglas was slain, and this stone is called to this day the Percy Stone; the battle itself formed the subject of one of the best-known of all the countless Border ballads, 'Chevy Chase'.

On a less martial, more domestic, note, it may be added that it is from the old mill at Otterburn that the rugs and heavy tweeds come that are so highly prized by their fortunate owners. Not the least interesting feature here is the mill that is to this day partly operated by the old water-wheel.

Reverting for a moment to the martial aspect: this Border Country is the country of pele towers. Only a bare stone's throw outside the perimeter, overlooking the little church at Elsdon, there is one of these. It came to be incorporated, centuries ago, in a fortified manor

Walkers on Hadrian's Wall

house, not unlike Ravenglass Manor though on a much smaller scale; this in turn came to be used as a vicarage, and it is now privately owned, a charming, gracious dwelling.

A little to the south and west lies Bellingham (you must pronounce the name 'Bell-injam' if you are to be understood locally!), a small market town near the headwaters of the North Tyne and beautifully centred between moorland slopes to north and south. There are no buildings here of real note, save for the Church of St Cuthbert, the oldest parts of which date from the early years of the thirteenth century. But it is worth more than a casual glance, especially its interior: for the barrel-vaulted roof is supported by hexagonal ribs of stone of a size and style that is more likely to be found in a cathedral or major parish church than in so small a building. Behind the church a path winds down to St Cuthbert's Well, whose waters (if you are prepared to believe what the older locals will tell you) have magical healing properties. On your way out, keep your eyes open for a very unusual shaped tombstone: pack-shaped, it commemorates an itinerant pedlar, or packman, a murdered youth and an attempt at a violent raid; all of this is recounted in the 'Legend of the Long Pack', which you may read to this day and believe or not as you will.

Some five miles to the south, on the other side of the river, you come soon to the hamlet of Wark, a cluster of small grey stone houses set about a charming village green. No more than a hamlet; yet eight hundred years ago it was the capital of Tyneside, named after its famous earth-'wark' or, as it would have been called in Norman times, its *motte*. This vast mound is alleged to have been built by the womenfolk of the district who carried the material of which it consists, mainly stone, from the bed of the river which flows close by. This, too, you believe or disbelieve according to your mood and the impression the place makes upon you. A farmhouse stands on its summit; at its foot is the Battlesteads Inn, so called, the landlord will tell you, because troops and their officers' horses were quartered here during one of the everlasting Scottish-Northumbrian wars. The date 1747 is inscribed on the stone lintel, but there is no doubt whatsoever that the building itself dates back a century or two further than that.

This minor road that runs southwards from Otterburn by way of Bellingham and Wark leads on, within a couple of miles or so, to Simonburn, in the second segment. This is a smaller and certainly more attractive hamlet than Wark, with its inevitable atmosphere of

Roman granary, Housesteads

Roman water trough, Housesteads

past military activity. It has charming, creeper-clad cottages, a tree-studded green, a miniature Stone Circle – which in fact now consists of no more than four rough pillars locally referred to as the 'Goat Stones', though no one seems able to tell you why. They are poised on a crag or outcrop of rock for all to see.

Most notable, however, is Simonburn's Church of St Mungo, which originated in the thirteenth century, though it has been much restored. Fragments dating from earlier centuries are to be seen, notably in its porch. St Mungo, strangely enough, is believed to have been the illegitimate son of a Pictish princess, but he survived the stigma and lived on to become Bishop of Strathclyde; he is better known by his baptismal name, Kentigern. As you walk down the little aisle towards the chancel you will perhaps be puzzled by the fact that you seem to be hurrying unduly. There is a rational explanation: the floor of this ancient church positively slopes downwards from west to east, the church having been built on a steepish hill and its first builders having apparently been amateurs who had difficulty with their levels!

Three or four miles farther south the road meets the line of Hadrian's Wall at Chollerford. With Chesters, the Roman Cilurnum, this offers a perfect blend of ancient and modern: the George Hotel, with all its up-to-date amenities (and they are many!), and the fascinating relics of the Roman bridge that they built to span the North Tyne when the river in spate caused the ford to be impassable. Immediately on the other side of the river, and overlooking it from the south close to its confluence with the South Tyne, is the aptly-named village of Wall: apt because it does not take an expert's eye to discern that much of the stone walling in the village derives from the Roman Wall itself rather than directly from any of the local quarries. This cannibalisation has been going on to a greater or lesser degree ever since the legionaries departed in the fourth century AD, leaving their monumental line of demarcation, with its spaced turrets and mile-castles, to the untender mercies of all who cared to seize upon the hewn stone of which it had been constructed. Barns and byres, cart-sheds and pigstyes: all bear witness to centuries of such activity.

The road winds on to High Warden and Warden itself, in our third segment. The latter hamlet is on the north bank of the South Tyne at the exact point where the two rivers meet and merge. In the graveyard of the Church of St Michael and All Angels, beneath a great yew tree, lie three graves, close to one another. They are unusual in that

St Mungo's Church, Simonburn

each is spanned by a row of wrought-iron hoops, fashioned by the local blacksmith at the request of the then rector's family when he, the Revd. W. T. Fields, his wife, and his eighteen-month-old child died. The child's grave, it will be noticed, required only three instead of four hoops; they were placed there to foil the activities of the unscrupulous body-snatchers who, a century and more ago, made a practice of digging up newly-buried corpses and selling them to the anatomists. A happier note is struck half a mile to the south, where the former bridge tollhouse, on the right bank of the river, but no longer required for the purpose for which it was built, now serves as a neat if circumscribed home for a small family who enjoy the musical meeting-of-the-waters at the foot of their sloping garden.

Hexham, a few miles downstream below the convergence of the two Tyne Rivers, has *multum in parvo* to offer. It is an old market town with a famous abbey church built in the late twelfth and early thirteenth centuries on a site that had held a church already for five centuries past; much of it was built of stone taken from the Romans' Corstopitum, only four or five miles to the east. It is rich in relics spread over many centuries, including the finest Anglo-Saxon crypt in all England. The town, too, is redolent of history, especially of medieval times. In themselves, the street names suggest this: Priestpopple and Hencotes, Quatre Bras and St Mary's Chare, for instance. Facing the ancient market place opposite the abbey church is the Moot Hall, or Court House, originally the gatehouse of the twelfth-century castle; near by is the fourteenth-century gaol, which was actually in use until the last century. It stands there to this day, a grim, haunting relic indeed, and a permanent reminder of a harsher way of life.

The minor road that runs southwards out of Hexham leads by way of Slayley Forest – less forest land, today, than empty, rolling moorland – to the village of Blanchland. This village, which can claim with some justification to be the most beautiful in this northernmost county, though there are of course others that will stoutly dispute the claim, lies almost on the periphery of the circle, and only just within the fourth segment. Here the River Derwent (one of the many rivers so named in the country, in Cumbria, for instance, and in Derbyshire, to name but two of them) flows into a kidney-shaped reservoir just to the east.

In Blanchland you will find perfection in a specific sense. Entry to the village is through a medieval gatehouse. You pass through this into an L-shaped open space which was almost certainly the Outer Precinct of Blanchland Monastery. As long ago as 1159 the Premonstratensians, or 'White Canons' as they were more familiarly known (and hence, in fact, the name of the village today), established themselves here, and the village as you see it today is built almost entirely of the stone they quarried and hewed for their monastery and ancillary buildings; it stands on the foundations they laid down some eight centuries and more ago. What was the frater, on the south side of the cloister, is now a neat row of cottages; the abbot's lodging immediately on the left of the gatehouse, together with the abbey guest-house, now forms the Lord Crewe Arms, one of the most famous hostelries in the whole of the North Country and reminiscent in some respects of its opposite number, The Luttrell Arms, in Dunster, far to the south-west in Somerset. Its gigantic fireplace is a reminder of those remote days, together with many other impressive

Iron-hooped graves, Warden, near Hexham

traditional features. You will not find anywhere else in the whole length and breadth of England a village that bears comparison with 'White Canons' Land'.

No road continues westwards from here. Now it is open moorland rising to 1,500 feet before you reach, by a tortuous but not unrewarding route, Allendale Town. It was, in olden times and until last century, a lead-mining centre of very considerable importance, and there is much evidence of the workings there to this day; but now it regards itself essentially as an attractive moorland holiday resort, a centre for excellent moorland walking and no less excellent trout-fishing. Indeed, it is now so conscious of its potential that it frequently wins the annual prize for the best-kept village in Northumbria. Blanchland, however, rises superior to such competitiveness.

A network of minor roads links East Allen Dale (in the fourth segment) with West Allen Dale (in the fifth segment) – rivals in their individual charms and also in the excellence of their trout-fishing amenities. Thence the road leads you to Alston. At a height of 921 feet above sea level it claims to be the highest market town in England, and no other town seems anxious to challenge this. It is a dour little place, somewhat turned in upon itself, you might say, and not openly welcoming. Its main street is so steep and so tortuous that you must concentrate on your driving, whether you are climbing or descending it. One driver in quite recent times failed in this respect; unfortunately he was at the wheel of a lorry, and the result was that the ancient market hall, for centuries its focal point, was badly damaged and will never be the same again. Within a very few hundred yards to the south, the road has climbed sufficiently to be well over 1,000 feet above sea level while still on the outskirts of the town. A bare five miles to the south-east on the A689 lies (or perches) Nenthead: at no less than 1,415 feet above sea level there is no question at all that this is the highest village in England. Not far away, but outside the periphery of our circle, is one of the highest road summits in the country, near St John's Chapel, which surpasses the 2,000-foot mark. Exalted country, this, for miles around. Without exception, the roads approaching townships and villages alike in this region carry a strong sense of combined purposefulness and isolation, not least the one that leads you into Nenthead.

But there are few roads indeed over these vast stretches of open moorland, an area that includes Gilderdale Forest, Snope Common, Whitfield Moor and Plenmeller Common, among others named on the map. Plenmeller Common leads us across into the sixth segment of the circle and on to Haltwhistle, a not particularly interesting township (in spite of a name which implies instructions to train drivers) lying astride the main east–west road that links Newcastle upon Tyne with Carlisle, just to the south of Hadrian's Wall, and in fact only seven or eight miles from our viewpoint, Housesteads. There is less to see here than you may have been led to expect. Thirlwall Castle, to the north-west and on the true line of the Wall, is of much greater interest; it is not, as you might be led to expect, one of the many Roman mile-castles, but a mid-fourteenth-century fortified house, much of the stonework of which almost certainly derived from adjacent sections of the actual Wall.

Now we are on the main A69, approaching Brampton, the westernmost limit of the circle. Just off the road, to the right, is Naworth Castle, which dates largely from the fourteenth century – a period in

Moorland road near Nenthead

which such a vast number of memorable buildings, whether castles, fortified manor houses, tithe-barns, bridges, or what have you seem to have been constructed in this country. Just to the north of this, and truly on the line of the Wall even though this is hard to pick out in this locality, where the Romans' purposefulness seems indeed to have been on the decline and they were often content with a massive turf wall rather than one built of solid stone, and so likely to last down the centuries but for the depredations of man, is Lanercost Priory. This was founded in the mid-twelfth century by monks of the Augustinian Order. Its gatehouse is very impressive, and it is recorded that Edward I was received here by the prior of the day. There has of necessity been a good deal of restoration at Lanercost over recent years. But this has been most skilfully and intelligently executed, and the famous Lanercost Cross, bearing the date 1214, will immediately catch the eye. Also memorable, particularly so, is the remarkable doorway in the massive wall of the west front. The priory is open to rolling, tree-clad pastureland to the east; if you approach it from the west, however, it is part-hidden by farm buildings. They constitute, in fact, Dacre Hall, though in their day they were occupied by the monks themselves, and include the cloister in which they meditated when they were not at work or at prayer.

The impact of Lanercost Priory is immediate. Not least because, unlike most ecclesiastical buildings of the period, it is largely built of russet sandstone of the region, though intermixed with greyer stone which is obviously from Hadrian's Wall. It contains relics, too, of the Roman occupation: altars and inscribed stones dedicated to the god Jupiter, among others, this particular one having been salvaged at some time from the neighbouring Roman fort, Birdoswald. As an interesting sidelight, the priory was founded, exactly a hundred years after the Norman Conquest, by Robert de Vaux, almost certainly a remote ancestor of the famous Northumbrian brewing family who thrive today in the trade. Its first occupants were a dozen or so Augustinian Canons. They were at once fortunate in the site of their priory, for it was in such beautiful country; and unfortunate in that it lay on a route much frequented by the English and Scottish armies that continuously fought their way northwards and southwards through this northern Borderland territory claimed by each. The priory was ransacked, partially destroyed, partly rebuilt, and ransacked again, throughout the twelfth and succeeding centuries. After the Dissolution (it was one of the first of Henry VIII's victims) it became the property of the then owner of Naworth Castle; he adapted much of what remained of the priory into a family residence and turned the nave into Lanercost Priory Church.

Little more than a mile across the fields to the west of the priory is one of England's countless beautifully-proportioned old stone bridges, now happily by-passed so that it should remain intact. It spans the little River Irthing and bears two iron plaques. One reads: 'This Bridge was Built in 2 Year of James II'; the other reads 'Unsafe for Traction Engines'. Like all bridges, new and old, it is eminently photogenic.

Two segments (one quarter of the Housesteads circle) remain. They are emptier than all the others; only a portion of the eighth segment has deserved the official appellation, Area of Outstanding Natural Beauty – the Wark Forest area. But a minor and very zigzagging road leads north from near Lanercost Bridge to Bewcastle

Lanercost Priory

Lanercost Bridge

(in the seventh segment), which fully justifies the tortuous approach. As its name implies, Bewcastle is of Roman origin; it is in fact a Roman site, though it lies several miles north of the Wall. Of greater interest, however, is the famous Bewcastle Cross in the churchyard: not merely famous but unique. It is a cross shaft (as at Gosforth, in Cumbria) rather than a full cross, and dates from the seventh century. The pagan and the Christian ideologies are blended: St John the Baptist and Christ himself appear on it; there are also runic inscriptions and traditional ornamentation, together with a mysterious figure locally known as 'The Falconer', not yet identified by antiquarians or other experts.

Just beyond Bewcastle the small road you have followed peters out completely. If you are an experienced walker, and enterprising, you could explore Whitelyne Common, which slopes westwards down to the small river of the same name. You could make your way farther northwards still, in the final segment, to reach the vast area of Kielder Forest, in the care of the Forestry Commission, and then pick up (if you get thus far!) the minor road which runs from the North Tyne valley by way of Falstone, crosses the perimeter of the circle just short of the foresters' village of Kielder, and almost immediately afterwards crosses the Border into Scotland – the least-used, most picturesque and interesting of all the roads that cross this historic border high on the undulating line of the Cheviot Hills.

Blanchland village

Rogan's Seat

As the crow flies, the focal point of our next circle, Rogan's Seat, high above the dales of the old North Riding of Yorkshire (now, to the regret of many, reduced simply to 'North Yorkshire', so that the age-old 'Thirding', corrupted to 'Riding', of this, the largest of our counties, is now irretrievably lost to us) is exactly forty miles due east of the Three Shire Stone on Wrynose Pass. The nearest points on the peripheries of the two circles are only five miles apart; they share portions of Westmorland (now incorporated in the new congeries of counties, Cumbria). A portion of County Durham lies in the north-eastern segments of the Rogan's Seat circle where the lovely valley of Teesdale forms a sinuous boundary-line. Half of the total area enclosed in this circle is shown on modern maps as one of those designated as of outstanding natural beauty – and small wonder, either – essentially Swale Dale and Wensleydale, with vast stretches of moorland to north, between them, and to the south. And immediately to the south of this area is the unsurpassed region of pot-holing, or caving, terrain, chiefly in what used to be known as the West Riding.

As with the Lake District, with Wrynose Pass arbitrarily taken as its focal point, here again there is a wide choice, even if it is not quite so wide as the first-named. As a viewpoint, Great Shunner Fell (2,340 feet), Middle Tongue (2,109 feet), Buckden Pike (2,302 feet), Wild Boar Fell (2,324 feet), and Knoutberry Haw (2,216 feet) – and, again, what splendid names these are! – all answer the purpose. A number of others easily top the 2,000-foot mark, and others again approach it closely. Many, indeed most, of them call for some

Richmond Castle, Yorkshire

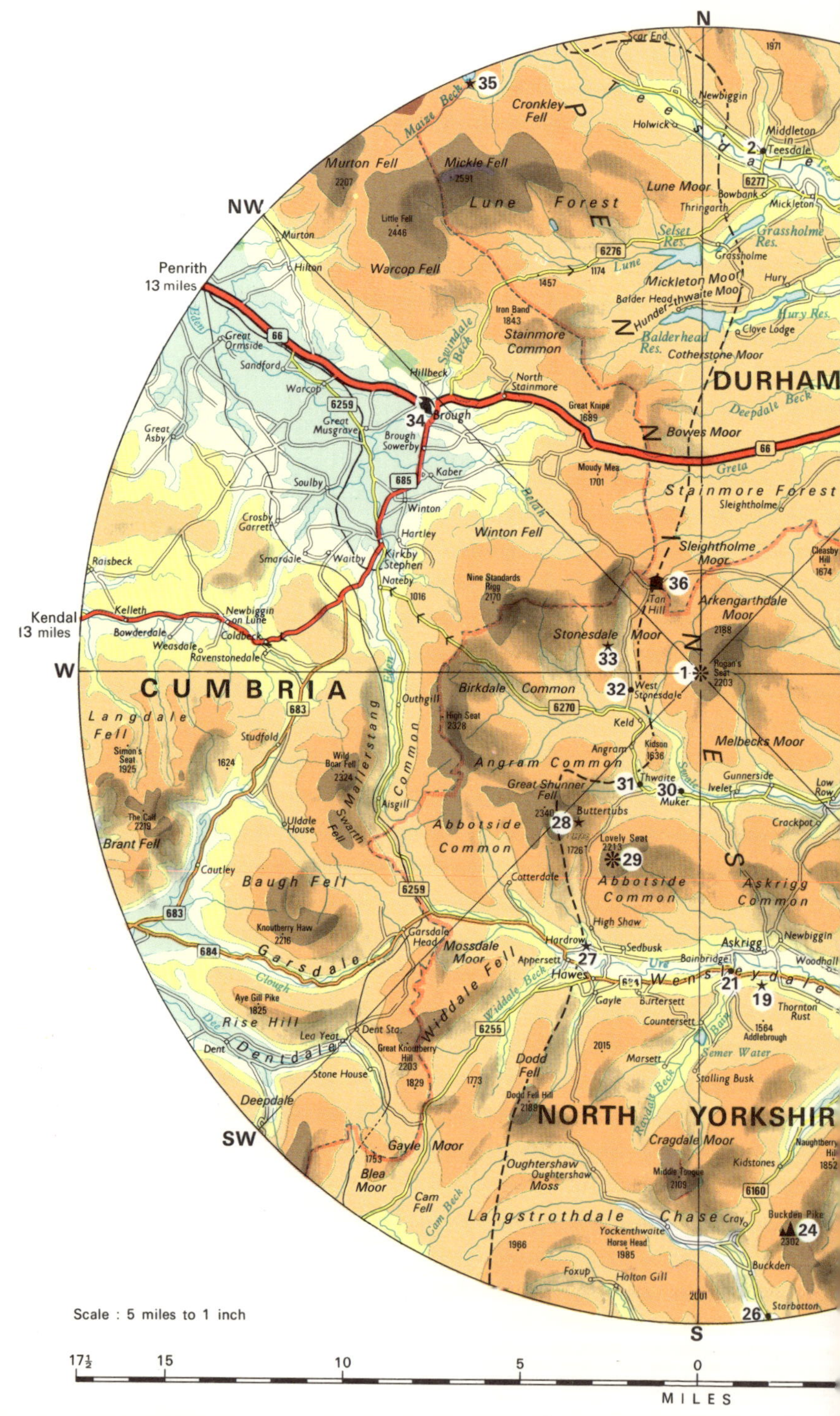
N
NW
W
SW
S
Penrith
13 miles
Kendal
13 miles
Scar End
1971
35
Maize Beck
Cronkley Fell
Newbiggin
Holwick
Middleton in Teesdale
2
Murton Fell
2207
Mickle Fell
2591
Lune Moor
6277
Bowbank
Mickleton
Thringarth
Lune Forest
Little Fell
2446
Murton
Hilton
Warcop Fell
Selset Res.
Grassholme Res.
Grassholme
6276
1174
Lune
1457
Mickleton Moor
Hury
Balder Head
Hunderthwaite Moor
Iron Band
1843
Hury Res.
Eden
Great Ormside
66
Stainmore Common
Balderhead Res.
Clove Lodge
Cotherstone Moor
Swindale Beck
Sandford
Hillbeck
North Stainmore
DURHAM
Warcop
6259
Brough
34
Great Knipe
1689
Deepdale Beck
Great Musgrave
Great Asby
Brough Sowerby
Bowes Moor
66
Moudy Mea
1701
Greta
Kaber
685
Soulby
Stainmore Forest
Sleightholme
Winton
Belah
Crosby Garrett
Hartley
Winton Fell
Sleightholme Moor
Raisbeck
Smardale
Waitby
Kirkby Stephen
Nateby
Cleasby Hill
1674
Nine Standards Rigg
2170
36
Tan Hill
Arkengarthdale Moor
1016
Kelleth
Newbiggin on Lune
2188
Bowderdale
Coldbeck
Weasdale
Ravenstonedale
Stonesdale Moor
33
1
Rogan's Seat
2203
CUMBRIA
Eden
Birkdale Common
32
West Stonesdale
683
Outhgill
6270
Langdale Fell
High Seat
2328
Keld
Simon's Seat
1925
Studfold
Kidson
1636
Melbecks Moor
1624
Wild Boar Fell
2324
Mallerstang
Common
Angram
Angram Common
Gunnerside
Low Row
Great Shunner Fell
31
Thwaite
30
Muker
Ivelet
Swale
Aisgill
2340
Buttertubs
28
Crackpot
The Calf
2219
Uldale House
Swarth Fell
Abbotside Common
1726
Lovely Seat
2213
29
Brant Fell
Cautley
Cotterdale
Abbotside Common
Askrigg Common
Baugh Fell
6259
High Shaw
683
Knoutberry Haw
2216
Garsdale Head
Mossdale Moor
Hardrow
Sedbusk
Askrigg
Newbiggin
684
Garsdale
Appersett
27
Bainbridge
Woodhall
Widdale Fell
Hawes
Ure
Wensleydale
21
19
Clough
Gayle
Burtersett
Thornton Rust
Aye Gill Pike
1825
Widdale Beck
Countersett
1564
Addlebrough
Rise Hill
Dee
Lea Yeat
Dent Sta.
6255
Bain
Dent
Dentdale
Great Knoutberry Hill
2203
2015
Marsett
Semer Water
Stone House
Dodd Fell
1829
1773
Stalling Busk
Raydale Beck
Dodd Fell Hill
2189
Deepdale
NORTH
YORKSHIR
SW
Cragdale Moor
Naughtberry Hill
1852
Gayle Moor
1753
Oughtershaw
Oughtershaw Moss
Kidstones
Middle Tongue
2109
Blea Moor
6160
Cam Fell
Cam Beck
Langstrothdale
Chase
Cray
Buckden Pike
24
2302
Yockenthwaite
Horse Head
1985
1966
Buckden
Foxup
Halton Gill
2001
Starbotton
26
Scale : 5 miles to 1 inch
17½
15
10
5
0
MILES

Rogan's Seat

1 Rogan's Seat
2 Middleton-in-Teesdale
3 Barnard Castle
4 Raby Castle
5 Greta Bridge
6 Rokeby Park and Hall
7 Scargill
8 The Stang Forest
9 Richmond
10 Easby Abbey
11 Swale Dale
12 Marrick Priory
13 Marrick
14 Arkengarthdale
15 Reeth
16 Leyburn
17 Castle Bolton
18 Middleham Castle
19 Wensleydale
20 Aysgarth Force
21 Bainbridge
22 Coverham Abbey
23 Braithwaite Hall
24 Buckden Pike
25 Cover Dale
26 Starbotton
27 Hardrow Force
28 Buttertubs Pass
29 Lovely Seat
30 Muker
31 Thwaite
32 West Stonesdale
33 Stonesdale Moor
34 Brough
35 High Force
36 Tan Hill Inn

experience, not to mention stamina, even to come within reach of their summits. Rogan's Seat has been selected, among many strong competitors, partly because it is less daunting than some of the others, but more particularly because it can be approached by road more easily. The twisting climb up and down West Stonesdale, to the west of Rogan's Seat, for instance, is now finely surfaced and the most hazardous of its bends ironed out – though the one at its foot still calls for care and anticipation as you approach it, especially on the descent towards the hamlet of Keld. Rogan's Seat, too, offers magnificent panoramic views, especially to the east and south, and sheer across Swale Dale to its counterpart and near-twin, Lovely Seat (2,213 feet).

You would need good eyesight as you stood on the summit and looked northwards over fifteen miles of moorland if you hoped to pick out the little township of Middleton-in-Teesdale, in the first segment. For though its old stone houses and cottages, many of them built originally for the lead-miners when the industry was being developed here in the mid-eighteenth century, are stepped, or terraced, upwards from the river on which the little town stands, it merges somehow into its background, self-effacing, self-sufficient. Nevertheless it is well worth a visit, and not only for its interesting layout of miners' and others' sturdy little dwellings. The Church of St Mary – focal point for those primarily interested in our myriad parish churches – will prove something of a disappointment, for it is barely a hundred years old. But it has two unusual features that will be memorable and justify the visit. It has a wholly-detached stone tower that is three centuries older than the main body of the church. And, more unusual still, many of the tombs in the graveyard have symbols carved on their stone lids which indicate the occupations followed by the men who were buried beneath them a hundred, two hundred years ago: agricultural implements such as forks and hoes and, in one or two cases, weaponry such as hilted swords. The Quaker fraternity who developed the lead-mining industry two hundred years ago would no doubt have strongly disapproved.

Ten miles farther downstream you will come to the ancient town of Barnard Castle, which must be approached by an impressive bridge that spans the river deep down below it, overlooked by the imposing ruins of the castle first built on its commanding site by Guy de Bailleul, but largely rebuilt and extended in the mid-twelfth century by his nephew Bernard, after whom, obviously, the town is named.

Rogan's Seat, from The Buttertubs

Few castle ruins, surely, make a more immediate impact, even from a distance, than these. The memorable Round Tower influenced Sir Walter Scott when he was writing his narrative poem *Rokeby*. History lies all about you, here in Barnard Castle, and it is for this reason that an exception is being made and emphasis laid on a town rather than purely on the rural scene. The past is to be savoured in St Mary's Church, dating from Norman times, though this was extensively restored only a hundred years ago; it is to be savoured in the eighteenth-century Market Cross; and perhaps even more at the King's Head, where Charles Dickens once stayed. If industrial activity is of interest, it is worth while searching for the traditionally-styled weavers' cottages with their characteristic long upper windows, for in olden times weaving was essentially a cottage industry. The weavers worked at home; the lead-miners worked in Teesdale, returning after their toil to their squat, snug, stone-built cottages. Nor, incidentally, should you leave Barnard Castle without a visit to its Bowes Museum, a massive building in French château style which contains one of the finest collections of paintings and other works of art to be found in England outside our major cities.

From Barnard Castle the main road (A688) will take you, in six miles or so, out of this segment and to Raby Castle, on the extreme periphery of the second segment. It is to be found a mile or two to the north of the village of Staindrop and is, in the opinion of many connoisseurs of castles and stately homes (call it which you will), among the half-dozen most impressive in the whole country. It is comparable in many respects, notably in its generally forbidding air, with Alnwick Castle, many miles to the north-east on the old Great North Road to Berwick and beyond. Portions of Raby Castle (it is open intermittently to the public from Easter until the end of September, and more consistently during the main summer holiday period) date from pre-Norman times; most of what you see today, however, dates from the fourteenth century and later. Home of the Nevilles for hundreds of years, it was in its Barons' Hall that the campaign to replace Queen Elizabeth by Mary was planned in 1569 – a plot that failed.

Seven or eight miles almost due south, in the second segment, lies Greta Bridge. It carries the A66 across a tributary of the Tees, the Greta, from which it derives its name. A stronger contrast with the menacing austerity of Raby Castle could hardly be imagined. On one side of the bridge a hotel stands on what (though you would never suspect it) was a Roman site seventeen centuries ago. Almost facing this is the entrance to the mellow beauty, light and shade and dappled turf, of Rokeby Park. At Rokeby Hall Scott actually wrote his poem *Rokeby*, which rivals in length his better-known *Lady of the Lake* and falls not far short of *Marmion* itself. Inspiration for the poem was born as he stood on Bernard Balliol's great Round Tower at Barnard Castle; ever a romantic, and appreciative of a site that has remained romantic to this day, he gladly accepted his host's offer of a tree-embowered 'hermit's cave' by the water side in which to write a hundred and more pages in close print – what must have been the labour of writing it with a quill pen in 1812–13!

A choice of very minor moorland roads now leads you southwards from the valley of the Tees and its tributaries uphill all the way to the

Aysgarth Force

fringe of Arkengarthdale Moor by way of Scargill and the emptiness of Stang Forest. Thence a valley road will lead you eastwards to Richmond, just over into the third segment and close to the eastern edge of this circle. Again, a town – though very soon we shall turn our attention away from towns to wilder, emptier scenes. But Richmond must not be ignored – the word 'overlooked' cannot be used here, for the town stands high on a rocky eminence, superbly sited above the steep gorge of the Swale; it is surely one of the most splendidly sited of all our smaller towns.

There is much here to see; perhaps even more to 'feel'. It possesses an astonishing eleventh-century castle, itself dominated by its 100-foot twelfth-century tower, one of the noblest in the country. From the castle walls the medieval market place – and even when buses and cars are drawn up in it this still has the feel of a Middle

Ages market place – slopes downwards like a cobbled skirt. Between the castle and the market place is Holy Trinity Church, which for hundreds of years served both as place of worship and venue for merchants and their customers in the ordinary way of barter and trade. Richmond possesses, too, its eighteenth-century Georgian Theatre Royal, apart from the one at Bristol the only survivor in the country from that period. L'Anson Road commemorates Frances, the original 'Lass of Richmond Hill'; and for a time Lewis Carroll attended the old grammar school opposite the Parish Church of St Mary. Though, inevitably, its tentacles spread, the heart of Richmond remains intact.

Just beyond the southern confines of this unusually beautiful North Country market town you will come upon the remains of Easby Abbey, which is open to the public. It is claimed that it is haunted – but then what ancient ruins are not? It is in Richmond itself, however, that the strongest conviction of a form of haunting prevails: according to local legend, King Arthur and the Knights of his Round Table sleep within the walls of Richmond Castle. They sleep, as did the Sleeping Beauty of the fairy tale. But they are not destined to wake at the summons of a love-smitten prince: rather, they will rise when the clarion call comes to save England's soul. Maybe the day and hour are nearer than some of us are willing to believe.

Farther inland in this third segment, with the soaring mass of Rogan's Seat ahead of you, you can travel leisurely up Swale Dale, by way of a farmstead that was formerly an establishment for nuns, shown on the map as Marrick Priory. From this a flight of some four hundred slabs of stone, all placed in position with infinite toil by the nuns themselves, will take you (if you have the will and strength) to the tiny hamlet of Marrick, high up on the valley side. The most devout of the nuns are said to have climbed those four hundred steps on their knees. Marrick Moor spreads out beyond the hamlet; on its lower, western slope, at the foot of Arkengarthdale, lies the old lead-miners' township of Reeth. A road climbs steeply and ever more steeply up this dale to Tan Hill; but we shall not be coming to this until later, indeed in the final stage of this clockwise circuit of Rogan's Seat.

Swale Dale, running almost exactly east–west, crosses the third, fourth, and fifth segments, approaching to within some three miles of this focal point on its south-east and southern sides. It is a much

'Green road', above Starbotton

more spectacular dale than Wensleydale, which runs roughly parallel with it some seven or eight miles to the south, on the farther side of Askrigg Common. From Marrick you may make for Leyburn, a market town as busy, and therefore as absorbing, today as it was in the Middle Ages. It possesses a sloping market place reminiscent of that of Richmond, though it is not immediately overlooked by a huge castle. It does, however, lie midway between two lesser castles. These are Bolton Castle, up the dale to the north-west, where Mary, Queen of Scots was once incarcerated, and Middleham Castle, just to the south, where tradition has it that she was recaptured and held only a few hours after she had escaped from Bolton Castle. Neither

Muker village

castle is particularly impressive – certainly not Bolton Castle, on the outskirts of the village of Castle Bolton; but Mary is a figure who always captures the imagination, about whom speculation never tires.

Wensleydale is wider and more welcoming especially in its middle reaches; it never constricts or imposes a sense of claustrophobia, as some would say that Swale Dale does between, say, Muker and Keld. Even its well-known 'force' (from the Scandinavian word *foss*, waterfall) at Aysgarth is kindly-disposed, picturesque, rather than menacing like High Force and Caldron Snout in Upper Teesdale. To High Force we shall come in our final segment, but Caldron Snout lies just beyond the perimeter.

Aysgarth Force is as pleasant and peaceful a spot as any to be found in Wensleydale: a spread of rocks forming a triple succession of dark sills, each lit and given life by the milky-white water that spills over it from the one above; trees line the banks, forming a frame to the running water – a picture, you might say, come alive yet held within bounds. There is the Upper, Middle, and Lower Force; a bridge crosses from one side to the other between two of them; overlooking this is an old, disused water-mill converted, somewhat unexpectedly in view of the remoteness of the site, into a museum of old vehicles, open freely to anyone interested enough to look in.

High above the old mill, set among trees, is the Church of St Andrew. Most of it is of comparatively recent date, but the west tower is largely medieval, its base having survived from the fourteenth century. Christianity came early to the North Country; only five or six years ago a Northumbrian cross head was found inset in the church wall, and it can now be seen by the main door. Inside, the vicar's stall is worth looking at carefully: it was constructed from two poppy-headed bench-ends taken, along with the ornamental screen, from Jervaulx Abbey, some ten miles away to the east, at the time of the Dissolution of the Monasteries.

A few miles up the wide valley from Aysgarth is Bainbridge, a curiously laid out village consisting of a spacious green sloping gently downwards, with cottages lining one side and the Rose and Crown at its foot. If you happen to be thereabouts at nine o'clock in the evening at any time between Michaelmas and Shrovetide you will hear the official Horn Blower sounding his three blasts apiece to each point of the compass, a tradition that dates from the era when shepherds on the surrounding fells relied on this to enable them to get their bearings

Thwaite village

Moorland farmstead

and find their way home after dark. The horn is kept permanently at the inn. Another reminder of an old tradition, less romantic perhaps but equally functional, is the set of stocks in the middle of the green. Unusually, they consist of two slabs of timber fitted into grooved uprights of stone. You will notice that, unusually again, they have only one pair of holes: perhaps vagrants and common felons were comparatively rare in the district, turning up only one at a time. The stocks are known to have been in use as long ago as the days of Elizabeth I.

If, instead of following the Ure (for that is the river's name) up Wensleydale from Middleham Castle and Coverham Abbey and the National Trust property Braithwaite Hall, you have chosen to explore the network of minor roads that run south-westwards from these in the direction of Buckden Pike (in the fourth segment) you will not be disappointed. Take the narrow, uncoloured road along Cover Dale towards Starbotton. This tiny stone hamlet lies on the extreme periphery, at its southernmost point. It is sheltered from the east winds by the mass of Great Whernside. Northwards from it there runs an alluring 'green road', steeply uphill between drystone walls, wriggling its way as though its builders, perhaps two hundred years ago, were almost defeated by the gradient. It is characteristic of the Pennines, and comparable with one that climbs over the fells from near Peak Forest to Castleton, to which we come in another circle.

Soon after leaving Bainbridge we cross into the fifth segment and, still following the Ure through Wensleydale, come to the market town of Hawes. It consists of one long main street (and a narrow side street or two) lined with dark grey stone buildings. On the north side, across a field or two, there is the glint of water. You cross this by a bridge carrying a minor road that twists and turns its way westwards to the village of Hardraw, after which it rejoins the main road, A684. There is space to park your car opposite the Green Dragon and, on payment of a copper or two, you may walk straight through the little inn and make your way along a grassy path which thrusts its way between ever-encroaching rocky cliffs forming a gorge at the end of which, shaped like a tight horseshoe (and somewhat reminiscent, though on a smaller scale, of the horseshoe formation known as Malham Cove, half a dozen miles or so to the south of the southernmost point on the present circle) is Hardraw Force.

It is immensely impressive, especially when the stream which

High Force

feeds the waterfall is in spate, in late autumn when snow has fallen, and in early spring when the snow on the upper slopes has been melting. But even in the summer it is memorable. There is not the sheer volume and weight of water that is so impressive at, for instance, High Force or Caldron Snout, where it seems to be abundant all the year round; but it takes on an ethereal, translucent quality in the summer that imparts to it a fairy-tale quality. There is a narrow (and permanently slippery) pathway round the concave face of the limestone cliff down which the water spills from a height not far short of 100 feet. It is possible to walk along this footpath, scraped out of the rock, sloping outwards and downwards, and too narrow for two people to pass one another on it. A sure foot is necessary; and even the lightest breeze will cause the intrepid passer-by to be sprinkled with spray. As you stand momentarily on the rock path, you look out, back along the narrow but now widening gorge, and see what there is to be seen through a misty veil which imbues it with the element of magic.

From Hardraw Force there is a glorious road, steep and tortuous, that climbs up and over the Buttertubs Pass at 1,726 feet, just to the west of Lovely Seat, which rises to some 500 feet higher still. It is from Lovely Seat, of course, that you obtain the finest view northwards to Rogan's Seat, its near-twin. But even if you do not feel inclined to make your way – on foot, of course – to the summit of Lovely Seat, you still obtain a splendid view of Rogan's Seat from the summit of Buttertubs Pass. You look out across the valley towards its rounded summit. Far down beneath it are the Swale Dale villages, hardly more than two miles apart, of Muker and Thwaite. They are typical dale hamlets: rows of snug stone-built cottages strung out along a road that twists its way through them. In Muker the majority of the modest buildings are all on one side of the curving road, and the tallish church tower stands proud behind them, its clock face looking steadfastly northwards to Rogan's Seat. A mile or two up the valley, where the narrow road has turned northwards, is the even smaller hamlet of Keld, at the foot of West Stonesdale (sixth segment).

Before leaving Buttertubs Pass, whether north- or south-bound, it is well worth while going in search of the 'butter-tub' pot-holes from which the pass derives its name. They are to be found on the west side of the road, but are not visible from the road itself, though there are some curious limestone formations right against the road side that the uninitiated assume to the 'butter-tubs' themselves. In fact, the real ones are to be found a hundred yards and more up the steepish slope, and must be approached over rough, hummocky turf. The map shows the word 'Pot', in association with a ring alongside, at this very spot; this symbol is to be found widely distributed in this carboniferous limestone country – just north of Keld, for instance; again on Stonesdale Moor and Birkdale Common, and throughout Langstrothdale Chase ten miles to the south. This is pot-holers' territory, and there is an even greater proliferation of this characteristic feature well to the south, in the former West Riding, notably in the area surrounding Malham Tarn and Cove. The 'pots' close to the side of the road on Buttertubs Pass are, however, no more than oddly-shaped, steep-sided hollows in the stone, with ferns and stunted trees growing out of them; no pot-holer or caver would accord them a second glance! Why, then, the odd name? It appears that at some time not recorded the suggestion was made that they resemble old-fashioned butter churns; the nickname caught on and became sufficiently recognised to merit insertion on the map.

Beyond the pots on Birkdale Common we pass, in the sixth and seventh segments, into the former Westmorland, leaving the lonely heights for the more sheltered district of the Eden Valley. We come

Tan Hill Inn

(seventh segment) to Kirkby Stephen, one of our older market towns and well worth lingering in, set about by moorland. Do not omit to take a look at the Church of St Stephen, from which saint the little town takes its name. Parts of it actually date back to Anglo-Saxon times, though most of it is in Early English style.

Only four miles north of the town is Brough, a village that lies low at the foot of the surrounding moors. It is a much older place than it may at first appear. It was a settlement in Roman times, during the period in which Hadrian's Wall was being built. As was their wont, the Romans constructed the road that climbs up and over Stainmore Common – no mean achievement even for those enterprising and determined civil engineers eighteen centuries ago. The remains of Brough Castle dominate the village from the natural bluff on which it was built. The ruins, which are well preserved and open to the public, date mainly from the thirteenth and fourteenth centuries; oddly enough, they are more impressive when seen from a distance, from any direction, than when you wander about among them, in the shadow of the high walls.

Brough lies on the junction of our last two segments. In the last of these, the features of greatest interest lie far apart from one another. One is right on the periphery not far from the pot marked just west of Scar End. This is the very famous waterfall known as High Force. It claims to be higher even than the near-100-foot Hardraw. Maybe it is – though it does not look to be so. And in any case, unlike Hardraw, it is not a sheer, unbroken fall but one that is stepped dramatically over more than one massive outcrop of rock. Here the Tees falls with immense power. You approach the falls along a tree-embowered, sloping, hand-railed pathway, picturesque in the extreme. There is no question, here, of passing behind the waterfall: to do so would be to commit certain suicide. It would be hard to find a more perfect contrast than that between Hardraw, at the upper end of Wensleydale, and High Force, in Teesdale; both are memorable, but in wholly different ways; the triple falls at Aysgarth, in Wensleydale, are not in the same league.

Close by the falls the Pennine Way (from Edale in Derbyshire to the Cheviots at Kirk Yetholm) passes out of our present circle, having entered it thirty-five miles to the south on Langstrothdale Chase and serpentined by way of Hardraw, Great Shunner Fell, Sleightholme Moor, and Lune Moor, northwards bound. Oak pointers set low on the ground mark the Way where necessary. One of these pointers is set in the ground at Tan Hill, immediately opposite the porched entrance to the Tan Hill Inn. This is to be located in our final segment, but only three or four miles north-west of Rogan's Seat. It proudly claims to be, at 1,732 feet above sea level, the highest inn in England. The Cat and Fiddle, on Axe Edge just to the north-west of Buxton, is only some twenty-five feet lower – but there is all the difference in the world, the landlord at Tan Hill will tell you, in twenty-five feet! Certainly, in addition to being the highest inn in England, it must be one of the loneliest and most isolated. Standing gaunt, four-square, and unprepossessing on the edge of Arkengarthdale Moor, it may be approached from Keld by the ascent of West Stonesdale, a narrow, steeply-climbing minor road that skirts the western flanks of Rogan's Seat – the focal point of the circle which we have now circumnavigated.

Middleham Castle

Byland Abbey

Blakey Ridge

More than three-quarters of our next circle, based on a viewpoint on Blakey Ridge, constitutes the North Yorkshire Moors, a National Park and designated Area of Outstanding Natural Beauty. Its two north-eastern segments are bounded by the coastline from Robin Hood's Bay to Redcar; apart from Middlesbrough, on its north-western perimeter, there are no towns of any real size. The Cleveland Hills range across the northern half; the Hambleton Hills dominate the south-western quadrant; Wheeldale and Goathland Moors, and Wykeham, Allerston, and Lockton High Moors the eastern quadrant; the gentle Vale of Pickering runs across the southern portion, bounded on the southern perimeter by the relatively modest Howardian Hills.

Two major roads cross the circle from east to west; but the lie of the land generally is such that the minor roads tend to follow the valleys or, in one or two cases, the intervening ridges, in a generally south-east to north-west direction. One such, Blakey Ridge, runs only some eight or nine miles before dipping at either end towards one or more of the innumerable vales so characteristic of this region. They are not major valleys such as those through which the Ure and the Swale run in the Rogan's Seat circle, whose centre lies some fifty miles to the west; even though they bear such names as Rosedale and Staindale, Eskdale and Bransdale, it is becks rather than full-grown rivers that run along them. Many are named even on this small-scale map: Baysdale Beck, Thornton Beck, and Costa Beck, for example.

Though there are higher individual summits on these moors – Stony Ridge, for example, at 1,422 feet, and Botton Head, three miles

N
NW
W
SW
S
Redcar
Marske-by-the-Sea
Saltburn-by-the-Sea
Brotton
Skinningrove
Dormanstown
Kirkleatham
Yearby
New Marske
Grangetown
North Ormsby
Lazenby
Lackenby
Wilton
Upleatham
Middlesbrough
Eston
Park End
Dunsdale
Skelton
Carlin How
Kilton
Loftus
Easington
North Skelton
Ormesby
Guisborough
CLEVELAND
Boosbeck
Lingdale
Stanghow
Liverton
Charlton
Marton
Nunthorpe
Stainton
Thornton
Hemlington
Maltby
Newby
Moorsholm
Scaling
Hutton Lowcross
Gisborough Moor
Newton
Roseberry Topping
Great Ayton
Little Ayton
Tanton
Hilton
Seamer
Stokesley
Tame
Easby
Kildale
Kildale Moor
Commondale
Castleton
Danby
Danby Low Moor
Beacon Hill
Lealholm Moor
Houlsyke
Scaling Res.
Crathorne
Hutton Rudby
Rudby
Enterpen
Battersby
Ainthorpe
Baysdale Beck
Broughton
Kirkby
Great Busby
Ingleby Greenhow
Westerdale
Church House
Street
Carlton
Potto
Faceby
Whorlton
Swainby
Baysdale Moor
Stony Ridge
Westerdale Moor
Danby High Moor
Glaisdale Moor
Egton
East Rounton
Ingleby Arncliffe
Ingleby Cross
Wiske
Urra
Botton Head
Cockayne Ridge
Farndale Moor
Blakey Ridge
Rosedale Moor
Seave Green
Chop Gate
Bransdale Moor
Cockayne
Cleveland Tontine Inn
Osmotherley
Whorlton Moor
Snilesworth Moor
Bilsdale East Moor
Church Houses
Hill Cottages
Thorgill
Rosedale
Rosedale Abbey
Ellerbeck
Thimbleby
Jeater Houses
Grange
Bilsdale West Moor
Fangdale Beck
Low Mill
Bransdale
Kirby Sigston
Over Silton
Nether Silton
Arden Great Moor
Spaunton Moor
Hodge Beck
Hambleton Hills
Leake
Kepwick
Cowesby
Arden Hall
Hawnby
Laskill
Helmsley Moor
Gillamoor
Fadmoor
Wether Cote
Lastingham
Hutton-le-Hole
Spaunton
NORTH YORKSHIRE
Knayton
Upsall
Kirby Knowle
Murton Grange
Old Byland
Carlton
Pockley
Kirkbymoorside
Keldholme
Appleton-le-Moors
Sinnington
Boltby
Felixkirk
Thirlby
Cold Kirby
Rievaulx
Beadlam
Nawton
Welburn
Kirkby Mills
Great Edstone
Wombleton
Scawton
Helmsley
Sutton-under-Whitestonecliffe
Harome
Southfield
Marton
Normanby
Sproxton
Riccal
Oldstead
Kilburn
High Kilburn
Wass
Ampleforth
Ampleforth College
Oswaldkirk
Nunnington
Stonegrave
Muscoates
West Ness
East Ness
Salton
Brawby
Coxwold
Newburgh Priory
Gilling East
Cawton
VALE OF
South Holme
Butterwick
Hovingham
Fryton
Slingsby
Barton-le-Street
Appleton-le-Street
Swinton
Oulston
Yearsley
Coulton
Scackleton
Brandsby
Stearsby
Howardian Hills
Terrington
Ganthorpe
Coneysthorpe
Dove
Seven
Rye
Seph
Leven
Stockton-on-Tees 3 miles
Stockton-on-Tees 6 miles
York 26 miles
Thirsk 1 mile
Scale : 5 miles to 1 inch
17½
15
10
5
0
MILES

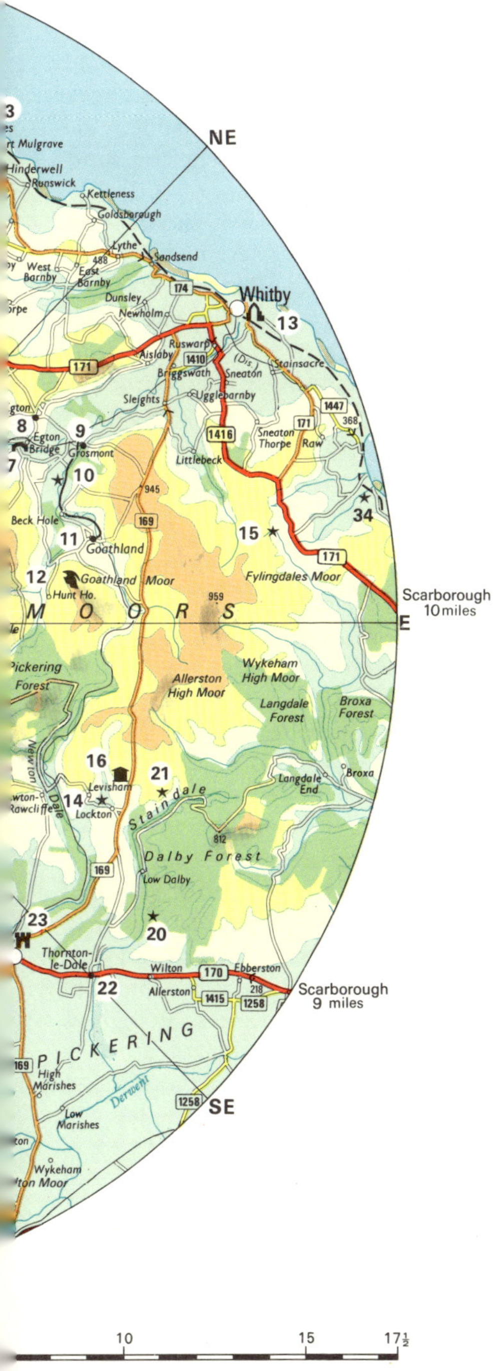

Blakey Ridge

1 Blakey Ridge
2 Boulby Cliff
3 Fishing town of Staithes
4 Beacon Hill
5 Danby
6 Scaling Reservoir
7 Egton Bridge
8 Egton
9 Grosmont
10 Railway route rehabilitated
11 Goathland
12 Roman road
13 Whitby Abbey ruins
14 Lockton High Moor
15 Early-Warning System radomes
16 Saltersgate Inn
17 Rosedale
18 Rosedale Abbey ruins
19 Blacksmith's Arms Inn
20 Thornton Beck
21 Staindale
22 Thornton-le-Dale
23 Pickering Castle
24 Castle Howard
25 Hutton-le-Hole
26 Lastingham village church
27 Duncombe Park
28 Byland Abbey ruins
29 Coxwold
30 Newburgh Priory ruins
31 Rievaulx Abbey ruins
32 Sutton Bank
33 Mount Grace Priory ruins
34 The Cleveland Way
35 Roseberry Topping Rock
36 Guisborough Priory ruins

to the west, higher by sixty feet and more – Blakey Ridge, at 1,256 feet above sea level, has a road and is easily negotiable by car. The point actually selected on it, though not the highest by seventy-odd feet, has been chosen for two good reasons. It is marked by an old (no one can say exactly how old) cross, with a shaft that has been broken in two places and most skilfully repaired; and it offers the finest long-distance view across the moor and down the most beautiful of its dales, Rosedale.

One more general point, which brings us conveniently to the start of our clockwise circuit, segment by segment. A long-distance walkers' route – a newcomer compared with the Pennine Way and Offa's Dyke – has recently been established here: the Cleveland Way. It follows the coastline from Robin Hood's Bay north-westwards, turns inland just short of Saltburn and then, serpentining generally south-westwards and south, skirts the North Yorkshire Moors to end at Helmsley in the fifth segment; almost all that is best in this region is contained within this great loop.

Small coastal villages are strung out like beads, no two of them alike, on this line. Many of them, and of the hamlets inland, bear the suffix 'by' – evidence of their origin as Danish settlements: Whitby is the best known of these names, with Grimsby many miles to the south. Much less well known is Boulby, in the first segment, undistinguished save for its Boulby Cliff which, at over 660 feet, is the highest cliff in England. Only a couple of miles to the south-east is the infinitely more picturesque fishing village of Staithes, North Yorkshire's answer to Cornwall's claim to possess the most picturesque fishing village of all, Port Isaac or Polperro. (You pays your money and takes your choice!)

The approach to Staithes is tortuous and steep; you feel you are plunging into a chasm from which there can be no escape. The cottage-fronts brush against you; a dog's-leg twist in the narrow road at first looks impossible. Then, with the Cod and Lobster inn on your left at the foot of the hill, you emerge at the harbour; it is dominated by a headland that you would be prepared to swear is as high as Boulby Cliff. Staithes is a quiet backwater today; but last century its fishermen could be counted in hundreds (though goodness knows where they were housed). Mackerel formed the main catch, but cod and lobsters too – hence the name of the inn on the water's edge, which has been damaged by high tides and onshore winds time and again, but happily survives, the focal point of the village. Within a

Wayside cross, Blakey Ridge

Staithes Harbour and village

stone's throw of it a lad named James Cook was apprenticed for a while to the grocer; like many lads before and since, he 'ran away to sea'. The move was to bring him fame, if not fortune, for he became one of the greatest sailor-explorers this island has ever produced, comparable with Vasco da Gama and Magellan.

Only ghost-trains run on what was once a busy railway line serving Staithes; a viaduct here, an embankment there, remind the visitor of the problems that faced the engineers who built the line. Again, its opposite number survives in the region of Luxulian in far-away Cornwall. Whitby, ten miles to the south-east, with more natural advantages, in due course took over from the fishermen of Staithes. Unexpected lengths of railway track are to be found inland, disused these many years; we shall see in the second segment how efforts have been made to revive them.

Inland, the moors rise and fall and rise again, attaining 988 feet at Beacon Hill, a superb viewpoint which you can reach from the west by way of Danby without leaving your car. If you are more enterprising (and aware of what moorland walking can entail) you can reach a smooth summit on Danby High Moor at 1,400 feet only five miles to the south; it is the source of three becks, running north, west, and south. Like a jewel in the sombre setting of these moors, and best viewed from Beacon Hill, lies the expanse of water named Scaling Reservoir, in the new county of Cleveland.

South of Beacon Hill flows the Esk, dominated by two craggy heights well known to climbers, though not severe. Following the Esk, we pass into the second segment and come to one of the most charming, intimate sites anywhere in the whole region, Egton Bridge. The hamlet is named from the lovely packhorse bridge that spans the Esk, dappled by the tracery of foliage on the trees that cluster about it; there is something quite magical about its setting. A mile or so to the north is the hamlet of Egton, probably the only place in England that holds an annual August Gooseberry Fair. A mile or two to the east is Grosmont, at the junction of the Esk and a tributary. For younger visitors to these moors, and perhaps no less for their fathers, the village's chief claim to importance is that it is one terminus of the newly rehabilitated North Yorkshire Moors Railway. This is a section of the old track along which passenger coaches are now steam-hauled some three or four enchanting miles along the valley by way of Beck Hole to Goathland. This delightful little railway is open to the public throughout the summer months daily.

Packhorse bridge, Egton

Goathland, a windswept moorland village, is the perfect centre for exploring the eastern part of the North Yorkshire Moors. The famous foss, seventy-foot Mallyan Spout, is easily reached from the village green. More interesting, however, indeed near-unique, is the mile-long section of a Roman road across the moorland two miles south of the village. It was laid there a hundred years before Hadrian built his Wall. Saved from being engulfed by the rough moorland all about it by the Ministry of Public Building and Works, it lies there just as it was laid, camber, drainage, and all; you can walk along it and get the true feel of what its worn stones were like beneath the feet of the legionaries who marched on it nearly two thousand years ago. It is easily approached, at its southern end, by car; the more satisfying approach is over the moors from Goathland to the north. A large-scale map will help, here.

This ancient road, most of which still lies beneath the shaggy turf, is believed to have run from Malton to Whitby, already briefly referred to. Whitby is a town packed with interest. It was a Roman signal-station before Hadrian's day; its abbey had been established for two hundred years before the Danes destroyed it in the ninth century, and it was rebuilt by the Benedictines soon after the Norman Conquest. No abbey ruins in all England are more superbly sited than those of Whitby Abbey, high on East Cliff, dominating the fishing port that lies low at its feet.

One major road spans the third segment, running south–north from Pickering to Whitby, the A169. Nowhere is it more impressive than where it crosses Lockton High Moor, some six miles north of Pickering. To the east are the monstrous 'golf-balls' – the Ministry of Defence's radomes, the dominant features of the Ballistic Missile Early Warning System that have to be seen to be disbelieved. A good view of them is from the famous Saltersgate Inn, or a little to the north of this. Square, uncompromising, the inn stands on the west side of the road just below a treacherous twist in it known (like so many others elsewhere in hilly country) as 'The Devil's Elbow'.

This 'devil', however, was a recluse who lived in the near-by Hole of Horcum. Locally known as 'The Owd Devil', he told the then landlord of the inn that if ever his peat fire went out the building would be destroyed. That was two hundred years ago. The fire has been kept alight ever since, through six generations of ownership. The name of the inn derives from the days of the Salt Tax. Fish caught along this coast was brought here by packhorse and 'salted' in secret with smuggled salt in the stone building that still faces the inn, before being carried on across the moors.

In this same segment a perfect contrast to this road is offered by Rosedale, which runs south-eastwards from Blakey Ridge. Part way along it is the hamlet of Rosedale; but of Rosedale Abbey, built as a Cistercian nunnery in the mid-twelfth century, little remains; Scots from the north ravaged it in the fourteenth century and its ruins were cannibalised for the building of farmhouses and cottages, and even the church. At Hartoft End, overlooking Rosedale, you will come upon the Blacksmith's Arms, once a farmhouse-cum-smithy. Here for generations the horses that hauled wagons along this road to and from the ironstone quarries first exploited seven hundred years ago by the monks from Byland Abbey, and still being worked until last century, came to be shod.

Saltersgate Inn, Lockton High Moor

Rosedale is the most open, indeed the largest, of all these many dales; it is certainly the loveliest of them all, in name and in appearance. From Staindale, to the east in this segment, Thornton Beck runs southwards, down to Thornton-le-Dale, a North Yorkshire 'show village' lying exactly on the boundary-line with the fourth segment. The village has running water channelled along its little streets, passing beneath individual stone bridges leading to the cottages and shops; a green, with a set of stocks; almshouses; all you might hope for. It is a little self-conscious.

And so into the fourth segment to the market town of Pickering. It lies at the junction of two important roads, the A169 northwards-bound for Whitby and the A170 east–west road linking Thirsk with Scarborough. All that is best in this old town lies (or rather tends to climb) on the north side of this road. Here it is terraced, no two of its narrow streets seeming to be either on the same gradient, or parallel

Rosedale, from Blakey Ridge Cross

or at right angles with one another. The stone cottages induce the sense that you have stepped back in time into some period not far removed from the Middle Ages. From almost any point it is easy to see the remains of Pickering Castle. The original castle was built at the time of the Norman Conquest; it was added to and elaborated over the centuries. Much of all this was destroyed by bombardment during the Civil War, but the shell keep still stands finely on its Norman *motte*, over forty feet in height, and there are the remains of the once-impressive curtain-walls.

Even more interesting is the Church of SS Peter and Paul. Its exterior alone declares its medieval origin, but you must go inside to find the feature for which it is virtually unique. The walls of the nave are covered with murals depicting, albeit somewhat crudely, episodes in the lives of the saints. The murals are not particularly beautiful, but they have the unmistakable hallmark of some medieval artist-craftsman – probably an itinerant, one of those who earned a precarious livelihood by tramping through Europe with their brushes and the raw materials from which they mixed their red, yellow, and black paints, seeking commissions here and there. These murals, among the most extensive to be found anywhere in England, have an odd history. They were discovered by chance under whitewash in the middle of last century. The then vicar disliked them, and had them whitewashed over again. A quarter of a century later the discovery was recalled by a parishioner: the vicar at that time was a more enlightened man than his predecessor, and had the whitewash carefully removed. As a result of his wisdom we can gaze our fill today on a surprisingly well-preserved series of murals, the handiwork of a medieval artist whose name will never be known, but who certainly left his brushmark in Pickering.

South of the town the landscape is mostly flat and uninspiring. Malton lies on the extreme periphery, a market town with a part-Norman church and records of Roman occupation a thousand years earlier. Six miles to the west and only just within this circle is the stupendous building, by far the largest in all Yorkshire and among the largest in the country, Castle Howard. It was built by Sir John Vanbrugh; and from that achievement he moved on to the masterpiece at Woodstock, Oxfordshire, for which he will always be remembered: Blenheim Palace. Like Blenheim Palace, Castle Howard is open to the public from Easter to the autumn.

Far, far to the north in this segment, close to Blakey Ridge, is the

Hutton-le-Hole village

moorland hamlet of Hutton-le-Hole. This is a village built seemingly at random on a slope, wide open to the skies, its trim stone cottages separated from one another by streamlets that do not run (as they do at Thornton-le-Dale) in stone channels at the edge of the roads but in deep clefts with rock and grassy banks and bordered by immaculately white painted railings. Small, windswept trees are dotted about the village, casting their shadows across roofs and chimneys; trim swards lie like neat aprons in front of many of the cottages, sloping downwards to the rivulets. There is a village school, an inn and, close to this, the Ryedale Folk Museum, housing exhibits of mainly local interest, but well worth looking at. Then the road divides: one branch continues northwards to Blakey Ridge viewpoint, five miles distant; the other goes eastwards to Lastingham, a smaller, less immediately attractive village, but one well worth visiting all the same.

It has its ancient Church of St Mary, which contains a crypt in which lie the remains of a Saxon bishop named Cedd. He founded a small monastery here in the seventh century; later he was canonised; and for hundreds of years afterwards, even after the Dissolution, this church was a place of pilgrimage to which the pious travelled across these lonely moors, in weather fair or foul, to pay their vows in the hope of attaining grace. Opposite the small, unobtrusive church is another Blacksmith's Arms, on the site of a much older building in which almost certainly these pilgrims sought refreshment and, if their purses allowed, overnight shelter from the sort of weather that can make these open moors so inhospitable and, at times, even frightening.

Between Lastingham and Hutton-le-Hole and the Thirsk–Scarborough road there is pot-holing for the enthusiast, though it is not in the same class as that to be found in the southern section of the circle based on Rogan's Seat. On this road, in the fifth segment, lies the delightful market town of Helmsley. It was built, as so many of these towns were, on a slope; its spacious market place slants downwards to the River Rye from the Black Swan Inn, which is a curious mixture of Georgian and the half-timbering from an earlier age. There is also Helmsley Castle, the oldest portions of which date from the twelfth century. Its most remarkable feature lies in its earthworks, which consist of a deep double moat and intervening banks, all surrounding the curtain-walls and remains of the towers and the keep. It is more impressive than the one at, say, Brough, but does not compare with Richmond. It has no tradition of ghosts; indeed, its garrison surrendered to the troops besieging it during the Civil War rather sooner than was deemed proper by the commanders of other garrisons whose ordeals had been of greater intensity and longer duration. The castle is in keeping with the quietude of this little market town, which in itself gives the impression that nothing very much has ever happened there, or is likely now to happen.

To the south is Duncombe Park, open to the public on one day a week during the summer months; it is one of Sir John Vanbrugh's lesser achievements, at least in comparison with Blenheim and Castle Howard. Beyond it, on the south-westernmost fringe of this Area of Outstanding Natural Beauty, lie the ruins of Byland Abbey. 'Lie' is not really the apt word, for in this low-lying meadowland the masonry of its superb west window and tower soars into the sky challengingly, as memorable as the ruins of Glastonbury, Tintern, or

Coxwold village

Fountains Abbey. Byland, the ruins of a Cistercian foundation dating back to the late twelfth century, has a haunting quality – not least because it appears so unexpectedly in this valley: you run down a hill road that twists its way among close-set trees, skirting Ampleforth with its famous college, and come upon it suddenly. It is best viewed from the small bridge or the slope of the road to the south of this; from here the remains of the huge rose window and the pinnacle that rises against it produce a breathtaking impact.

Two miles farther on is the village of Coxwold, another of Yorkshire's show villages, but less self-conscious than, say, Thornton-le-Dale. Like Milton Abbas in Dorset, it consists of a climbing street with greensward interspersed with cobbled terraces on either side, and two rows of neat stone cottages, with a tree or two here and there to interrupt the horizontal and slanting man-made lines. At the top of the street is the church. Its incumbent, for a while, was Laurence

Sterne, and it was here that he wrote much of his rambling masterpiece, *The Life and Opinions of Tristram Shandy*.

To the south of Coxwold, overlooking a charming expanse of still water, is Newburgh Priory; but after the splendour of Byland (especially when seen with the light of a westering sun illuminating it) you may not feel that it merits more than a passing glance from the road. But Rievaulx Abbey, in this same segment, three miles to the west of Helmsley, is a very different matter indeed. Here, truly, is one of North Yorkshire's most memorable ruined abbeys and priories – and the county seems to possess more than any one other county does. Some connoisseurs maintain that Rievaulx ranks with Fountains and Byland in beauty and 'presence', though different from both.

You come upon it, as on Byland, after descending a twisting, tree-clad road that opens out suddenly into the valley of the Rye. Like Byland, this was a Cistercian foundation; the buildings you see today are more substantial than those at Byland, even if there is no one single feature quite comparable with that soaring, ruined west window. Almost the whole of the buildings were completed before the end of the twelfth century; in its heyday there were nearly a hundred and fifty monks at Rievaulx and more than three times that number of lay brothers in addition. It must have been one of the most flourishing monasteries anywhere in the whole country.

Rievaulx lies (and the word is apt enough here) almost on the boundary-line between the fifth and sixth segments. If you turn due west along the main road (A170) just south of the abbey, you come in a mile or two to a point where it drops with startling suddenness down to the hamlet of Sutton-under-Whitestonecliffe (in the sixth segment). The 'edge' over which the road falls is Sutton Bank, a favourite haunt of glider enthusiasts, comparable with the one on The Long Mynd in Salop, or at Great Hucklow in Derbyshire; here, too, the thermals afford them the necessary lift for their wings.

North-westwards from Rievaulx, between the main road running northwards to Middlesbrough and the Hambleton Hills to the west, is another district of pot-holes; the last sections of the Cleveland Way pass southwards through it, to curve eastwards below Ryedale and come to an end at Helmsley itself. Moorland all about you: parts of it named, such as Arden Great Moor, Bilsdale West and East Moors; dales with becks trickling through them – among which, notably, Seph Beck calls for exploration. And thence northwards again into the last segment but one, with its outcrops on the moors,

Rievaulx Abbey

rocky masses, some of them named, like Botton Head (1,489 feet).

Close to the western periphery of this seventh segment lies Mount Grace Priory. This is one of the nine Carthusian priories established in this country (known also as Charterhouses). In its low-lying unobtrusiveness it is in perfect contrast to the high moorlands, hill tops, and rock eminences that characterise the landscape to the east. These priories were noted for their extreme austerity. The monks lived in silence and total isolation from one another; each had his private cell in which he meditated, and a tiny garden which he cultivated for the good of the community; he even had his own private lavatory. His cell was so designed that he could not, even if he wished, catch even a glimpse of the lay brother who brought him his sparse daily ration of food and water. One cell, and one or two of the ancillary buildings, have been rehabilitated; you can now see, and even more feel, what life must have been like for members of this extraordinarily strict order of monks, who settled here, later than most, in the fourteenth century.

From a point close to Mount Grace Priory the traditional Lyke Wake Walk, eastwards, up and over the moors, a sort of pilgrimage, took place; on a larger-scale map much of its route may still be traced and followed. It crosses the westwards bulge of the Cleveland Way, which in this segment curves north-eastwards over the moors, and among the outcrops of rocks on and northwards of Bransdale Moor. Then, on Westerdale Moor, with its rock summit at 1,409 feet close to the line of Blakey Ridge in the eighth segment, the Way curves north-westwards again over Kildare Moor, skirting more of these rocks, including one that bears the charming name of Roseberry Topping, 1,057 feet above sea level. It is a favourite 'easy climb' for the fairly energetic, approached from the road that runs from Stokesley to Guisborough; from its summit one obtains a fine moorland view, notably to the south and east. Northwards lies industrial Middlesbrough, but in the middle distance is Guisborough, a stone-built market town with a long tradition and, once again, the remains of a noble priory.

Guisborough Priory was founded by the Augustinian Order early in the twelfth century. Largely because it lies within the periphery of the town, which has expanded considerably, it lacks the splendid isolation of priories and abbeys such as Byland, Fountains, and Rievaulx. Nevertheless it is imposing, and its great east front dominates the little town at the top of the climbing main street, thirteenth century in date. There is a gatehouse still standing which is a century or so earlier. Its survival, in relatively good repair, is doubtless due in part to the fact that, like the gatehouses of most monasteries, abbeys, and priories, and castles too, it was massively constructed; being less high and less elaborate in design, it has stood up to wind and weather and the passing of the centuries more successfully than the loftier portions of the priory have done, though this end still stands up proudly. It is perhaps fitting that our circuit of an area based on a natural feature, Blakey Ridge, should end with this noble relic of the handiwork of dedicated men.

Guisborough Priory

Chatsworth House

Mam Tor

Three-quarters of the circle centred upon Blakey Ridge consisted of an Area of Outstanding Natural Beauty. In this next circle, centred upon Mam Tor, in Derbyshire, an even higher proportion of the terrain is similarly designated. Discount the tentacles of Sheffield which encroach upon it from the east, and those of Manchester and Stockport from the north-west, and virtually the whole of this area constitutes the Peak National Park. The contour colouring on this map, not unlike that of the well-known two-miles-to-the-inch maps, consists largely of brown and ever darker brown, representing consistently high ground, even though it may be intersected by relatively low-lying valleys. It is proper to open this section of the book with the warning that north Derbyshire contains some of the most desolate moorland in the whole country, often treacherous, and comparable with the remoter parts of Dartmoor.

This potentially dangerous moorland lies mainly to the immediate north of Mam Tor: The Peak, Kinder Scout, Featherbed Top or Moss; if ever there was a misnomer, here it is! Nevertheless, as the map clearly shows, the terrain is not completely desolate. It is ringed to the north by a major road linking Sheffield with Manchester, the A628; a lesser but still good road, the A57, spans it nearer to the centre, running over Hallam Moors to the Snake Pass and thence to Glossop; two other main roads, the A6 and A623 run north-westwards across its lower portion, from Matlock and Chesterfield, to join at Chapel-en-le-Frith and continue as one north-westwards, crossing the perimeter of the circle beyond Stockport. This is emphasised to make the point at the outset that almost all that is

N
S
W
NW
SW
Huddersfield
9 miles
Oldham
2 miles
Manchester
6 miles
Manchester
2 miles
Altrincham
6 miles
Stoke-on-Trent
26 miles
Knutsford
8 miles
Congleton
4 miles
Leek
6 miles
Leek
2 miles
Ashbourne
6 miles
WEST
YORKSHIRE
GREATER
MANCHESTER
DERBY
HIGH PEAK
HOPE
FOREST
CHESHIRE
STAFFORD
Meltham
Meltham Mills
Netherthong
Holmfirth
Thurstonland
Shepley
New Mill
Scholes
Hepworth
Holmbridge
Austonley
Holme
Upperthong
Wooldale
West Nab
1641
Black Hill
1908
Britland Edge Hill
1717
Hade Edge
Carlecotes
Dunford Bridge
Flouch Inn
Diggle
Dobcross
Saddleworth
Saddleworth
Moor
Grasscroft
Lees
Greenfield
Mossley
Carrbrook
Chew Res.
1762
Woodhead
Crowden
Longdendale
Arnfield Brook
Torside Res.
Ashton under Lyne
Hurst
Stalybridge
Droylsden
Dukinfield
Newton
Audenshaw
Denton
Haughton Green
Hyde
Gee Cross
Hollingworth
Hadfield
Padfield
Mottram
Broadbottom
Glossop
Charlesworth
Chisworth
Chunal
Compstall
Woodley
Bredbury
Romiley
LEVENSHULME
REDDISH
BURNAGE
HEATON
STOCKPORT
HEAVILEY
Cheadle
Marple
Hazel Grove
Hawk Green
Mill Brow
Mellor
Rowarth
Little Hayfield
Hayfield
Thornsett
Birch Vale
Low Leighton
New Mills
Cheadle Hulme
Bramhall
High Lane
Kitts Moss
Poynton
Disley
Newtown
Handforth
Woodford
Dean Row
Adlington
Furness Vale
Buxworth
Whaley Bridge
1213
Chinley
Chinley Head
1480
Slackhall
Chapel-en-le-Frith
Sparrowpit
Sponds Hill
1348
Pott Shrigley
Taxal
Kettleshulme
Lower Crossings
Whiteley Green
Bollin
Kirkleyditch
Prestbury
Bollington
Kerridge
Bollington Cross
Rainow
Brockhouse
Fernilee
Combs
Dove Holes
1662
Black Edge
Tytherington
Macclesfield
Hurdsfield
Broken Cross
Shining Tor
1834
Goyt's Moss
Buxton
Burbage
Macclesfield Forest
Langley
Warren
Sutton Lane Ends
Oakgrove
Shutlingsloe
1659
Wildboarclough
1324
1118
740
Allgreave
Wincle
Danebridge
Flash
Axe Edge
Brand Side
Harpur Hill
Chelmorton
Taddington
Blackwell
Hollinsclough
Earl Sterndale
High Wheeldon 1383
Sparklow
Longnor
Fawfieldhead
Newtown
946
1074
1658
Heaton
Upper Hulme
1603
Sheen
Pilsbury
Brund
Hartington
Warslow
Hulme End
Upper Elkstone
Thorncliff
769
1113
Alstonefield
Heathcote
Biggin
Wolfscote Hill
1272
Newhaven House
Pikehall
1253
Flagg
Monyash
1166
Bleaklow Hill
2060
Howden Moors
Margery Hill
1793
Howden Res.
Derwent Res.
Derwent
Langsett Res.
1785
Featherbed Top
Snake Inn
Mill Hill
1761
Kinder Res.
Kinder Scout
2088
Edale Moor
Edale
1937
Nether Booth
Brown Knoll
1866
Barber Booth
Mam Tor
Castleton
Hope
Aston
Thornhill
Brough
Bradwell
Ladybower Resors.
1523
1280
Noe
Eldon Hill
1543
Peak Forest
Little Hucklow
Windmill
Wheston
Lane Head
Peak Dale
Upper End
1322
Tideswell
Hargatewell
Wormhill
Litton
Miller's Dale
Dane
Scale : 5 miles to 1 inch
17½
15
10
5
0
MILES

Mam Tor

1 Mam Tor
2 Road
3 Reservoirs
4 Abbey Brook
5 River Ashop
6 Hope Forest
7 Vale of Edale
8 River Noe
9 Wigtwizzle
10 Ringinglow
11 Back Tor
12 Ladybower Reservoir
13 Hope Valley
14 Grindleford bridge
15 Froggatt Edge
16 Great Hucklow
17 Riley Graves
18 Eyam
19 Peveril Castle
20 Peak Cavern
21 Winnats Pass
22 Blue John Caverns
23 Chatsworth House
24 River Derwent
25 Edensor
26 River Wye
27 Haddon Hall
28 Miller's Dale
29 Packhorse bridge
30 Litton
31 Sheepwash Bridge
32 Anchor Inn
33 Wildboarclough
34 Cat and Fiddle Inn
35 Pennine Way
36 Nag's Head Inn

best in this beautiful and often spectacular region can be approached without hazard or even difficulty by car. The determined walker will exercise caution if he wants to explore the moors on foot.

The 1,696-foot summit of Mam Tor has been chosen as the viewpoint for several reasons. It can be attained without undue effort from an easily-negotiable road, it offers probably the finest long-distance view that can be obtained anywhere in this whole region. From it you can look westwards along Rushup Edge; north-westwards across the Vale of Edale to Kinder Scout, at 2,088 feet; due northwards to The Peak, whose grouped summits are all just below or just above the 2,000-foot mark; and north-eastwards to the glinting waters of the Ladybower and other reservoirs that have been expertly landscaped in such a way as to trap the waters necessary for large conurbations like Sheffield without materially altering the contours of the moors from which they spring.

Mam Tor is interesting, too, in itself. It is nicknamed 'Shivering Mountain', and the name is apt. Look at its great bulk from the road that skirts it to the north, and you will readily see that it is largely composed of alternating strata of shale and harder grit. Because of this formation it gives the curious illusion – especially in certain light conditions – of being 'on the move'. Nor is this entirely an illusion. From time to time portions of its steeply-sloping surface do literally 'shiver', and miniature, often dangerous, landslides are the result. This phenomenon must have been more than disconcerting to the occupants of the Iron Age camp, the extensive remains of which are to be found almost on its summit.

Do not expect any great area of true forest land, for all that the map indicates Peak Forest to the south of Mam Tor and, in even bolder lettering, Hope Forest to the north. This is not forest country, as ordinarily understood, even if perhaps in remote times trees abounded here; no, this is open, rolling moorland, its seemingly limitless extent often given dimensions, and character too, by the network of drystone walling, mainly of off-white carboniferous limestone, but also of the more sombre gritstone that abounds in such vast quantities in the Pennines that range northwards from Edale and terminate not far short of Hadrian's Wall.

It is time, now, to abandon the general for the particular and to consider the circle based on Mam Tor in detail. The terrain close to the perimeter must largely be ignored, passing as it does through areas lacking in beauty, and gradually becoming engulfed by the

Drystone walling landscape, near Litton

spread of population centres. Happily this cannot now befall the Peak National Park itself.

In the first, north-eastern, segment there are not many minor roads. One small but well-engineered road follows the great expanses of water, both curiously shaped, the Howden and Derwent Reservoirs; fed by interlocking becks, notably Abbey Brook, which enters the Howden Reservoir right on the South Yorkshire–Derbyshire border. This is a small area of scenic beauty sufficiently outstanding, even in an area of general dramatic beauty, to have come under the aegis of the National Trust.

A bigger road, the A57, cuts across this segment only three or four miles from Mam Tor, serpentining its way north-westwards, climbing ceaselessly, with the River Ashop running beside it, but deep down below it and usually out of sight, from its twin sources on Featherbed Top, to skirt the southern end of Ladybower Reservoir and continue on south-eastwards to join the larger Derwent and Wye near Rowsley. The further lengths of this road, in what will be the final segment, beyond the Snake Inn, run through forest land, so that the name Hope Forest does come into its own; alas, however, this is Forestry Commission land: countless acres of regimented conifers, planted in serried ranks, stiff as sentinels in Kendal green, with the regulation broad firebreaks designed to prevent fires from spreading from one battalion to the next.

A much smaller road, one of the pleasantest to be found anywhere among these moors, twists and turns its way across the narrowest part of this first segment within a mile or so of Mam Tor, passing from Hope, in the second segment, by way of Nether Booth to the hamlet of Edale, which we shall come to in the final segment. It follows the curving line of the Vale of Edale, but the stream that waters it is the Noe, with its echo of the medieval Mystery Play, *Noe's Flude*; this runs soon into Hope Valley, a few miles on to the east. With understanding of high moorland walking and its potential hazards you could follow this stream to its source on the slopes of Kinder Scout.

Lying exactly on the boundary-line between the first and second segments, two or three miles inwards from Stocksbridge, is the improbably-named hamlet of Wigtwistle – a name that one feels should come from the diminutive pages of Beatrix Potter. It lies on the eastern edge of Broomhead Moor; to the south of it there is a network of minor roads, some of them skirting more Forestry Commission land, a feature that one is nowadays forced to accept, though the true lover of forests, as in the Chilterns or Hampshire, will never accept them as natural, let alone desirable.

The South Yorkshire–Derbyshire border zigzags across this second segment from Ringinglow north-westwards to Back Tor (1,765 feet). No road follows this, but larger-scale maps indicate a track which could be followed by the experienced walker. Midway between this line and Mam Tor lies the complex of Ladybower Reservoir, perhaps the most beautifully shaped of all our reservoirs. Its designers must have been aware of its potential, for they have established waterside viewpoints where one can park and gaze one's fill at the blue and shimmering water so exquisitely and elaborately framed. At one of these an inscribed plaque records that the Ladybower Dam was inaugurated in 1945 by King George VI.

'Plague Cottage', Eyam

At Ringinglow we pass into the third segment and the environs of Sheffield reach out towards us; Dore and Totley, within living memory no more than isolated villages, are now dormitories for those who work in the city five miles beyond them. So, we turn our backs on them and look inwards at Hathersage, on the A625, and the Hope Valley beyond; at Grindleford and Eyam and Froggatt Edge to the south; and at Castleton, where the segment narrows to a point at the 'Shivering Mountain', Mam Tor.

Hathersage is an overgrown village, its stone-built cottages scattered about the hillside. It has a much-restored fourteenth-century church visited, by the romantically-inclined at any rate, not so much for its famous brasses as for the fact (no Hathersage native calls it mere legend) that the churchyard contains the grave of Little John, Robin Hood's henchman and closest friend. After his master's death, Little John – so named for his great height and girth – left Sherwood Forest and came here to Hathersage, lodged awhile in a widow's cottage, and died beneath her roof. Before dying he took up his bow, long disused, and, summoning up the last of his former great strength, shot an arrow into the air; where it fell, he said, he wished to be buried.

The grave marks the exact spot; a headstone testified to the fact that Little John (whoever he may have been) lies beneath the sod; the grave is lovingly tended by the Ancient Order of Foresters. In the eighteenth century the grave was opened and the skeleton of a man revealed, the thigh-bones of which measured no less than thirty-two inches in length. If it was not Robin Hood's friend, then certainly the skeleton must have been that of a comparable giant.

Hathersage is the 'Morton' of Charlotte Brontë's *Jane Eyre*. The author spent some time here, becoming imbued with its atmosphere and that of the surrounding moors, and made use of this when, two years later, she wrote her novel. Grindleford and its well-known bridge lie just to the south, National Trust property; it was at a point just above the bridge that Jane Eyre was set down by the coachman after she had run away from Thornfield Hall.

The Derwent flows southwards here, spanned by the bridge; to the east of it is the rocky escarpment so typical of this part of Derbyshire, Froggatt Edge. These 'edges' are cliff-like eminences rising with dramatic abruptness, often from relatively low-lying ground. Many of them afford good practice in rock climbing; the higher ones, as at Great Hucklow to the west, are made good use of by gliding enthusiasts. The best time, for the photographer at any rate, to look at Froggatt Edge is when the sun is overhead (not usually the best time to use a camera), for then the deep clefts, some of which resemble promising caves, are cast into strong shadow by the mass of overhanging gritstone.

To the west of Froggatt Edge is the so-called 'Plague Village' of Eyam. The indication that there is something unusual here is the map entry 'Riley Graves'; but the story of Eyam must be generally well known. In 1665 the Great Plague, which was decimating London, reached this hamlet, allegedly in a parcel of clothes from a tailor. The rector, the Revd. William Mompesson, took charge of the situation. He realised that the villagers were doomed; his own wife was among the victims; but by persuading the villagers to isolate themselves from 'the rest of the world' he hoped to spare the in-

Peveril Castle, Castleton

habitants of other Derbyshire villages. He caused a 'curtain-wall' of stones to be laid around the village, and beyond it no Eyam man, woman, or child was to pass. Food was to be brought to one or other of these mark stones and laid there in return for coins deposited in running water. As a result of this action the plague spread no farther, though more and more of the stricken villagers of Eyam died agonising deaths. Within a few months some eighty per cent of them succumbed.

Mompesson held his services throughout, not in the church just behind 'Plague Cottage', allegedly the cottage to which the parcel had been delivered, but in the open air at a spot known as Cucklet Dell. Here, on the last Sunday in August, an annual service is held in honour and remembrance of the self-denying people of Eyam. The churchyard was too small to contain the graves of all who died in that terrible year, though Mompesson's wife and many others were buried there. More were buried beyond the confines of the village to the east, at Riley Graves. Eyam, like Tissington and other Derbyshire villages, is the scene of an annual well-dressing ceremony, held always on the Sunday preceding the Service of Remembrance. Mompesson's Well, as this one is naturally called, is where the parcels of food contributed by villagers spared contamination by the people of Eyam were laid, in exchange for the coins 'sterilised' by being placed under water; the simple belief seems to have proved not unfounded – perhaps by a kindly dispensation of Providence.

Farther in towards the centre of this third segment we come to Castleton, only two miles or so short of Mam Tor. It is a typical Derbyshire dale village of stone-built cottages standing shoulder to shoulder. The Church of St Mary is of Norman origin but has been much restored; it does, however, possess one of the comparatively rare 'Breeches Bibles', with the date 1611 inside. For those primarily interested in church architecture, its outstanding feature is its Norman chancel arch, practically the sole relic of the original building.

More impressive by far is Peveril Castle. Though largely ruined, it nevertheless dominates the village of Castleton, named after it. Standing well back from the main street, the church, and small square, it towers grimly on its huge mound, which you must climb by a tortuous and steep path. Built by Sir William Peveril immediately after the Norman Conquest (he was William the Conqueror's illegitimate son), it was added to by that great builder of castles, Henry II, a

Winnats Pass, near Mam Tor

hundred years later: the great keep is Henry's work. Sir Walter Scott immortalised the castle in his novel *Peveril of the Peak*. As always, its builders had chosen the site with an eye to its natural advantages: it is naturally protected on three sides, and they designed the fourth so that it was virtually impregnable. Its site and appearance fired the imagination of the romantically-inclined Sir Walter.

Castleton is famous not only for its above-ground features but for those unseen save by the determined pot-holer. Within a hundred yards of the village, to the west, is Peak Cavern. Unlike the remote moorland pot-holes, this has a huge, gaping entrance into which the non-spelaeologist can enter with ease. Water flows by, and it is not until you have covered quite a distance between its enclosing walls and lowering roof that you begin to recognise Peak Cavern's potential. Dedicated pot-holers have penetrated far into its bowels; they believe that one of the labyrinthine passages that branch eastwards may

Packhorse bridge, near Bakewell

connect with the subterranean portions of Peveril Castle itself. But today's pot-holer is by no means the first to enter. Centuries ago when, after the departure of the Romans, this part of England became increasingly subject to forays from the north, this was a place of refuge for the population of the whole district; the smoke from the fires they lit to warm themselves and cook their food may be seen on the blackened rock ceilings of some of the side chambers.

The cavern has inevitably become somewhat commercialised. Its main great chambers have been dubbed: The Devil's Cavern; Bell House; Roger's Rain House (in which water continuously seeps through the roof); Orchestra Chamber – sometimes the setting for various types of concert today. You can imagine the reverberating effects!

A few hundred yards farther on, beneath the very shadow of Mam Tor, just short of Winnats (or Wind-Gates) Pass, there is another complex of caverns that should not be missed. One of these is Speedwell Cavern, first hewn out by the eighteenth-century lead-miners in search of the precious ore that was already known to the Romans. The route they cut is now filled with water, and you make the journey not on foot but by boat. The climax is reached when the boat comes to a stop and the silence is broken only by the sound of water falling into a hollow deep down and completely out of sight and known, inevitably, as 'The Bottomless Pit'.

There are other caverns near by, strongly commercialised. Notable among them are the Treak (or Tray) Cliff and the Blue John Caverns. They are set at the foot and the top of Treak Cliff, to the east of Mam Tor and Winnats Pass. It is from the Blue John Caverns that the unique Blue John stone has been quarried for centuries: a crystalline spar, mainly amethystine in hue, found nowhere else in the world, its best specimens being virtually priceless. The Romans sent great blocks of it home for Italian sculptors to shape into ornamental vases, bowls, and urns. If Pliny is to be believed (and he was a romancer, as well as a historian), the Emperor Nero coveted one such vase so greatly that he paid the equivalent of, by today's values, £250,000 for it. At Treak Cavern you can today buy souvenirs in almost every conceivable design, made out of small, relatively valueless (but still beautiful) fragments of this spar. An 'egg' of Blue John (the words are a corruption of the French term *bleu-jaune*) is one of the author's most valued minor possessions, obtained some forty years ago and suitably mounted on a small wooden ring he created for it. Some of

Sheepwash Bridge, Ashford-in-the-Water

the finest specimens in the world are to be found at the Vatican, including possibly the very vase for which Nero paid so impressive a sum.

The finest specimens of worked Blue John in England are to be found at Chatsworth House, ten miles from Mam Tor and almost on the border-line between the third and fourth segments. Exteriorly at least, its main fabric a dingy brownish-grey, this is by no means among the most beautiful of England's great houses, though it is beautifully sited in its own spacious parkland to the south of the picturesque village of Baslow. The Derwent flows through its grounds close to the house, which has for generations been the country seat of the Dukes of Devonshire. Water, indeed, is its key-note. Thanks to the imagination of the sixth Duke and his friend and adviser Joseph Paxton (who was later to design the Crystal Palace), cascades of water, ornamental pools, and ornate waterfalls abound;

a fountain jets nearly 300 feet into the air, its explosive force generated entirely by the head of water developed in the rocks behind and above it. The water dominates the scene, and to some extent mitigates the austere aspect of the house. It is open to the public from early April until the end of September, easily approached by a parkland road. An odd (and revealing) fact is that an earlier Duke of Devonshire caused the entire village of Edensor to be removed from its site to another, so that it could not 'offend the eyes' of distinguished guests, and himself, in his palatial residence.

Over the border into the fourth segment, on the bank of the Wye just above its confluence with the Derwent a mile or two south of Bakewell, is Haddon Hall. It is lovelier by far than ever Chatsworth House could be, and older by a great deal. What you see today when you have crossed the 300-year-old bridge is an Elizabethan manor house, within a containing wall which itself dates back to the twelfth century. In fact, the earliest building work here was done by that same William Peveril who built the fortress at Castleton, and if you know how and where to look for them, the remains are still to be seen. The outstanding feature here is the Banqueting Hall, with its fifteenth-century tapestries; much of the place remains furnished as it was in its heyday four hundred years ago. It is one of the most romantic of our great houses; the story of Dorothy Vernon of Haddon Hall is one of the great *true* love stories of all time. It has been for generations the country seat of the Dukes of Rutland; like Chatsworth, it is open to the public from April to September.

Westwards through the remainder of this fourth segment and well into the next lie the Derbyshire Dales, of which Monsal and Miller's are the best known, though there are others – lesser, remoter – that call for exploration. To reach them you should go to Bakewell, whence a complex of minor roads turn westwards off the A6 to take you to them. Before branching off along them, however, have a look at the packhorse bridge just beyond Bakewell; it is an unusually fine specimen of the type, having no fewer than seven arches, with cutwaters on the upstream side, in strong contrast with, say, the single-span Egton Bridge over the Esk among the North Yorkshire Moors.

To obtain the best among the Derbyshire Dales you really need the walkers' one-inch Ordnance Survey map, or its slightly larger-scale modern counterpart. Tiny hamlets abound: Monyash, Little Longstone, Hassop, Litton, and Flagg, for example; typical of the

Anchor Inn, near Tideswell

county in their off-white, stone-built, close-set cottages occupying hollows among the open moors and usually watered by one or other of the many streams that flow through these dales. If one of the meandering roads should lead you back to the A6 again, a few miles beyond Bakewell, do not omit to explore the unusually charming village of Ashford-in-the-Water. It is well named, for the Wye twists and turns its way through it, passing as it does so beneath no fewer than three bridges, one of which is the lovely Sheepwash Bridge; the origin of its name becomes apparent as you look over its parapet at the drystone pound on the river bank nearest to the road.

Farther northwards in this fourth segment you will come to Tideswell, with its huge church, popularly known as the Cathedral of the Peak. It is so large, especially in relation to the size of the community it serves, that it has been estimated that if every recess and every buttress along its walls is taken into account it measures a mile, no no less, in girth. The two villages of Great and Little Hucklow lie beneath the 'edge' from which the gliders operate, making use of the capricious thermals, four or five miles to the north. Between them and Tideswell, at the crossing of the A623 and a lesser road at Lane Head, you will come upon the Anchor Inn. It is so named, the story goes, because a sailor, tired of serving before the mast, jumped ship one day and walked inland till he reached this spot, which he considered to be roughly equidistant from the Irish and the North Seas, and there 'dropped anchor' for the last time.

The western half of this circle does not deserve such ample treatment as the eastern side. The dales continue on into the fifth segment, down which the boundary-line with Staffordshire meanders, as the South Yorkshire–Derbyshire border does twenty miles to the east. Axe Edge cuts across this from the south towards Buxton, to branch away westwards skirting Wildboarclough (and there's an evocative name for you!); on it lies Tan Hill Inn's closest rival, the Cat and Fiddle, at 1,707 feet, almost exactly on the line between the fifth and sixth segments. Shining Tor (1,834 feet) – a misnomer indeed – dominates the wild and rolling moorland hereabouts (sixth segment).

Then you descend into the sliver of country which, as you see at a glance from the map, is excluded from the Area of Outstanding Natural Beauty. Whaley Bridge is there, and Chapel-en-le-Frith (less attractive than its name suggests), where the brake-linings that restrain your car on these steep slopes may well have been made. And so on, up and over by way of the seventh segment to Hayfield, on the western slope of Kinder Scout, and to Glossop, in the last segment at the crossroads of the A624 and the A57. Manchester's environs loom near. You skirt them, to reach the sinuous expanse of Longdendale Reservoir, which accepts the waters of the innumerable becks that flow ceaselessly down off the moors from all directions. If you are a true walker, you may well choose to walk northwards out of this final segment along the Pennine Way, first and finest of our long-distance routes. It leaves the segment just to the east of the rock summit shown on the map as West Nab, 1,641 feet above sea level; its beginning is at the Nag's Head Inn, Edale, within a long stone's throw of Mam Tor, 'Shivering Mountain', our viewpoint.

Haddon Hall

The Wrekin

Barely thirty-five miles separates the north-eastern perimeter of this circle from the south-western perimeter of that based on Mam Tor, but it would be hard to find any two adjacent circles more contrasted. Almost all of the Derbyshire area was high moorland; north Salop (formerly Shropshire) is low-lying, flattish terrain and not until the south-western quadrant is reached do you come to high ground. There is, however, one exception: our viewpoint, The Wrekin.

Though in fact it is not Salop's highest point, it gives the immediate impression of being so; this is because the terrain all about it is in such strong contrast. From its summit, at 1,334 feet, on a clear day you can see to the north-east Kinder Scout, 100 miles distant as the crow flies; to the north-west you can descry the summit of Snowdon, 120 miles distant; looking to the horizon full circle, your eye covers part at any rate of no fewer than seventeen counties. No other viewpoint in all England can match these figures.

In geological terms, The Wrekin ranks among our most ancient formations: pre-Cambrian volcanic rock considerably more than 500 million years old. From the south-west, seen from the track leading to The Long Mynd, it gives the impression of being a cone or pyramid. This is because, in common with the other high ground in the southern part of Salop, the general lie of the land here is on a south-west to north-east axis – The Wrekin is in fact a ridge-like formation with this same major axis, appearing foreshortened from this angle. It is deceptively gentle in outline, even from close up. Climb to the summit, however – which you may do without great effort along a number of tracks – and you will come to rock formations standing

Wenlock Priory

Whitchurch 4 miles
N
Market Drayton
Llangollen 20 miles
Welshpool 9 miles
Ludlow 10 miles
NW
W
SW
S
SALOP
Shrewsbury
Wellington
Wem
Prees
Baschurch
Pontesbury
Church Stretton
Much Wenlock
Broseley
Bayston Hill
Meole Brace
Frankwell
Harlescott
Shawbury
Hodnet
Longslow
Moreton Say
Longford
Almington
Bletchley
Darliston
Faulsgreen
Ternhill
Edstaston
Pressgreen
Sutton
Rosehill
Newtown
Lowe
Wollerton
Marchamley
Wistanswick
Loppington
Tilley
Aston
Weston
Millgreen
Noneley
Hopton
Stoke upon Tern
Petton
Burlton
Lee Brockhurst
Preston Brockhurst
Booley
Ollerton
Hinstock
Child's Ercall
Weston Lullingfields
Alderton
Clive
Grinshill
Stanton upon Hine Heath
Moreton Corbet
High Hatton
Peplow
Myddle
Eyton
Harmerhill
Eaton upon Tern
Ellerdine Heath
Brownhill
Walford
Merrington
Edgebolton
Muckleton
Great Bolas
Prescott
Little Ness
Walford Heath
Preston Gubbals
Hadnall
Cold Hatton
Cherrington
Tibberton
Great Wytheford
Rowton
Waters Upton
Nesscliffe
Great Ness
Yeaton
Bomere Heath
Astley
Grafton
Leaton
Albrighton
Poynton Green
Walton
Grudgington
Sleap
Pentre
Felton Butler
Ensdon
Fitz
Roden
High Ercall
Kynnersley
Longdon upon Tern
Sleapford
Eyton upon the Weald Moors
Shrawardine
Forton
Montford Bridge
Bicton
Montford
Rodington
Marsh Green
Alberbury
Ford
Uffington
Withington
Admaston
Donnington
Trench
Shelton
Upton Magna
Wrockwardine
Hadley
Cardeston
Stretton Heath
Walcot
Ketley
Yockleton
Nox
Weeping Cross
Arleston
Cluddley
Oldpark
Westbury
Crockmeole
Nobold
Great Hanwood
Norton
Stoney Stretton
Edge
Lea
Rushton
Farley
Hinton
Annscroft
Upper Pulley
Wroxeter
Horsehay
Westley
Asterley
Pulley
Pleaaley
Cross Houses
Longwood
Little Wenlock
Longden
Berrington
Eaton Constantine
Leighton
Dawley Magna
Condover
Coalbrookdale
Stapleton
Cound
Wrentnall
Ryton
Pitchford
Golding
Cressage
Sheinton
Iron Bridge
Ploxgreen
Habberley
Dorrington
Acton Pigott
Snailbeach
Castle Pulverbatch
Church Pulverbatch
Acton Burnell
Homer
Wyke
Longnor
Frodesley
Kenley
Harley
Barrow
Ruckley
Willey
Pickescott
Woolstaston
Leebotwood
Church Preen
Hughley
Ratlinghope
Plaish
Presthope
Bridges
All Stretton
Enchmarsh
Cardington
Gretton
Eastshope
Haughton
Wall under Heywood
Brockton
Aston Eyre
Tasley
Morville
Hope Bowdler
Weston
Monkhopton
Shipton
Little Stretton
Rushbury
Upton Cressett
Minton
Ticklerton
Stanton Long
Chetton
Hatton
Broadstone
Middleton Priors
Acton Scott
Eaton
Holdgate
Ditton Priors
Ape Dale
Wenlock Edge
Harton
Middlehope
Munslow
Tugford
Neenton
Middleton Scriven
Henley
Felhampton
Munslow Aston
Cleobury North
Abdon
Sidbury
Upper Heath
Westhope
Diddlebury
Burwarton
Corfton
Bouldon
Clee St. Margaret
Aston Botterell
Red Brook
Peaton
Stottesdon
Great Sutton
Corve
Stoke St. Milborough
Loughton
Weston Hill
Farlow
Oreton
Roden
Tern
Severn
Cound Brook
Mor Brook
Scale : 5 miles to 1 inch
17½
15
10
5
0
MILES

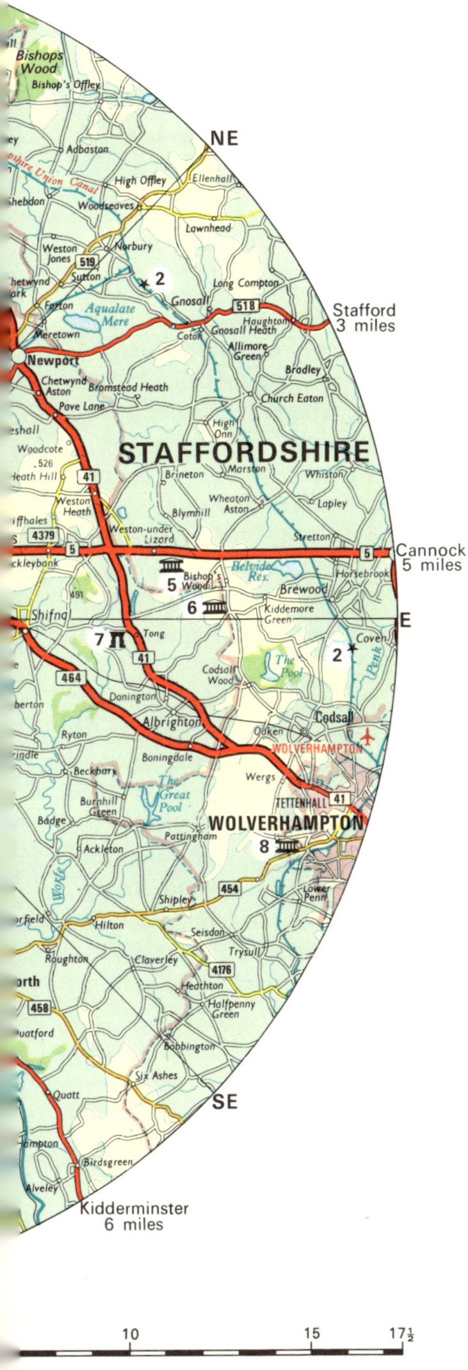

The Wrekin

1 The Wrekin
2 Shropshire Union Canal
3 River Tern
4 Edgemond
5 Weston Park
6 Boscobel House
7 18th-century 'folly' at Tong
8 Wightwick Manor
9 Coalbrookdale
10 Ironbridge
11 Benthall Hall
12 Buildwas Abbey ruins
13 Wenlock Priory ruins
14 Guildhall, Much Wenlock
15 Corve Dale
16 Wenlock Edge
17 Hughley
18 Wilderhope Manor
19 Shipton Hall
20 The White House, Munslow Aston
21 The Long Mynd
22 Carding Mill Valley
23 East Onny river and valley
24 Stiperstones
25 Ratlinghope
26 The Edge
27 Rock near Pontesbury
28 Acton Burnell
29 Uriconium
30 Atcham bridge
31 Shrewsbury
32 Haughmond Abbey ruins
33 High Ercall
34 Myddle
35 Wem
36 Hodnet Hall

clear of the turf and bearing impressive names: The Gate of Hell; The Needle's Eye; The Raven's Bowl. The last of these is the true summit. The legends surrounding them are innumerable. Here you will find, if you know where and how to look, relics of an Iron Age settlement. Though you will find no relics of a much later historic event, it is interesting to know that from the summit of The Wrekin there flared, in 1588, a beacon warning of the Spanish Armada's approach.

Apart from the A5 – substantially the Romans' Watling Street – which crosses the circle from just north of Wolverhampton on the eastern periphery to Shrewsbury near the western periphery, a number of other major roads such as the A41 and the A49 give easy access to the area from many points of the compass. More interesting and certainly more beautiful than these communication-lines is the Shropshire Union Canal, which enters the first segment just north of Market Drayton and leaves the third segment at Wolverhampton. Whether you travel along it by boat or are content to wander at will along its towpath, crossing its many small bridges and lingering at the locks, it offers you a welcome feature only rarely to be met with in any of the viewpoint areas in this book. It forms just part of a complex of canals with which the name of Thomas Telford will be for ever associated. One of the branch canals of this system curves round barely five miles from The Wrekin.

Though generally speaking it is the rural scene rather than the town that is discussed in these pages, an exception must be made for Market Drayton, in the first segment. It is a small market town of unusual quality which was granted its Charter by Edward I, so that its market has been in existence for some 700 years; it still takes place every Wednesday, in the High Street. Not far from it is the grammar school, founded thirty years before that beacon was lit on the summit of The Wrekin. Here Clive of India went to school, and the desk may still be seen on which he carved his initials. But he made a name for himself many years before his association with India, for as a young schoolboy he climbed the tower of the fourteenth-century Church of St Mary and sat in triumph astride one of its gargoyles.

South of the town there are many scattered hamlets, accessible by a network of minor roads, some in the shallow valley of the Tern and its tributaries. Few of them possess any specific notable feature, but they possess one in common: the russet sandstone of which church and cottage, farm and walls are built, a colour particularly easy on the eye. It is the picture that is painted by these small congeries of modest buildings in russet-red that creates the dominant impression of a serenely warm composition. Among them perhaps Edgemond, to the west of Newport, calls for special mention. The fifteenth-century embattled and pinnacled tower of St Peter's soars above the Old Rectory on its outskirts; not far from these will be found the Provost's House, antedating the church by a hundred years, and in itself an interesting example of a small manor house complete with great hall, solarium, and private chapel. The warm, mellow stone-work charms the eye; even the nineteenth-century additions blend reasonably well with the original.

A branch of the Shropshire Union Canal marks the boundary with the second segment; Newport, another market town, and one notable for the generous breadth of its main street, lies just beyond. One of Salop's few stretches of open water, apart from rivers and canals, lies just to the east: aptly named Aqualate Mere, it is, so far as the writer knows, the only piece of water in England to bear a name that includes the Latin word *aqua*. Beyond it is the long reach of the canal, which will be taken by many as the eastward limit of their peregrinations, for Wolverhampton and Stafford lie on and immediately beyond this part of the perimeter.

Almost on the A5, midway between the perimeter and The Wrekin, is the imposing mass of Weston Park, country seat of the Earl of Bradford, and open most days of the week from April to the end of September. It does not rank among our oldest great houses, for it dates only from the late seventeenth century; but it deservedly claims to be among the finest examples of Restoration-style houses. The so-called Marble Room, the Tapestry Room with its magnificent examples of the craftsmanship of the Gobelin weavers, and the gallery of paintings by such artists as Gainsborough, Holbein, and Van Dyck, are among the treasures to be admired within its walls; but it could be that the strongest impression will be made on the visitor by the beauty of the parkland in which the house is so beautifully sited, the work of 'Capability' Brown.

Some three miles to the south-east of Weston, on the boundary-line between the second and third segments, lies Boscobel House. Dating from somewhat earlier in the same century, it is famous primarily as the house in which Charles II first took refuge from the Parliamentarians after his defeat at the Battle of Worcester in September 1651. It is open to the public daily, all the year round, and

Weston Park, Salop

you will be shown one of the many built-in hiding-places in which the unhappy monarch secreted himself; you will see also an oak tree in the grounds, successor to the oak in which Charles sought refuge while Cromwell's men searched both house and grounds.

Just over the boundary-line, on the A41, is the hamlet of Tong. Its disproportionately large church is jocularly called 'The Village Westminster Abbey'. It dates back to 1410, but prior to this Lady Pembruge had founded a chantry college for 'Four Preests, Two Clerks and Thirteen Poore Peeple'. Here, three and a half centuries later, one George Durant – whose family motto was a pun, *Beati Qui Durant,* or 'Blessed are the Enduring (Durants)' – an eccentric who established his own private hermit in a cell especially designed for him, built, among other 'follies', the curious, ugly Egyptian Aviary, a pyramid-like structure that has to be seen to be believed. It stands at the end of a farm approach-lane, visible from a minor road branching westwards off the A41.

There are few villages of special interest in the outer portions of this third segment; the tentacles of Wolverhampton reach uncomfortably close to it. But near as it is to that town, Wightwick Manor should not be overlooked. What Brantwood, in the Lake District, is to devotees of John Ruskin, Wightwick Manor is to devotees of William Morris. With its massive half-timbering and leaded windows, its great gables and ornate chimney-stacks, you might feel perfectly justified in assuming it to be Tudor or Jacobean; but you would be very wrong! In fact the house was built a good deal less than a century ago, for one Mander, a name borne to this day by a well-known firm of paint manufacturers. Ignore, if you wish, the pseudo-Jacobean exterior; but do not ignore the quintessential William Morris interior. Timberwork, plasterwork, tapestries, furnishings, wallpapers, tiles, paintings and drawings: all these are examples of Morris-created, or at least Morris-inspired, art and craftsmanship and, in general, the work of the Pre-Raphaelites. As National Trust property it is secure for all time.

The Staffordshire and Worcester Canal runs into and out of this third segment, close to its perimeter; a welter of minor roads, intersecting and linking unremarkable hamlets like those in the first segment, can be ignored. You will do better, now, to turn in towards The Wrekin, for here is terrain infinitely more rewarding. It straddles the boundary-line between the third and fourth segments. The stripling Severn, originally known hereabouts as Coldbrook, runs

Egyptian Aviary, Tong

southwards through Coalbrookdale to the Bristol Channel; here, for some distance, through a gorge whose sides reach upwards a couple of hundred feet or so above its surface.

Coalbrookdale was once an industrial centre of immense importance. Coalport had its famous potteries, and there are relics of its bottle-kilns to this day, most of them sadly dilapidated, though once they fired the porcelain for which the little town became famous; the name echoes in the minds of those who collect rare porcelain today. Here, too, there were ironworks: it was in Coalbrookdale that Abraham Darby, the first man in England to smelt iron with coke instead of charcoal, operated, and the district claims, not without justification, to be 'the cradle of the iron industry'.

It was the ironmasters Darby and Wilkinson who in 1779 designed and built the world's first cast-iron bridge. It spans the Severn, here in this spectacular gorge, a work of art as well as of craftsmanship in a new medium. The township that stands exactly on the dividing-line between the third and fourth segments, Ironbridge, took its name from this masterpiece of originality and skill, this 'ancient monument' unlike any other in the country. But the most interesting feature of this relatively constricted area is that it is now being skilfully rehabilitated and reconstructed so as to recapture its late-eighteenth-century image. Here, awaiting you, is the Ironbridge Gorge Museum, incorporating the Blists Hill Open Air Museum. Here you may see the gigantic twin beam 'blowing engines' designed to force air into the blast-furnaces then operating at a foundry near Wellington, a few miles to the north. Named Samson and David, they have now been re-erected here, a pair of monsters to delight old and young alike. And they are only two – if the most spectacular – of the many exhibits on display here, exhibits *in situ* very often, laid bare by the picks and shovels and tackle of a band of enthusiasts whose passion is what we have recently come to know as industrial archaeology.

In complete contrast, a mile or so to the west (in the fourth segment) is Benthall Hall, a sixteenth-century stone-built manor house owned by the National Trust, and open to the public three days a week from Easter until the end of September. Outstanding among its features are the immensely tall clustered chimneys, the gables, the mullioned bow-windows rising through two of its three storeys, and the topiary work that sets it off so perfectly.

A little nearer to The Wrekin, in a hollow among low, tree-clad

Wightwick Manor

hills, lie the ruins of Buildwas Abbey. Close by it runs the Severn, not yet confined between the rock walls of the gorge downstream. Perhaps its sheltered position is partly responsible for its excellent state of preservation after more than eight centuries. It contrasts strongly with, say, Whitby Abbey, which has stood for a comparable period, but high on a windswept cliff top, and shows clear signs of the challenge it has had to meet down these same centuries. Buildwas is Norman, and its most impressive feature is its nave, nearly 200 feet long, with huge round pillars and intervening arches. By an unhappy chance it has to endure the presence, all too near, of a multi-chimneyed power station; but that is a fact of life which we are all having to come to accept.

Just over the border-line in the fifth segment, and two or three miles to the south, are the ruins of Wenlock Priory, on the northern fringe of Much Wenlock. Even compared with Buildwas it is ancient, for it was founded as a convent by St Milburga in the seventh century. It was destroyed by the Danes two hundred years later, and piously rebuilt a hundred years after that, on the instructions of Lady Godiva of 'Peeping Tom of Coventry' fame. Yet once more it was destroyed, and yet once more rebuilt; this time as a Cluniac priory at the end of the eleventh century. Today it is largely in ruins, but the ruins are beautifully sited in what resembles more a garden than (as, say, at Glastonbury) a huge monastic precinct. The most impressive feature may well be the massive wall of the chapter house, but the most truly beautiful is the west face of the wall of the north aisle. There is a serenity here matching that of Tintern.

A very different type of structure, this time in the heart of this small town, is the Guildhall. This triple-gabled, half-timbered building is supported on two rows of massive oak pillars, among which for centuries the weekly butter market was held. At the far end is the part-stone-built portion which for some hundreds of years served as a gaol. Above the market hall and gaol are the Court Room and Council Chamber, still in use today. It is recorded that the whole of this extensive upper storey was 'Reared over the Prison House in the Space of Onlie Two Days', in the year 1577. Considering the quality of the workmanship still to be noted after almost exactly four hundred years, quite apart from the sheer size of the structure, it is hard to credit that any number of craftsmen, however skilled and well organised, could have achieved such a feat in so ridiculously short a time.

From Much Wenlock a ridge of high ground runs south-westwards between Ape Dale and Corve Dale; you can follow it, by car or on foot, for nearly ten miles, until it dips down on to the A49 just short of Craven Arms. Tree-lined, gently undulating, with views to either side that offer intimate glimpses of snug farmsteads, spacious meadows, scattered steeples in tiny hamlets, it constitutes one of the most enchanting short-distance ridge walks anywhere in England – a complete antithesis to, for example, Blakey Ridge on the North Yorkshire Moors. You are now in an Area of Outstanding Natural Beauty, even if not extensive enough to be dubbed a National Park.

This is 'Housman country', of course. He wrote of Wenlock Edge and of Hughley church's steeple, hidden on the north side of the

The Guildhall, Much Wenlock

Edge until you come upon it at the foot of a steep, narrow lane. He did not mention the fine specimen of a half-timbered house on the outskirts of Hughley, its massive timbers enclosing exact squares of plasterwork; perhaps built as a small manor house, it is now a farmhouse of distinction. Nor did he write of Wilderhope Manor, at the end of a track that drops off the Edge south-eastwards, making for Corve Dale. This splendidly gabled building of grey stone is poised on a terrace overlooking the River Corve beyond the meadowland that slopes skirtwise from its base. There is a notable cluster of chimneys at one end. Built in 1586, it is rightly National Trust property; but you may be disturbed to find that it is now a Youth Hostel, its vast rooms echoing to the sound of walkers' heavy boots.

Two other houses along Wenlock Edge call for special mention before we cross over into the next segment. The first is only a couple of miles beyond Wilderhope Manor, in Corve Dale. This is Shipton Hall, an Elizabethan manor house of almost exactly the same age. It is notable for two features: the unusual star-shaped chimney-stacks, first and foremost, and its dovecote. This last was a feature of medieval manor houses, and monasteries too, when food 'on the wing' supplemented food 'on the hoof', centuries before the era of the refrigerator and the deep-freezer.

The other, and even more interesting house, is at Munslow Aston, a few miles down the dale and close to the perimeter. Here, at The White House, the owner has been building up over the years a most interesting type of open air museum on a modest scale. She has the initial advantage that the house itself presents a cross-section of architectural development: the site is medieval; there is a dovecote dating from Norman times; the main hall is cruck-built – a style of building relatively rare and always worth more than a casual glance; there is a half-timbered cross-wing whose date has been established as 1570; and there are additions to the main structure manifestly of the more elegant eighteenth century. Inside and out there are well-ordered displays of domestic and agricultural implements in wide variety.

To the north-west, beyond Church Stretton in the sixth segment, is the invigorating highland region covered by the name The Long Mynd. You may reach this afoot by a track that ascends Carding Mill Valley; or you may take the steep and tortuous road alongside the valley. Two, or say three, miles – and you are very literally on top of the world. This is moorland. It does not, as from Rogan's Seat or Mam Tor, extend in all directions to the horizon; nevertheless it offers a strong impression of being limitless. The turf is stretched tightly over pre-Cambrian rock. Here and there the rock breaks through the turf and you have, for example, the spectacular grouping of naked crags five miles to the west on the far side of the valley of the East Onny and right on the periphery, known as the Stiperstones.

The Stiperstones stand at a height of 1,731 feet, 400 feet higher than The Wrekin; but because all the terrain hereabouts is lofty, they do not stand out in the same way as our viewpoint does. To reach them (and they are worth the effort!) you must either strike out boldly, compass in hand, across the moor, or take the narrow road that drops down into the valley at Ratlinghope. This tiny hamlet (locally its name is pronounced 'Ratchup') is set about with relics of prehistoric camp sites. From it you continue on for two or three

Wilderhope Manor, near Wenlock Edge

miles to your objective, right on the perimeter, climbing all the time. There is more than a chance that you will see overhead one or two – or even a covey of – sailplanes which on a good day are catapulted off the 'edge' on The Long Mynd some four miles west of Church Stretton and then perform their leisurely, silent convolutions in the empty sky, returning to base sooner or later according to the degree of co-operation of the thermals and the skill of the pilots.

Locally known as 'The Devil's Chair', this rock mass does not rate the rocks-for-climbing symbol of the cartographer, though parts of it can be testing enough, especially if you arrive breathless after tramping into the wind across the open country. It is, however, spectacular in its own way, resembling a lesser Derbyshire 'edge' that has somehow contrived to fall apart and never since got itself properly reassembled. If you want an upstanding rock that offers more of a challenge, there is one about five miles to the north-east, near Pontesbury, which tops the 1,000-foot mark but, like The Wrekin, appears much higher because it rises from much lower-lying ground.

Before leaving this sixth segment, cross the A49 Shrewsbury road near the excellently thatched Pound Inn and make for Acton Burnell. In this secluded hamlet you will find, unexpectedly, the Castle, considered to be among the oldest fortified houses in England. With its corner towers of the local russet sandstone, though partly ruinous, it has the air of a small manor house; it is older than it looks, having been built in the late thirteenth century by Henry I's chaplain, Robert Burnell. Adjacent, strongly contrasting in its grey stone, is the Early English Church of St Mary, in which you can see one of the comparatively rare Lepers' Windows affording a view of the altar.

Wroxeter lies on the boundary-line with the seventh segment; close to it is Uriconium, a Roman site which was once the fourth-largest Roman town in England, covering an area more than half that of their Londinium itself. Excavation there has been in progress for more than a century, and more and more of its treasures are being revealed. Unhappily, much of what Hadrian had built was later demolished by the Anglo-Saxons and only fragments of its walls are left standing, though the foundations have been uncovered and intelligently displayed and explained, as at Housesteads. Among the major features still in evidence is the great entrance-way of Roman brick and stone that gave access to the all-important *frigidarium*.

Stonework of much more recent date, and of much greater elegance, is to be found two or three miles to the west and close to the A5, which now, fortunately, by-passes it. This is the multi-arched bridge at Atcham designed by John Gwynne of Shrewsbury in 1777. Beautiful in itself, that quality is enhanced not only by the limpid waters of the Severn that glide through its arches, but because its pale stonework is in contrast with the red brick of the Georgian Mytton and Mermaid immediately alongside it, and with the red sandstone Church of St Eata beneath its chestnut trees a hundred yards away.

Westwards of the bridge lies the county town of Shrewsbury, often referred to as the finest Tudor town in all England; here whole days could be spent, something new and appealing discovered with every passing hour. Just beyond its northern outskirts is the site of the

Uriconium Roman site, Wroxeter

John Gwynne's Bridge, Atcham

Battle of Shrewsbury at which, in 1403, Henry IV defeated the rebels led by Harry Hotspur, son of the Earl of Northumberland. Eastwards are the remains of Haughmond Abbey, a twelfth-century Augustinian foundation. Secluded beneath a tree-clad hill, it seems to have escaped the ravaging that befell so many monastic establishments after the Dissolution; much of it has survived and has been used for periods of varying length as a private dwelling. The chapter house, with a fine Norman doorway, contains a display of abbey relics, including a quite charming piece of statuary representing the Virgin Mary and the Child Jesus.

The final segment of this circle, like the first, consists largely of open, low-lying country with many scattered hamlets of no great distinction, though usually charm due to their russet stonework. High Ercall is of historic interest because it was in Ercall Hall that the last Salopian garrison, except that of Ludlow, held out against the Royalists during the Civil War. Myddle's church has an early seventeenth-century tower with an unusual hexagonal clock-face, but its fourteenth-century castle survives only in the form of a delicately-proportioned stair turret, to be approached with care.

Without question, Wem is the most interesting township. It was almost totally destroyed by fire shortly after the Great Fire of London, so that it has few buildings of earlier date. Wem was once wholly owned by Judge Jeffreys of the 'Bloody Assizes' of 1685; he assumed the title Baron of Wem, and spent some time at his house there, Lowe Hall, dated 1666 – the year of the Great Fire of London.

Eastwards of Wem, almost at the limit of this final segment and close to its perimeter, is Hodnet Hall. The Hall itself is not open to the public, but the great glory of the place is the sixty acres of landscaped gardens, open to the public from April until September. The gardens include ornamental waters, and also a seventeenth-century building in which you can not only obtain refreshments but also look at a notable display of Big Game trophies. For lovers of fine trees and exotic and other plants and shrubs in profusion perfectly tended, Hodnet could well prove the most rewarding feature of this northern quadrant of the circle based on our viewpoint, The Wrekin.

David and Samson

Charlecote Park

Broadway Tower

Broadway Tower stands on Fish Hill, a summit 1,048 feet above sea level three miles to the south of Broadway village, in the 'tongue' of the new county of Hereford and Worcester that probes into Gloucestershire. It can be approached within a hundred yards by road; a field path leads to it; a climb of seventy-five steps up one of the spiralling flights contained in two of its four corner turrets will bring you to its battlemented roof, sixty feet above ground. Built as a 'folly' towards the close of the eighteenth century, it affords a view over almost as many counties as may be seen from The Wrekin. The figure usually quoted is thirteen; now that there is the new county of Avon maybe it is fourteen, but with recent changes in county boundaries across the Welsh Border perhaps neither of these figures is today correct.

But who cares? Suffice it that on a clear day the view from the top of the tower is breathtaking, especially to the north, across the Vale of Evesham, and to the west, where the valley of the Severn, the Vale of Gloucester, permits an extensive view into Wales, with the Black Mountains on the horizon a hundred miles distant. Did the old lady named Mrs Hollingsworth, who lived here as caretaker until as recently as 1972, bringing up her family on these three floors, relish that view? If all the stone steps she must have climbed during her occupancy were added together they will surely entitle her, eventually, to the threshold of Heaven!

Near the boundary of the first segment the River Alne flows in across the perimeter west of Little and Great Alne. In the latter you will find the flower-basket-hung inn, Mother Huff's Cap: its sign-

N
S
W
NW
SW
Redditch 3 miles
Birmingham 19 miles
Birmingham 17 miles
Worcester 4 miles
Worcester 4 miles
Birmingham 33 miles
Worcester 6 miles
Ross-on-Wye 18 miles
Gloucester 3 miles
Gloucester 3 miles
Bristol 38 miles
Stroud 8 miles
Cirencester 8 miles
Cirencester 4 miles
HEREFORD & WORCESTER
VALE OF EVESHAM
GLOUCESTER
Alcester
Evesham
Pershore
Tewkesbury
Cheltenham
Winchcombe
Broadway
Chipping Campden
Bidford-on-Avon
Prestbury
Andoversford
Cleeve Common
Chedworth Woods
Bishop's Cleeve
Inkberrow
Coughton
Upton upon Severn
Mickleton
Northleach
Scale : 5 miles to 1 inch
17½
15
10
5
0
MILES

Broadway Tower

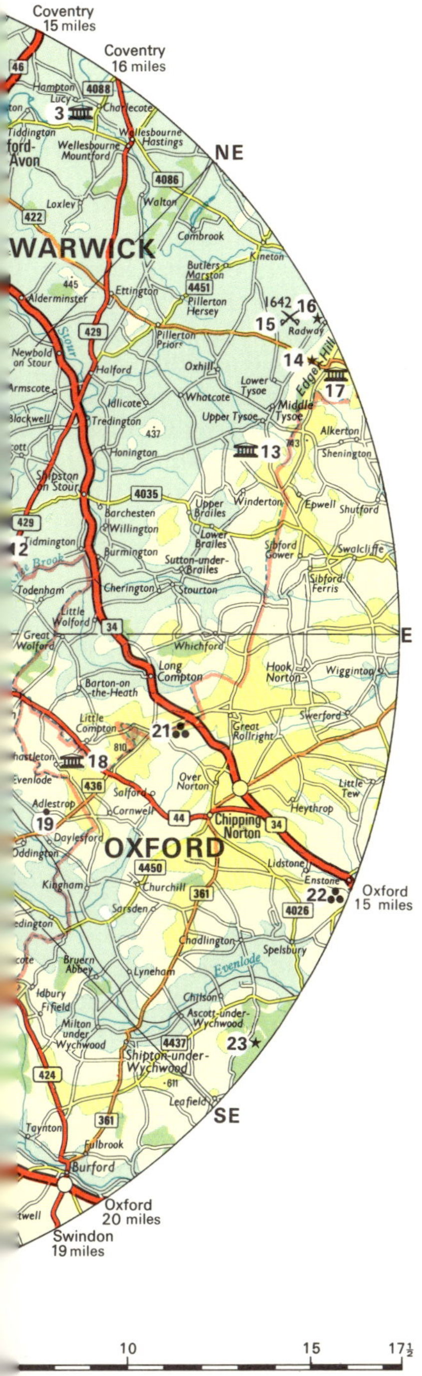

1 ❋ Broadway Tower
2 ★ River Alne
3 🏛 Charlecote Park
4 • Welford-on-Avon
5 ☗ Upper Quinton
6 ❋ Meon Hill
7 ✺ Hidcote Manor Gardens
8 • Weston Subedge
9 ★ Coachman's signpost
10 • Blockley
11 • Ebrington
12 • Stretton on Fosse
13 🏛 Compton Wynyates
14 ★ Edge Hill
15 ⚔ Battle of Edgehill
16 ★ Radway Tower
17 🏛 Upton House
18 🏛 Chastleton House
19 • Adlestrop
20 🏆 Evenlode
21 ♣ Rollright Stones
22 ♣ Enstone
23 ★ Wychwood Forest
24 ★ Fosse Way
25 ★ Arlington Mill, Bibury
26 ◗ Roman Villa
27 ★ Devil's Chimney
28 ❋ Cleeve Hill
29 ★ Belas Knap long barrow
30 ♜ Sudeley Castle
31 ∩ Hailes Abbey
32 🏆 Snowshill Manor
33 ❋ Bredon Hill
34 ☗ Bull Inn, Inkberrow
35 🏛 Ragley Hall
36 🏛 Coughton Court

board depicts a buxom lady with a foaming tankard in hand, and a doggerel verse tells you all about her and her famous brew. Like so much of Warwickshire, this corner is filled with fine examples of half-timbered buildings large and small, private and public. An admirable specimen of the latter is the Bull's Head at Wootton Wawen, just beyond Little Alne, but a few hundred yards outside the perimeter.

One place-name in this first segment stands out head and shoulders above all the others in the whole circle, and even farther afield: Stratford-upon-Avon is the first place to which the overseas visitor goes when he has seen the sights of London. To describe it here would be a gesture of supererogation, so it will be deliberately ignored. A novel approach to it, however, would be along the canal that shares its name and enters it from the north, having wisely left Birmingham far behind; it joins the River Avon in the town; the river continues placidly on its way westwards to Evesham, then southwards by way of Tewkesbury, to pass out of our circle at its junction with the Severn five miles north of Gloucester, having spanned just half of the circle.

Between Stratford and the perimeter north-eastwards lies Charlecote Park. According to tradition it was in this park that the young Shakespeare was arrested for poaching deer – the remote ancestors, perhaps, of those grazing in our photograph. Behind them rises the beautiful Elizabethan house, Charlecote Hall, home of the Lucy family for 800 years. House and park are open to the public most days of the week from April until October. The adjacent village of Hampton Lucy perpetuates the name of this ancient family. It is here that the stripling Avon enters the circle, with only five miles to flow before it passes beneath the fourteen-arched, fifteenth-century Clopton Bridge and on beneath the walls of the Royal Shakespeare Theatre at Stratford.

Part of the lovely Vale of Evesham lies in this segment, near the boundary between Warwickshire and Gloucestershire, the county that occupies the greater part of this circle, emphatically an area of outstanding natural beauty. Where the Avon loops close to the A439 road linking Stratford with Cheltenham lies the miraculously unspoiled village of Welford-on-Avon. Perhaps its chief claim to distinction is the fact that here may be seen at its best (unsurpassed even at Ickwell Green, in Bedfordshire) the annual May Day ceremony. The spiral-striped maypole permanently dominates the village green, tipped with a weathervane. On May Day you may see not only the traditional ribbon-plaiting dance round the maypole but morris dancing too, and at its best. Look also for the Four Alls Inn, with its signboard depicting a soldier, a parson, a farmer, and a king; a doggerel verse clarifies the meaning of the group.

This is all low-lying ground. Just south of Upper Quinton, however, is Meon Hill, from the summit of which, at 637 feet, you can obtain a splendid view westwards across the Vale of Evesham. You must climb it on foot, and if this exhausts you, you can refresh yourself at the College Arms, Quinton, facing the green. Though it lies outside the limestone belt of the true Cotswolds, the inn is nevertheless partly built of that incomparable stone. The explanation of the sign will be understood at once by any Oxford man whose college was Magdalen, for it bears the arms of that college, 'Lozengry Sable and Ermine and a chief Sable charged with three garden lillies proper'. Building and site were a gift from no less a patron than Henry VIII himself.

Just south of the county boundary lies a National Trust property that is a Mecca for all lovers of great gardens, of flowers, trees, and shrubs. Hidcote Manor Gardens are in fact some twenty gardens, one leading into another, varying in their landscaping and essential content, as their names suggest: White Garden, Camellia Corner, and Fuchsia Garden are three examples. They are open daily from April until October. They are landscaped on sloping ground between a ridge to the east that rises to over 800 feet, and highish ground to the west pinpointed by revelatory names such as Aston and Weston Subedge; but now, inevitably, your eye will be drawn away from these to one of the best-known Cotswold names of all: Chipping Campden.

What can one say of this serene and almost completely unspoiled town that has not already been said a thousand times – and never better than by H. J. Massingham in his classic *Cotswold Country*? It would be presumptuous of any man to think he could write as well as that strange, difficult character whose topographical pen possessed a magic peculiarly its own. Safer, then, just to content oneself (albeit unwillingly) with a brief mention of what there is to see, and let the visitor find and savour it for himself. Fortunate the man or woman who comes here for the first time; the initial impact is unlikely ever to be erased from the memory.

Chipping Campden is a market town, largely built by the wool merchants of the fourteenth, fifteenth, and later centuries. It was their pride as well as delight to transmute some part of their wealth into mason-wrought oolitic limestone – the basic raw material of the Cotswolds, whether the paler stone of western Gloucestershire or the richer, iron-permeated stone of Oxfordshire and parts of Warwickshire and the old Worcestershire (notably Broadway). Look for the great 'wool' church, Perpendicular in style, its Norman stonework partly rebuilt by William Grevel, one of the important Campden names, whose own beautiful house stands in the main street, notable among its peers for its great gabled bay-window; look for the William Hicks Almshouses, set back from the main street on a raised stone terrace; look for the Woolstaplers Hall, built in 1340 by the Calf family, whose name is perpetuated in Calf Lane near by. It was from here that the bales of wool from the sheep of the surrounding wolds were carried by pack-pony train to the Channel ports. It is now a museum of essentially local interest, one of the ever-growing number of such museums. And of course look, from every angle, at the town's best-known (though not, in the author's opinion, most beautiful) building, the seventeenth-century stone-arched, timber-roofed Market Hall. Look – but the buildings of Chipping Campden, like those of virtually every township, village, and hamlet in the Cotswolds, will catch and hold the eye; like Rome and Venice, the Cotswolds make return visits inevitable; their lure is wholly irresistible.

Two and a half miles south-west of the town and just over the boundary-line into the second segment is an odd feature that you will almost certainly miss if you are (unwisely) hurrying along the A44 between Oxford and Evesham, especially if travelling southwards. It stands beneath overhanging trees at the junction with the the B4081: an old-style signpost dating from the era of the stage-coach and still, happily, *in situ*, the only one of its kind, to the author's knowledge. It is of the type known as a 'coachman's signpost', ten feet high to enable him to read its directions from his lofty perch, in strong contrast to the modern signposts at its feet. It carries four wrought-iron arms, disproportionately slender, each with a pointing finger; the distances are given in Roman figures, familiar, no doubt, to long-distance drivers of former days, but, one wonders, would they be understood by today's lorry-drivers?

The hamlet of Blockley lies a mile or two to the south-east. It is not one of the Cotswold 'show places', but worth a visit if only for the

'Coachman's signpost', near Chipping Campden

unique tombstone – not in the churchyard but in a cottage garden, and erected to the memory of – of all creatures – a trout! It had spent its whole life in a streamlet flowing through the garden of Fish Cottage:

> Under the soil the old Fish do lie;
> 20 years he lived, and then did die.
> He was so tame, you understand,
> He'd come and eat out of your hand.

Ebrington, a few miles to the north, is another of the lesser-sung Cotswold hamlets. Snug, unpretentious, unassuming, lying in a hollow, it is easily overlooked. Like Gotham in Nottinghamshire and Heathfield in East Sussex, it has accumulated a modest tradition of the absurd: here too, apparently, the inhabitants leave their hedges untrimmed 'to keep the cuckoo in'. In a region noted for its stone roofs, it has much thatch. A few miles to the east is Stretton-on-Fosse; the last part of its name reminds us of the Roman road that crosses England from near Axmouth north-eastwards to Lincoln and beyond, never deviating more than six miles from a rule-straight line; the 'Stretton', like the many 'Strattons', emphasises the 'street' element.

North-east again is Shipston-on-Stour, straddling the busy A34 but happy in the possession of the Old Mill Inn, formerly, as its water-wheel shows, a water-mill operated by a leat from the Stour that flows beneath its mellow walls. Five or six miles farther to the east, still in this segment and near the perimeter, you will come to what many hold to be at once the most beautifully named, and most beautiful, as well as the most beautifully sited of all our great houses. Compton Wynyates (the name is reminiscent of Winnats in the Mam Tor circle), the country seat of the Marquess of Northampton, dates from the late fifteenth century. It is as perfect an example of Tudor domestic architecture as may be found anywhere in this part of England, where stone predominates over half-timbering. Its ornate, castellated façade, its great side tower, its variegated chimneys of mixed spirals and bandings, the whole topped by a windmill on the crest of the hill beneath which the gracious house shelters, and the foreground filled with some of the finest topiary work in the country: this adds up to a perfect composition of man's work and nature's blended as one. Compton Wynyates is open to the public on several days of the week from April till September.

On the very perimeter of this segment a ridge runs northwards out of the circle. It is Edge Hill, and it was at the foot of its north-western slope that the battle signalling the commencement of the Civil War was fought, the Battle of Edgehill, in October 1642. King Charles is said to have unfurled his standard here on the ridge close to the hamlet of Radway. And on this spot, a century later, one Sanderson Miller erected a 'folly' known as Edgehill, or Radway, Castle. It dominates the Edge, as it was intended to do, though today it forms part of a small country inn. Eastwards of it is Upton House, with its terraced gardens and an interior filled with porcelain, paintings and rare tapestries, open twice weekly from May to September.

On the perimeter of the third segment, the first just outside, the second just inside, are the twin villages of Great and Little Tew. They are notable especially for their exceptionally rich colouring, due to iron in the limestone, and for their thatch. Three miles west of them lies Chipping Norton, a market town (as the first half of the name implies) with a tradition dating back to the thirteenth century. Its spacious market place is evidence of its importance in its heyday, but its market hall, unlike the beauty at Chipping Campden, is little more than a hundred years old, though happily it was built to match the true Cotswold style.

Radway Tower, on Edge Hill

Nearer to our viewpoint by five miles is Chastleton House, which dates from 1603 and is especially notable for its Long Gallery and for its State Rooms, in which period furniture and furnishings, including tapestries, are displayed in such a way as to give the impression that the house is still occupied by its original Jacobean owners. In the grounds facing the house is a most unusual dovecote, set there in the eighteenth century, yet not unduly conflicting with the design of the house it was built to serve. Chastleton is open to the public most days of the week and all the year round.

Not far away to the south-west is the hamlet of Adlestrop in the valley of the River Evenlode, known to all who remember the poetry of Edward Thomas; westwards in the valley is Evenlode itself, with its 'one-woman museum of bygones' in the Old School. Beyond is Moreton-in-Marsh (non-Cotswold folk almost always insert an intrusive 'the'); there is no marsh, as seems to be implied, but the little town straddles the Fosse Way at a point which was originally the meeting-place of four 'marches', or county boundaries.

Do not leave these townships and hamlets without taking a minor road to the north of Chipping Norton. You will come soon to the Stone Circle known as the Rollright Stones. Dating from the Bronze Age, it is at least 3,500 years old and ranks almost with Avebury's Stone Circle, though none of the stones in this 100-foot-diameter circle is as large as those in the Wiltshire one. There is an additional interesting feature: on the opposite side of the road from 'The King's Men', as the stones are called, is a single isolated menhir known as the 'King Stone', though it has rather the silhouette of the witch who pronounced judgment on a mythical king and his men. The Rollright Stones have become the objective of vandals and it is up to the caring public to support the valiant efforts of their owner in ensuring their preservation. In the field a hundred yards beyond the circle is the trio of menhirs known as 'The Whispering Knights'; they are simply the tilted uprights of a Bronze Age dolmen that has lost its capstone, but they add a fascinating detail to the mythical episode. There is another of these collapsed dolmens at Enstone on the perimeter of this segment to the south. It is less easy to find than the Rollright Stones, being tucked in a hedge beneath a tree, and road works, alas, threaten its future after more than three undisturbed millennia; the Hoar Stone's days may well be numbered.

Southwards again you will come to a length of the little Evenlode – a stream which shares with the Windrush a few miles to the west in

'The Whispering Knights', Rollright Stones

the fourth segment the claim to be the most beautifully-named of all Cotswold waters. On the edge of the map, here, is the name Wychwood Forest. Do not expect a forest in the accepted sense, any more than you did at Peak Forest and Hope Forest in the Mam Tor circle. True, there once was an extensive forest here, the hunting preserve of a succession of monarchs; not so, however, any longer. Names such as Ascott-under-Wychwood and, in the next segment, Shipton-under-Wychwood and Milton-under-Wychwood stress the fact that formerly trees grew in this region in sufficient abundance to shelter game.

The fourth segment contains some of the best-known of all the Cotswolds' many villages, hamlets and townships. On the perimeter lies Burford, with a High Street as famous as any in the country for its breadth and gradient and the beauty of the old houses, shops, and inns that line it on either side, especially the eastern side. If an individual building must be singled out, then it is the fifteenth-century Tolsey, now a museum, though it was built, as the name implies, for the collecting of tolls where such were due. Here the prosperous wool men of the region held their meetings, prices were fixed and arguments settled among them. At the foot of this lovely street the Windrush flows beneath a beautiful bridge; and hard by, close to the river, stands the church, of which the porch and main body of the tower are Norman, though most of what you see today is of fifteenth-century origin.

Two or three miles to the west you cross from Oxfordshire into Gloucestershire. Clustered or scattered on or near the Windrush are the villages beloved by devotees of the Cotswolds: Great and Little Barrington (but do not ever be deceived by the appellation 'Great'!) and Great and Little Rissington; Bourton-on-the-Water, too, with its main street spaced-out by miniature stone bridges spanning the Windrush, flowing alongside. Bourton, like Broadway, has unhappily become commercialised; it is just *too* perfect, and therefore somewhat aware of itself. It may be seen, reproduced in scaled-down miniature, correct as to every detail, behind the New Inn – a labour of love and pride indeed. But both township and miniature version will unfortunately involve you in jostling and elbowing, for Bourton is a magnet that draws sightseers to the ineptly-named 'Venice of England' by the coach-load.

North of Bourton are Lower and Upper Slaughter, neither of them spoiled in the way that Bourton tends to be; the same may be said for Lower and Upper Swell. It is in and among villages such as these, and by the roadsides, that you will see many of the finest examples of Cotswold drystone walling for which the region is famous. Usually it is plain, functional, and all the better for being so; occasionally, where such a wall forms the boundary of a private house, it may be ornamented in one or more of several ways: ploughs set along the top, or odd-shaped stones inset in it.

Beyond these delectable villages is Stow-on-the-Wold, at 800 feet the highest of all the Cotswold townships. It stands at the meeting of no fewer than eight roads that run radially outwards across the Wolds, tacit (though no longer silent) witnesses to the former importance of this wool-marketing town which attracted traders in many other commodities as well, and from far and wide, from the Middle Ages onwards. This place is indeed one to linger in. Its Parish Church of St Edward has Norman stonework in it, a fourteenth-century

Ornamented drystone walling

The Red Lion, Northleach

Snowshill village

chancel, and a fifteenth-century tower. In the seventeenth century Cromwell made use of this church as a place of incarceration for no fewer than a thousand Royalists captured by his army. It even contains some nineteenth-century stained glass that contrives to harmonise with the general ambience of the church.

Just over the borderline with the fifth segment is another wool town, Northleach. It stands within half a mile or less of the Fosse Way at the point where the Roman road is intersected by the A40 Oxford to Cheltenham road. There is Cotswold stone here, but there is also more half-timbering than is to be found in most towns in the region. Sometimes the two materials are blended, and a good example of this is to be seen in the façade of the Red Lion, an old inn that overlooks the slanting market place. Northleach is fortunate in that the heavy Fosse Way traffic by-passes it; but its ancient peace is inevitably disturbed by the traffic on the busy A40 that passes through it.

In this same fifth segment, nearer the perimeter, lie many of the best-known villages and hamlets: Bibury, with its trout hatchery, its National Trust-owned Arlington Row and Mill; Coln Rogers, and Coln St Dennis, and the lesser-known Winson, all three in the Coln Valley. At Winson you may be surprised to see peacocks occasionally deigning to strut among the more plebeian fowl. Just north of Chedworth and west of Yanworth, in the same valley, is the National Trust-owned Roman Villa, one of the most remarkably preserved relics of a prosperous Roman's abode to be found in all England.

But now the eastern outskirts of Cheltenham Spa begin to encroach; we shall do well to steer north-eastwards for such scattered hamlets as Naunton, with its fine dovecote and church, Guiting Power and, just up the hill beyond it, Temple Guiting, Cutsdean and Ford a mile or two farther on still. On the south-eastern outskirts of Cheltenham, above Leckhampton, there is the impressive rock spire known as the 'Devil's Chimney', which requires stamina rather than rock-climber's skill to tackle; you can approach it only on foot. It forms an outlier of the limestone scarp that is the westwards limit of the Cotswolds as a whole; in general they slope eastwards into Oxfordshire, where they end.

North of Chedworth Roman Villa, still skirting Cheltenham, you will come by road to Cleeve Hill (in the sixth segment) which offers a stupendous view westwards over the Vale of Gloucester almost at your feet; this is a continuation northwards of the escarpment, and

Cottages in Broadway

if you leave the road you can climb soon, and easily enough, over smooth turf, on to Cleeve Common, where you will find the megalithic long barrow, Belas Knap, with its superb ogee-shaped entrance, regarded by experts as perhaps the noblest in England.

Bearing north-eastwards from here, you will come to Sudeley Castle, just south of Winchcombe, the twelfth-century home of Catherine Parr, sixth and last of Henry VIII's wives. With its Elizabethan Garden it is open most days of the week from March till October.

Cistercian Hailes Abbey ruins, worth visiting if only for the beauty of their setting, lie on your route to Snowshill, within two miles of our viewpoint in this sixth segment. The village is built on a slope; its manor house, National Trust property, long served as a farmhouse, but now contains furniture and other features depicting Cotswold rural life of olden times. Having accepted 'Ratchup' as the local pronunciation of Ratlinghope (in Salop) you must now remember that Snowshill is locally pronounced 'Sno'zl'. On your way there you should have branched off to Stanton and Stanway. Of the two, perhaps the first is the more memorable for the simple beauty of the stonework in every building, large and small; but each has its devotees, and rightly.

In the seventh segment we cross into Hereford and Worcester. Ahead of us is the Vale of Evesham, especially lovely in fruit-blossom time. Midway between Evesham, serenest of market towns, and the perimeter is the hamlet of Elmley Castle. It is dominated by Bredon Hill, which must be climbed on foot. It is worth the effort, for from its 961-foot summit you have a superb view across the Severn to the Malvern Hills.

Maybe the final segment is the least rewarding, over all; but it has its features. The half-timbered village of Inkberrow, for instance, whose Bull Inn is the original of the Old Bull known to all followers of the interminable BBC 'Archers' programme; here the folk of Ambridge fictionally meet. Much more distinguished, if less plebeianly popular, is Ragley Hall. This, the late-seventeenth-century country seat of the Marquess of Hertford, notable for its furniture, pictures, library, and *objets d'art*, is open, with its gardens, most days of the week from May to the end of September. Just north of Alcester, near the perimeter, is Coughton Court, a National Trust property open to the public several days a week from April to October; its outstanding feature is its huge central gatehouse, dated 1509, though the main fabric is Elizabethan.

Finally we turn inwards to our viewpoint, which overlooks the beautiful if highly self-aware village of Broadway itself, in the 'tongue' of Hereford and Worcester. You must simply accept Broadway as a 'show village' *par excellence*. Whichever way you turn, incomparable stonework confronts you, set off by the greensward spread like an apron at its feet. The larger buildings, like the seventeenth-century Lygon Arms, are matched by rows of dormer-windowed cottages no less beautiful, if humbler in origin; all were built by skilled native craftsmen working in the material lying so lavishly to hand; such a feast of stonework, perfectly set off by nature, is almost more than can be assimilated. So climb once more to the viewpoint, Broadway Tower, and take one final look down over the rooftops, and then outwards at the glory of the Cotswolds, of which this is so perfect a focal point.

Compton Wynyates

Market Cross, Malmesbury

Silbury Hill

Looking at the map, you may wonder why Silbury Hill has been chosen as a viewpoint. Why not Milk Hill (964 feet), a few miles to the south-west? Or Hackpen Hill (892 feet), the same distance to the north? Or Oldbury (852 feet), an Iron Age camp a similar distance to the west? Reasonable questions. But one fact alone supplies the justification: Silbury Hill is the largest *man-made* hill in all Europe. It rises to some 130 feet above the level landscape all about it; it is more than 200 yards in diameter, and covers more than five acres. Strictly, it is the upper three-quarters of this extraordinary mound that is man-made: excavation has shown that its builders used a natural mound, cut an enormous U-shaped trench round it, and carried the material they dug from it, probably in basket-loads, up the steep slope to fashion the whole into the rounded conical shape Silbury presents today.

No one knows who they were, these men of such diligence and stamina; or when they built. Only the fact that the old east-west Roman road (today's Bath Road) had to curve round its southern slope proves that it was there 2,000 years ago. Burial-place of some Iron or Bronze Age chieftain of super-importance? Excavators have not yet found an answer. They started work here in the mid-nineteenth century, sinking a shaft vertically from the summit; nothing significant was found. In 1877 a shaft was driven in from the south side and made contact with the earlier shaft; again, nothing was found. As recently as 1967 the BBC, in collaboration with certain archaeological organisations, embarked on a more elaborate, and camera-monitored, excavation; yet again, nothing of significance came to

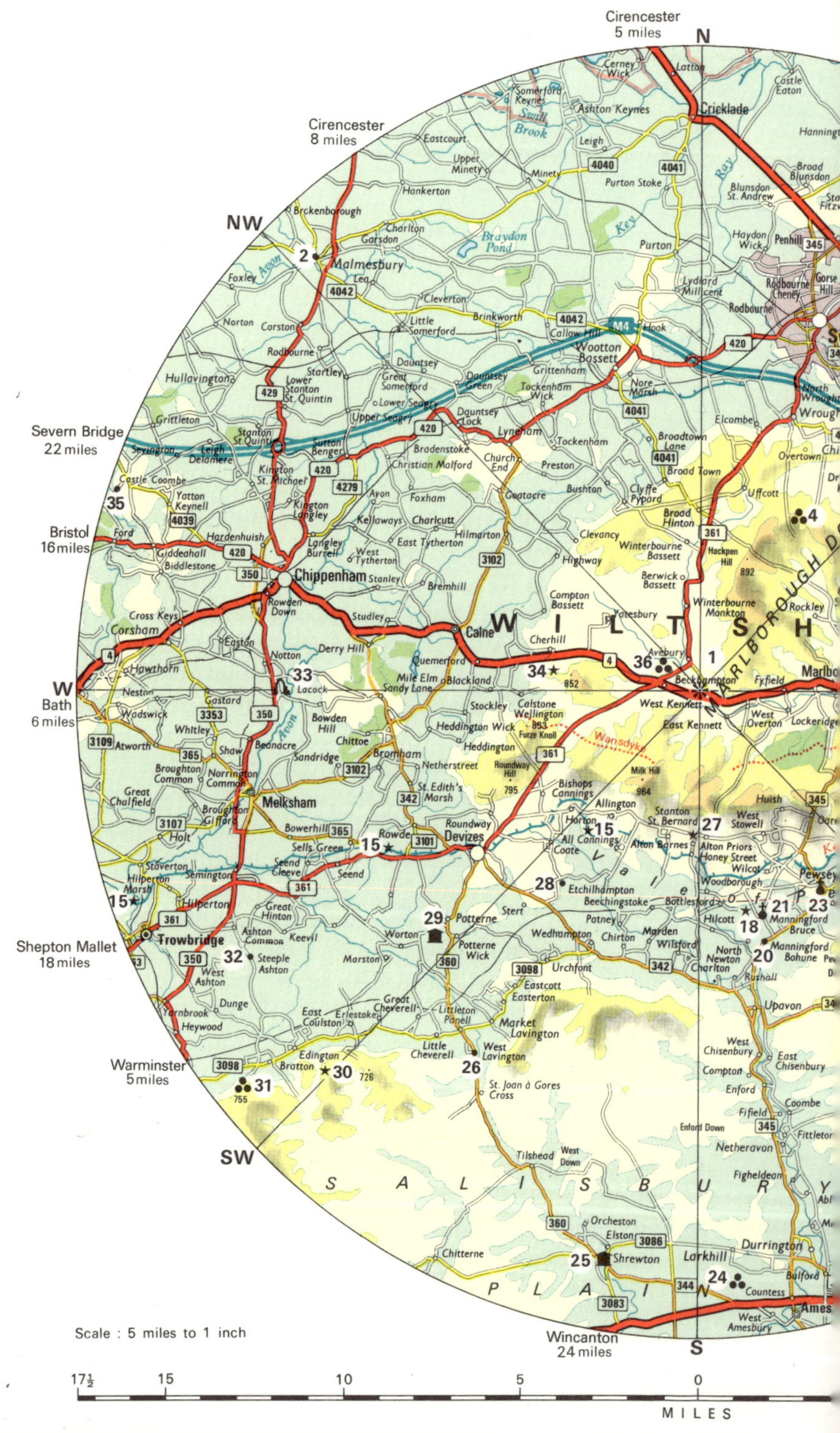

Cirencester
5 miles
N
Cirencester
8 miles
NW
Severn Bridge
22 miles
Bristol
16 miles
W
Bath
6 miles
Shepton Mallet
18 miles
Warminster
5 miles
SW
Wincanton
24 miles
S
Cerney Wick
Latton
Castle Eaton
Somerford Keynes
Swill Brook
Ashton Keynes
Cricklade
Hannington
Eastcourt
Leigh
Upper Minety
Minety
4040
4041
Purton Stoke
Ray
Broad Blunsdon
Blunsdon St. Andrew
Hankerton
Brokenborough
Charlton
Garsdon
Braydon Pond
Key
Purton
Haydon Wick
Penhill
345
2
Malmesbury
Foxley
Avon
Lea
4042
Cleverton
Lydiard Millicent
Rodbourne Cheney
Gorse Hill
Rodbourne
Norton
Corston
Little Somerford
Brinkworth
4042
Callow Hill
M4
Hook
Rodbourne
Wootton Bassett
420
Dauntsey
Startley
Lower Stanton St. Quintin
Great Somerford
Dauntsey Green
Grittenham
Tockenham Wick
Hullavington
429
Lower Seagry
Upper Seagry
Dauntsey Lock
Nore Marsh
North Wroughton
Wroughton
Grittleton
Stanton St. Quintin
420
4041
Elcombe
Sevington
Leigh Delamere
Sutton Benger
Bradenstoke
Lyneham
Church End
Tockenham
Broadtown Lane
Kington St. Michael
420
Christian Malford
Preston
4041
Broad Town
Overtown
Castle Coombe
4279
Avon
Foxham
Goatacre
Bushton
Clyffe Pypard
Uffcott
35
Yatton Keynell
Kington Langley
Broad Hinton
4
4039
Kellaways
Charlcutt
Clevancy
Winterbourne Bassett
361
Ford
Hardenhuish
Langley Burrell
East Tytherton
Hilmarton
Hackpen Hill
Giddeahall
420
West Tytherton
3102
Highway
Berwick Bassett
892
Biddlestone
350
Chippenham
Stanley
Bremhill
Compton Bassett
Rowden Down
Winterbourne Monkton
Rockley
MARLBOROUGH D
Cross Keys
Corsham
Studley
Yatesbury
Calne
W I L T S H
Easton
Cherhill
Derry Hill
4
Avebury
1
Notton
Quemerford
36
4
Hawthorn
33
Lacock
Mile Elm
Sandy Lane
Blackland
34
852
Beckhampton
Fyfield
Marlb
Neston
Gastard
Stockley
Calstone Wellington
West Kennett
Wadswick
3353
350
Bowden Hill
Heddington Wick
853
Furze Knoll
East Kennett
West Overton
Lockeridge
Whitley
Chittoe
Wansdyke
3109
Atworth
Shaw
Beanacre
Heddington
365
Sandridge
Bromham
361
Broughton Common
Norrington Common
3102
Netherstreet
Roundway Hill
Milk Hill
Great Chalfield
Melksham
342
St. Edith's Marsh
795
Bishops Cannings
964
Huish
345
Broughton Gifford
Allington
3107
Holt
Bowerhill
365
Rowde
Roundway
Devizes
Horton
15
Stanton St. Bernard
27
West Stowell
Sells Green
15
3101
All Cannings
Alton Barnes
Alton Priors
Honey Street
Wilcot
Staverton
Seend Cleeve
Coate
Semington
Seend
Pewsey
Hilperton Marsh
15
361
28
Etchilhampton
Beechingstoke
Woodborough
Hilperton
Great Hinton
Stert
Bottlesford
18
21
23
361
29
Potterne
Manningford Bruce
Trowbridge
Ashton Common
Keevil
Worton
Wedhampton
Chirton
Patney
Marden
Hilcott
18
350
32
Steeple Ashton
Potterne Wick
Wilsford
North Newton
20
Manningford Bohune
West Ashton
Marston
360
3098
Urchfont
342
Charlton
Rushall
Eastcott
Easterton
Dunge
Upavon
Yarnbrook
Heywood
East Coulston
Erlestoke
Great Cheverell
Littleton Panell
Market Lavington
West Chisenbury
East Chisenbury
Little Cheverell
West Lavington
Compton
3098
Edington
Bratton
30
726
26
31
755
St. Joan à Gores Cross
Enford
Coombe
Enford Down
Fifield
345
Fittleton
Netheravon
Tilshead
West Down
Figheldean
S A L I S B U R Y
360
Orcheston
Elston
3086
Durrington
Chitterne
25
Shrewton
Larkhill
24
Bulford
P L A I N
344
Countess
3083
West Amesbury
Scale : 5 miles to 1 inch
17½
15
10
5
0
MILES

Silbury Hill

1 Silbury Hill
2 Malmesbury
3 Liddington Castle
4 Barbury Castle
5 Coate
6 Vale of White Horse
7 Alfred's Castle
8 Ashdown
9 Ashdown House
10 Uffington Castle
11 Uffington White Horse
12 The Ridge Way
13 Littlecote Manor
14 Savernake Forest
15 Kennet and Avon Canal
16 Great Bedwyn
17 Chisbury
18 Vale of Pewsey
19 Crofton
20 Manningford Bohune
21 Manningford Bruce
22 Collingbourne Ducis
23 Pewsey
24 Stonehenge
25 Shrewton
26 West Lavington
27 Alton Barnes White Horse
28 Etchilhampton
29 Porch House, Potterne
30 Westbury White Horse
31 Bratton Castle
32 Steeple Ashton
33 Lacock village and Abbey
34 Cherhill White Horse
35 Castle Coombe
36 Avebury

light. If some great chieftain was honoured by the construction of this mound-to-end-all-mounds, then his skeleton and all his prized possessions, presumably buried with him, were located and removed by the British equivalent of the tomb-robbers who have operated so efficiently among the pyramids of the Pharaohs along the banks of the Nile. The secret of Silbury will never be known.

Modest as it is, the Hill offers a magnificent viewpoint. There is only one way, the hard way, up on to its summit, along zigzagging paths worn through the thin turf to the underlying chalk. On a clear day you can see to far horizons: northwards to Barbury Castle, the high undulations of the Marlborough Downs lending character to the vista; eastwards and westwards along the Bath Road, which bisects this circle exactly, and is roughly paralleled by the M4 motorway several miles to the north. Southwards, beyond the lovely Vale of Pewsey, extend the limitless acres of empty Salisbury Plain, all too much of it virtually 'owned' by the Army. In all this circle there is only one town of any size: Swindon. The worthy inhabitants of Chippenham, Trowbridge, Devizes, Malmesbury, Marlborough, and Hungerford must not take exception to this statement, for these towns have qualities all their own, of a type that Swindon lacks: they are market towns with centuries-old traditions of which to be proud.

There is little to be said in detail about the first segment, for it is dominated by the 'railway town' of Swindon. Railway enthusiasts will make for its Railway Museum, with its splendid exhibition of locomotives and rolling-stock, especially that of its 'own' Great Western Line. Somewhat nearer to the viewpoint, however, there are two of the many prehistoric sites for which Wiltshire and neighbouring Dorset are unmatched. The first is to be found just south of the M4: an Iron Age site named on the map Liddington Castle after the village that it dominates from its eminence just to the south. Like the others, though they vary in size and design, it consists essentially of earthworks carved out of and heaped up upon high ground that offered a wide view in most (if not all) directions, and so security against the potential enemy. Most of these sites date from the last few hundred years BC. They are difficult to photograph successfully, save from the air; but they possess atmosphere, one and all.

The second such camp – the map word 'castle' is deceptive, for these are earth-constructed, not stonework – lies four miles nearer to Silbury Hill. On the slope of the ridge running north-east from

Silbury Hill, from the west

Hackpen Hill, Barbury Castle's twelve-acre site is enclosed within earthworks consisting of a double ditch and wall of turf. It is of a pattern that is to be seen at its most extensive, most elaborate at Maiden Castle in Dorset. At Barbury you may see one of the innumerable sarsens that are so characteristic a feature of the open Wiltshire landscape. It is not a 'native' of Barbury but was specially selected and brought here from Overton Down, and inscribed with the name of the country writer Richard Jefferies, who was born at Coate, on the outskirts of Swindon; Barbury was one of the places he knew and loved best of all in his native Wiltshire.

From both Barbury and Liddington Castle there is a glorious view north-eastwards over the Vale of White Horse, which flows out across the perimeter between Faringdon and Wantage, with its close association with King Alfred the Great. Just over the border into the second segment you come to explicit reminders of Alfred. The

Castle that bears his name is one of the smaller Iron Age sites, curiously enclosed within a larger one, so that archaeologists have been able to establish links between Iron Age and Romano-British occupants. It was never one of Alfred's strongholds, but it was not far from here, on these Berkshire Downs, that he fought one of his greatest battles with the Danes, in the year 871 AD.

As strong a contrast as can be imagined is afforded by Ashdown House, a National Trust property not a mile to the south. This late-seventeenth-century house, together with its grounds, is open to the public on one or two days a week only from May to September. Access is permitted to its roof, which offers a superb view across the downs. An even better view, and one certainly in less sophisticated surroundings, may be obtained from Uffington Castle, yet another Iron Age camp three or four miles to the north and close to the perimeter. From its ramparts you look northwards over the Vale of White Horse, and across to Whitehorse Hill itself; at 856 feet this is the highest point on the Berkshire Downs.

It takes its name from the extraordinary segmented, dragon-like chalk-cut figure of the Uffington White Horse, easily the most famous, and mysterious, in England. You can walk over and along it at will, all 374 feet of it from nose-tip to the tip of its elongated tail, and down its oddly detached foreleg and hindleg; but to take it in at a glance you need a helicopter or balloon. No one knows for sure who carved it, or when, or why; it is almost certainly of prehistoric origin. For centuries past it has been re-edged, cleaned, and maintained; Thomas Hughes, of *Tom Brown's Schooldays* fame, who was born in Uffington a century and a half ago, wrote of this in his *Scouring of the White Horse*. Not far from Uffington Castle is one of the best-known of all megalithic long barrows, popularly known as Wayland's Smithy. Wayland, or Vieland, was a character in Norse mythology and it is a traditional belief that he shod horses that used the Ridge Way that runs close by this burial-place.

To the south are the Lambourn Downs: this is racehorse-stable country. More important, to some of us at any rate, is the fact that along the northern fringe of these downs that most ancient of trackways, the Ridge Way, runs westwards and south-westwards to Liddington Castle and on, southwards, to Old Sarum. It has always been loved and respected by long-distance walkers; the present writer walked its whole length some thirty years ago, then picked up the South Downs Way and walked from Butser Hill to Birling Gap;

A stretch of the Kennet and Avon Canal, near Pewsey

in all, the finest long-distance walk he ever did in this country, with the possible exception of the Pennine Way. This Ridge Way has very recently (September 1973) been 'officially' opened – eighty-five miles of it at any rate – from Ivinghoe Beacon to Silbury Hill. You could walk out of this circle and enter the Ivinghoe Beacon circle by its south-western quadrant: the perimeters are not thirty miles apart. As you left the present circle you would come immediately to Kingston Lisle, where you may try your luck with 'King Alfred's Blowing-Stone', with which, allegedly, he summoned his troops to battle. You would probably evoke not the slightest whisper; but a child in the adjoining cottage can manage a blast on it every time!

Littlecote, a Tudor manor with notable ceilings and a Great Hall displaying arms and armour from Cromwellian times, is to be found on the southern edge of this second segment. Long-roofed, triple-chimneyed, and boasting three fine gables with unusually large mullioned windows, it stands in a serene stretch of parkland, backed by trees on the downland slope; it is open to the public during summer weekends only.

Immediately beyond the boundary-line between the second and third segments, marked also by the A4, is Savernake Forest. Here are more than 3,000 acres of elms, beeches, and oaks. They grow so thickly that they afford cover for deer to roam at will. Parts of the forest have been 'organised': the Grand Avenue, for instance, consists of lines of stately beeches, planted in the eighteenth century as a great through-way running from south-east to north-west. From this there radiate no fewer than eight forest rides along which you can walk or ride (but not, of course, drive). Though so very close to a major trunk road, within minutes you would believe yourself to be in some other world; indeed, you have stepped back in time, for Savernake was royal property long, long before the advent of William of Normandy.

The border with Hampshire zigzags southwards through this segment close to the perimeter. The area contains a scatter of villages and hamlets linked by very minor roads indeed, along which no one in his senses would wish to hurry. Close to the A4 the Kennet and Avon Canal enters the circle, to meander leisurely westwards through the succeeding segments and make its quiet exit not far from Bradford-on-Avon. For anyone asking for real quietude, but in open country as opposed to the cathedral-like atmosphere of Savernake Forest, this is the answer. The canal was designed by the great John Rennie in the earliest years of the nineteenth century; the development of the railways led, as it did elsewhere, to the desuetude of the canal; much of it has since fallen into almost hopeless disrepair. Happily, under the auspices of the Kennet and Avon Canal Trust large numbers of enthusiasts are working like beavers (almost literally in some sections) to restore as much of it as is practicable. The canal's outstanding feature has always been its extraordinary 'staircase' of no fewer than twenty-nine consecutive locks on the outskirts of Devizes; this feature offers as good an excuse as any to visit this busy town in the sixth segment of the circle.

Follow the line of the canal and you can hardly go wrong. Silence lies all about you, save for the song of birds, the lowing of cattle, the distant bark of a dog, the susurration of water spilling gently over dilapidated lock gates; this is pure paradise – and all hardly more than five miles from that east–west highway with its incessant hum of

Ornamented thatch, near Great Bedwyn

speeding traffic along its length. The villages too, small and scattered as they are, have their individual mites to offer. The Bedwyns, Great and Little, lie alongside the canal, each with its distinctive charm. Great Bedwyn has some lovely thatch, the ridge ornamented with pheasants of straw, very lifelike. It has, too, a church built substantially of flint, with a fourteenth-century tower, a chancel a century older, and some interior features that date back to Norman times.

Between the Bedwyns is the Iron Age site of Chisbury: from its 600-foot summit there is an entrancing view along the gentle Vale of Pewsey and the canal that waters it. South of Great Bedwyn, in a crook of the canal, there is Crofton, a Mecca for canal enthusiasts and indeed for all admirers of early nineteenth-century engineering projects. For here, as long ago as 1812, a pumping station with two gigantic beam-engines was built; the engines could pump no less than eleven tons of water per minute into the canal at its highest point

(400 feet) above the source of the River Kennet. As at Ironbridge, enthusiasts are labouring to rehabilitate these splendid memorials to enterprise of a bygone age.

The fourth segment, particularly as you approach the viewpoint, abounds in charming little places, often with resounding names that belie their smallness. Manningford Bohun is one such; another is Manningford Bruce, which has an interesting early-Norman church with a rounded apse. They match in resonance two villages on the boundary-line with the third segment: Collingbourne Kingston, and Collingbourne Ducis, which has a thirteenth-century flint-and-stone church, the upper portion of whose tower was built to form a dovecote, a function it has fulfilled for centuries.

Pewsey itself, from which the Vale takes its name, is the largest of these villages. It has some half-timbering, but its most remarkable feature is its church, some parts of which date back to the thirteenth century at least, and are particularly unusual in that they were founded on sarsen stones, miniatures (if massive ones) of those which form so large a part of Stonehenge. Here, as at Wantage, King Alfred is commemorated; his statue, less impressive than that in the Berkshire town, stands in the heart of the village – the statue of a scholar-king. It is in and between villages such as these, and others farther to the south, that you will come upon a feature peculiar to Wiltshire and neighbouring Berkshire, the thatched wall. Composed of friable material such as chalk reinforced with flint, these are easily destroyed once water penetrates them: hence the 'roof' of close-knit thatch.

To explore this segment southwards is to become involved in areas of Salisbury Plain that have been monopolised by the Army; names like Bulford, Larkhill, and Tidworth are uncomfortable reminders. But almost at the nadir of this perimeter is Stonehenge, the most famous prehistoric monument in the country, perhaps anywhere in the world. Two roads lead southwards to the A303 at Amesbury; the lesser one, east of and parallel with the A345, is the more attractive by far, made lively by the flow of the little Avon and virtually traffic-free save in its scatter of hamlets south of Upavon. At Amesbury you turn west along the main road, and Stonehenge awaits you at the fork three miles along the road where the A344 branches north-westwards off the A303.

There was a day when you could simply turn off either road and walk leisurely across the turf and right into the heart of this breath-

Thatched Wiltshire cob wall

taking complex of megaliths, unimpeded. But we live in an age of commercialism and, alas, ever-increasing vandalism; now Stonehenge must be at once exploited, and protected from those who would daub the monoliths with their ideological and other slogans; money must be taken at turnstiles, and barricades must be erected so as to make approach difficult if not impossible without strict authorisation. The day might well come when every visitor will be searched with the sort of devices now becoming increasingly evident at airports: the X-Ray Eye will check every would-be visitor to this monument to our heritage.

It has no parallel anywhere else in the world. Popularly accredited to those 'Druids' of indeterminate date whose Ancient Order celebrates there every Midsummer Eve (thus perpetuating a fallacy!), Stonehenge is known to date back at least 4,000 years; but its construction was spread over some 700 years, representing more than twenty successive generations of builders. The temptation to write

Westbury White Horse

much more, even in the limited space available, is strong indeed. How were the eighty colossal so-called 'blue stones' transported from their known place of origin, the Prescelly Mountains of Pembrokeshire, more than two hundred miles distant even in a straight line? How did prehistoric man shape the mortises and tenons by which the giant lintels were fitted to the even larger upright stones? How were those capstones lifted into place? Why, anyway, was this complex of concentric ovals and circles ever designed and constructed? What brain was behind it to produce that alignment which means that the sun rises on 21 June exactly over the stone at the eastern end of the major axis? These and other questions are of inexhaustible interest; some have been tentatively answered, but others 'abide our question' still.

There is little in the fifth segment that merits much attention, though the beehive-shaped lock-up at Shrewton is well worth a photograph for any collection of odd aspects of England that you may be compiling for your own interest. West Lavington, on the A360, is worth a visit for its seventeenth-century Parsonage, Dial House, and Old Manor, while its neighbour, Market Lavington, has a church nicely poised on a steepish mound, its chancel dating from the thirteenth century. Farther north is another stretch of the Kennet and Avon Canal, with Alton Barnes astride it and, near by, another White Horse, on a slope of the downs, carved in 1812. If you want to ask the way to Etchilhampton, do not forget that, locally, it is pronounced 'Ashelton'!

Devizes, Melksham, and Trowbridge dominate the sixth segment – of interest to you if market towns appeal; but if it is the rural scene that you are after, there is plenty here too. On the boundary-line with the fifth segment lies the hamlet of Potterne. It is dominated by a fine church built in 1220 (the same year as Salisbury Cathedral was begun), though it has been restored here and there since. Beneath it lies one of the outstanding examples of half-timbering in a county where stonework predominates. This is Porch House, a small fifteenth-century house that has been intimately connected with the church, but has also been an inn, though now it is privately owned. It is open to the public on one day a week only, from May to September, and you will be impressed by its oriel-windowed dining-hall but could miss, if you were not told in advance, the curious battery of spy-holes in the ceiling through which the goings-on below could be watched unseen – and restrained if necessary!

Herringbone brickwork at Steeple Ashton

Westbury itself lies half a mile outside the perimeter of this segment, but gives its name to the neighbouring White Horse, easily the finest in Wiltshire. A minor road from Bratton runs up the downland slope, offering an excellent long-distance view of this chalk-cut and very realistic horse, allegedly carved to celebrate one of King Alfred's victories over the Danes. It is well worth while taking the track up this slope to the Iron Age camp known as Bratton Castle, at a height of 755 feet, above the slope on which the White Horse was carved. In spite of smoke from a cement works below, the camp offers a glorious view northwards over the Kennet and Avon Canal.

There are more roads to choose here than in the fifth segment. A minor one will take you to Steeple Ashton – the first half of the name is a corruption of 'staple', evidence of its former connection with the wool trade. In fact, there is no steeple to the fine Perpendicular-style Church of St Mary, for the spire was destroyed by lightning in

1670, and never replaced. Overlooking the triangular green, with its little domed lock-up, reminiscent of the one at Shrewton, and the ancient market cross, said to date from the eleventh century though it has been repaired several times during its eight centuries of existence, is a beautiful example of mixed-style architecture. The house has a slabstone roof such as is ordinarily found in the Cotswolds; it has a massive stone plinth; and between these, half-timbering inset with mellow brickwork in delightful and unusual herringbone style.

A few miles to the north, fortunately by-passed by the A350, though only by a few hundred yards, is Lacock. This is, deservedly, National Trust property; with Castle Combe, six miles to the north-west, it can claim to be the most beautiful village in all Wiltshire, and one of the half-dozen most beautiful in all England. Buildings here range from the fourteenth century to the Georgian era, and even later; astonishingly, they do not conflict with one another but blend harmoniously into a composite picture. Lacock Abbey dates from even earlier than the village itself, but has been much altered since the Dissolution and is now a private house; it is open to the public on most week-days from April to October. There is a fourteenth-century barn which originally formed part of the abbey estate; The Sign of the Angel, half-timbered and steeply gabled, reminiscent of The Star at Alfriston with its projecting upper leaded windows, dates from the sixteenth century, and the Red Lion dates from the eighteenth century, its mellow brickwork in pleasant contrast with stonework and half-timbering inset with plasterwork. The most interesting building in Lacock, however, is the cruck-built cottage standing at right angles to The Sign of the Angel; its enormous adze-hewn tree-trunk gable supports threaten to crush the small windows inset beneath; but it has stood there since medieval times, and should last as long again. The relatively few surviving examples of this building technique are always worth a visit.

To enter the seventh segment you must cross the Bath Road. If you do so near Calne you can obtain a rewarding long-distance view of the Cherhill White Horse three miles to the east; it is less impressive at close quarters, as is always the case with such features. If you cross by way of Chippenham, then branch off north-westwards, you will come in five miles or less to Castle Combe – Lacock's only true rival among Wiltshire villages – right on the perimeter. The village is set on a steepish slope that climbs upwards from Bye Brook, the street lined with seventeenth-century cottages, and culminating in

Corner in Lacock village

Avebury Stone Circle and ditch

an exceptionally-fine market cross, two lovely inns, a manor house, and the Church of St Andrew, which was built by the wool men of the region and is a match for many of the Cotswold 'wool' churches.

And so to the final segment. All of this to the north of the motorway will be ignored, also the greater part between the motorway and the Bath Road, though there are scattered hamlets of varying degrees of interest. Avebury, close to our viewpoint, is our final goal. The village lies athwart the A361, which does a dog's-leg turn through it. The dominant feature, of course, is the Stone Circle. Originally there were a hundred of these gigantic sarsens. Unlike those at Stonehenge, they were not worked by hand, so every individual one is distinct, and different from every other. They were transported here from the Marlborough Downs at about the same time as work began on Stonehenge, some 4,000 years ago. As with Stonehenge, its purpose has not yet been established, though a variety of inspired guesses have been made down the years. Unhappily, unlike Stonehenge it has been cannibalised in the way in which Hadrian's Wall was cannibalised: many of the megaliths were broken up for building material, fragments of them being discernible in cottages and even in the church's fabric. Avebury Manor, dating from Elizabethan times, is open to the public most days of the week from April to September; girdled by trees, it overlooks the Stone Circle and the enormous bank and ditch enclosing the stones that remain.

But – and here we come full-circle back to our viewpoint – the best way to approach Avebury is by way of the great avenue of sarsens that runs alongside a minor road almost the whole way from Silbury Hill. Strictly, its starting-point is at West Kennet, where you will find the 350-foot-long burial-chamber, a long barrow constructed about 2700 BC and almost comparable, except in its siting, with Belas Knap on Cleeve Common. Not all the sarsens of this avenue survive; but the positions of those that have been removed by farmers and builders down the years have been marked out so that the whole of this ancient, mysterious route can be followed today. To walk down from the top of Silbury Hill, join the Stone Avenue, and follow it through to Avebury Stone Circle is an experience that will leave an indelible impression.

Avebury Manor

The Banqueting Hall, Knebworth House

Ivinghoe Beacon

Inevitably, with a viewpoint only thirty miles in a straight line from the heart of London, the contents of a circle thirty-five miles in diameter drawn round it must be to some extent urban. Hatfield, St Albans, and Hemel Hempstead are in it; Barnet and Harrow are only a few miles outside it; and Greater London creeps inexorably towards the southern perimeter. High Wycombe lies on the circle's south-west perimeter; Stevenage and Welwyn Garden City lie on its eastern perimeter. You may well ask, 'Is there no escape?'

But of course there is! A glance at the map shows that four major trunk roads encourage swift transit into rural areas. The M1, first of our motorways, stands out clear and bold among them; the A5 – the Romans' Watling Street – darts across four segments in an almost straight line; the A6 heads due north across three of them, Manchester-bound; the A41 passes through four segments, Oxford-bound. Leading off all of these, a hundred minor roads will take you into unexpectedly quiet byways, each of them holding promise. Less obvious, but in fact – if time is little object – more promising still, is the existence of the Grand Union Canal, which serpentines its leisurely way north-westwards across this circle from its southernmost point through five segments towards the most north-westerly point of the perimeter.

Hertfordshire, Bedfordshire, and Buckinghamshire are almost equally represented within this perimeter; they meet within a mile or so of the viewpoint, high on Dunstable Downs. To stand on Ivinghoe Beacon, at a height of 807 feet, is to be offered an astonishingly wide panorama, especially to the north-east, north-west, and north. If you

N
Northampton
15 miles
Towcester
8 miles
NW
Bicester
7 miles
W
SW
Oxford
19 miles
Oxford
26 miles
Reading
18 miles
S
London
21 miles
Milton
Keynes
Bletchley
Far Bletchley
Fenny Stratford
Leighton
Buzzard
Linslade
Dunstable
Aylesbury
Tring
Berkhamsted
Chesham
Amersham
High
Wycombe
West
Wycombe
Beaconsfield
Princes Risborough
Thame
Chorleywood
Cranfield
Woburn
Winslow
Wendover
Great Missenden
Hazlemere
Waddesdon
B
U
C
K
S
B
E
D
F
OXON
The Three Hundreds of Aylesbury
Chalfont
St. Giles
Chalfont
St. Peter
Jordans
Seer Green
Ivinghoe
Dagnall
Whipsnade
Studham
Haddenham
Long
Crendon
Stoke
Mandeville
Great
Kimble
Monks Risborough
Little Kimble
Ellesborough
Hughenden
Valley
Penn
Wooburn
Cheddington
Marsworth
Pitstone
Stewkley
Wing
Whitchurch
Quainton
Botolph Claydon
Middle
Claydon
East
Claydon
Bierton
Hartwell
Weston
Turville
Aston
Clinton
Halton
Hastoe
Wigginton
Northchurch
Cholesbury
Ashley
Green
Latimer
Little
Chalfont
Coleshill
Winchmore
Hill
Knotty
Green
Loudwater
Wycombe
Marsh
5130
4033
4034
4032
488
557
418
528
5140
5120
4146
489
4541
4540
4506
413
41
4544
4011
4010
4009
4129
4445
4128
4010
404
474
485
416
355
404
4442
4505
40
413
M1
14
13
3
1
2
3
10
14
15
16
17
18
19
20
21
22
23
24
25
26
27
28
29
30
31
32
33
34
35
36
Scale : 5 miles to 1 inch
17½
15
10
5
0
MILES

Ivinghoe Beacon

1 Ivinghoe Beacon
2 ★ Grand Union Canal
3 ★ Chalk-cut lion, Dunstable Downs
4 • Clophill
5 • Ampthill
6 • Flitwick
7 Knebworth House
8 Shaw's Corner
9 Luton Hoo
10 ★ Whipsnade Park Zoo
11 Verulamium
12 Hatfield House
13 Gorhambury House
14 Berkhamsted Castle
15 ★ Berkhamsted Common
16 ★ Ashridge Park
17 Little Gaddesden
18 Aldbury
19 Chalfont St Giles
20 Jordans
21 • Penn
22 • Penn Street
23 Hughenden Manor
24 West Wycombe Park
25 Ellesborough
26 ★ Nature Freeway
27 ★ Coombe Hill
28 • Thame
29 • Long Crendon
30 • Haddenham
31 Waddesdon Manor
32 Claydon House
33 • Ivinghoe
34 The Globe Inn
35 ★ Leighton Buzzard Narrow Gauge Railway
36 Woburn Abbey

do not wish to make the effort of climbing you can drive up a well-engineered if narrow road that winds from the northern side up the slopes of the downs to a smooth turf area where you can park your car (free) for as long as you like while you walk leisurely along an undulating chalk-cut path a couple of hundred yards to the actual summit. The ground falls away from you, notably to the east, where a giant chalk-cut lion glares out from this northern slope of the downs. Its eye may be directed towards the animals roaming in Woburn's Safari Park not ten miles away; or it may be more concerned with the inmates of Whipsnade's Open Zoo that roam at apparent liberty virtually at its feet – living animals oblivious of the inanimate King of Beasts.

The very flat county of Bedfordshire occupies much of the northern part of this circle. The county has been termed 'a dear old lump of mud, stuck all over with steeples', an unkind, unfair description. There are, it is true, steeples galore, because there are so many small villages and smaller hamlets scattered about between the arterial roads, and well removed from busy industrial centres like Luton. Clophill, for example in the first segment, with its street sloping gently down to its old water-mill, against whose walls two huge millstones lean, their labours past these many years, while a trickle of water still flows from beneath the massive brick arch of the east wall.

Just across the A6 is Ampthill, larger than Clophill, and once a staging-point of some importance. Nestling close to its Church of St Andrew, built in dark-russet ironstone, is a trio of almshouses dating from 1690; their end wall, overlooking the churchyard, is half-timbered; the façade is painted white and picked out in sky-blue. Named the Feoffee Almshouses, they are as charming a little group as you may ever have seen, not forgetting those in Norfolk's Castle Rising. They overlook a diminutive square, with stonework-surrounded flowers and shrubs in an ornamental bed; facing them are some gracious eighteenth-century dwellings. The whole place seems to be asleep. The tapering stone obelisk signpost at the cross-roads, incorporating an old pump, dates from 1784 and is a tacit reminder of coaching days. Near here, Catherine of Aragon sojourned while awaiting her divorce from King Henry VIII. Though small and unpretentious, there is a truly historic feel about little Ampthill.

In almost every village hereabouts you will find thatched cottages and farmsteads. On the western outskirts of Ampthill are two linked cottages, twins bearing the names respectively of Hatters' and Cob-

Chalk-cut lion on the Dunstable Downs

blers' Cottages, an enormous brick chimney running up the whole of the end wall. Flitwick, a few miles away, with its charming village green watered by the streamlet Flitt, which gave this 'wick', or settlement, its name, is just one of innumerable others in the area.

Over the boundary-line into the second segment the rural scene tends to become overshadowed by the urban: Luton dominates, and three major arterial roads close in on one another. To escape, you must cross the border into Hertfordshire, preferably steering clear of the sprawl of Stevenage, right on the perimeter. It is well worth going close to this area, however, to visit one of the county's two best-known great houses, Knebworth House. Though the first structure on the site owes its origin to Sir Robert Lytton, who was building here as long ago as 1492, the year when Columbus discovered America, most of what you see today is the result of the efforts of a later member of this historic family, the novelist and statesman Sir Edward Bulwer-Lytton. Five centuries, give or take a couple of decades, of constant occupation and development may be seen here. It is not only the display of paintings by great artists and furniture by great craftsmen that will delight the eye but the much older

Banqueting Hall; in addition, there are the gardens and aptly-named Country Park, the herds of deer and the Aviary, and much, much else besides. Knebworth is open to the public daily from May until the end of September.

On a much more modest scale, but of interest especially to his admirers, Shaw's Corner, at Ayot St Lawrence three miles to the south, is also in this segment. It is National Trust property. Here 'G.B.S.' lived and wrote from the beginning of the century until his death in 1950. He chose well. The village, with its half-timbered buildings, is charmingly rural, though it lies between two motorways. The house itself, a late-Victorian edifice, is wholly lacking in distinction; but there is 'character' enough in the mere ghostly presence of this controversial figure, and more than one visitor to Shaw's Corner has been convinced that because the dramatist's ashes were buried in the garden where he did so much of his writing, he haunts the whole place still. It is open to the public daily for eleven months of the year.

If you follow the boundary-line with the third segment in towards the viewpoint, you will come to Luton Hoo, an eighteenth-century mansion the exterior of which was begun by the great Robert Adam, though little of his work now survives. The interior was later remodelled in the French style. Among the many treasures here are some priceless examples of the artist-craftsmanship of Fabergé and many *objets d'art* of Russian origin. These form the famous Wernher Collection; the house and its treasures are open to the public on four days a week from mid-April until the end of September. The house lies in parkland laid out by 'Capability' Brown.

Nearer still to Ivinghoe Beacon is Britain's most famous, indeed unique, open air game reserve, Whipsnade Park Zoo. Some two thousand animals range widely on the slopes of Dunstable Downs and the Chilterns, enclosed for their own safety as well as for that of the public, but in an area so spacious that they have the air of being wholly untrammelled. You can walk, or drive, within easy view of them, in a countryside that seems ideal as a habitat for them all. Whipsnade can claim a very remarkable record for the breeding of wild animals in (strictly speaking) captivity.

The third segment is dominated by St Albans and Hemel Hempstead. On the outskirts of the cathedral city of St Albans is the Roman 'suburb' Verulamium, a Mecca for every archaeologist and antiquarian, amateur or professional. Much less ancient but more

Thatched cottages, Ampthill

Black rhino and young at Whipsnade

Overleaf, *Hatfield House*

picturesque, overshadowed by the hill on which the cathedral stands and close to the stripling River Ver, is the allegedly 'oldest inn in England', Ye Olde Fighting Cocks. It claims to have been 'built before the flood'; but 'the flood' was that of the Ver which, three hundred years ago, rose in spate and inundated this low-lying area. At that time the inn was known as The Rounde House (being, in fact, octagonal), and also, more appropriately, The Fisherman. It was already old in the late-sixteenth century; close to it were the fish-ponds from which the monks from the abbey extracted their Friday fare. Its closest rival in age is Nottingham's Ye Olde Trip to Jerusalem, allegedly built in 1189; well, you pay your money (for the beer) and take your choice!

East of St Albans, on the perimeter, is Hatfield House; it has been the country seat of the Earls of Salisbury since it was built by Robert Cecil, the first Earl, in 1608. As a blend of Tudor and Jacobean, it has few rivals either in scale or in beauty. Elizabeth I spent much of her childhood here. The Banqueting Hall extends over two floors, with Jacobean carving perhaps unmatched elsewhere in the country; equally difficult to match are the Long Gallery and the Great Staircase. The house is superbly sited in a great park and gardens that were deliberately laid out afresh only a century or so ago, so that it is impossible, save from pictures, to know what they were like when Elizabeth I knew them. But you can still see the oak beneath which, according to tradition, she was sitting with her lady's maid when the news was brought to her that Mary had died and the throne was now hers – the commencement of perhaps our most glorious reign. The house and West Garden are open at intervals from March to October.

Between St Albans and Hemel Hempstead is Gorhambury House, country seat of the Earl of Verulam. Compared with Hatfield, whether as to date or as to distinction, it is much less impressive. For all that it is worth a visit, if only for the subtle pleasure of contrasting styles. For this is a late-eighteenth-century mansion in what is technically called 'modified classical' style. Though its immediate impact conforms to this, there is in fact much older stonework in its fabric: in the porch and in a projecting wing, for instance, are portions of the original house, built in 1568. It was the home of Sir Francis Bacon, statesman and writer ('Baconians' believe he wrote the plays of Shakespeare); after his term of imprisonment in the Tower of London he came here to Gorhambury to spend the last years of his life. The place is open to the public on

Thursday afternoons only, from May until September.

Just over the boundary-line with the fourth segment you will come to the Grand Union Canal. It is now a sadly-declining through-way between the Midlands and London for industrial traffic, but is increasingly used today by those who take to the canals, large and small, for pleasure, as the present writer was doing nearly forty years ago. The canal follows the A41 closely across this segment into the next, and there are scores of points along its length here and elsewhere, that offer views of craft negotiating the locks, or slipping quietly through open country and under arched brick bridges only a stone's-throw from a major road. Here the canal runs close beneath the ruins of Berkhamsted Castle, of which there is little to be seen but the double moat, the bailey, and the *motte* on which the castle was built by William the Conqueror before being handed over to his half-brother Robert. Two centuries later the Black Prince was to end his life here.

The Grand Union has here to climb the Chilterns' south-east slope, which it does in an impressive 'staircase' of huge locks, similar in principle to the smaller ones near Devizes on the Kennet and Avon Canal. Beyond Northchurch it skirts that beautiful Chiltern area shown on the map as Berkhamsted Common. A minor road climbs up to the National Trust property of Ashridge Park; beyond this is the enchanting hamlet of Little Gaddesden, backed by some of the Chilterns' most famous stands of beech: National Trust property again, and a wildlife sanctuary too. The half-timbered building with the overhanging upper storey so characteristic of the fifteenth century was the home of John Gaddesden, the Royal Physician. The Manor House is noted for its fine collection of early keyboard instruments, and for its ornamental gardens, periodically open to the public. Near by, at yet another Chiltern 'show village', Aldbury, is a sixteenth-century 'little manor house' overlooking the green with its medieval stocks alongside the pond, overshadowed by a giant elm tree.

The border between Hertfordshire and Buckinghamshire to the west zigzags along the boundary-line between the fourth and fifth segments. Close to the perimeter on the Buckinghamshire side you are on the southern fringe of the Chiltern Hills, with a scatter of villages every one of which calls for a visit. Here, for instance, are Chalfont St Peter and Chalfont St Giles; in the latter you will find Milton's Cottage. Here, in 1665, the year of the Great Plague, the poet, nearing sixty and now grown blind, sought refuge and embarked on the dictation of the greatest epic in our language, *Paradise Lost*. Close to the cottage is the parish church, flint-built like so many buildings hereabouts (though the cottage is predominantly of red brick). Parts of it date from the twelfth century, though the tower was added three centuries later. The church, of course, is open to the public; so, on most days of the week, is Milton's Cottage, now both memorial and museum to this great poet and pamphleteer.

Only a mile or so away is Jordans, a tiny, neat hamlet consisting of little more than a green part-surrounded by trim cottages. The name is familiar world-wide, for here was buried William Penn, the Quaker who founded Pennsylvania. Only a few hundred yards down the lane from the green is the brick-built Friends' Meeting House, built in 1687, with its portraits and relics of those early days of 'free-thinking'; beneath its windows are the simple headstones of Penn himself, the two women who became his wives, and a handful of other Quakers who made their mark on their times. Beyond again is the 'Mayflower Barn', part brick, part timber, overlooking a quiet rectangle of turf; some of its timbers are believed to have come from the ship of that name, part of the lettering being still visible in one of the beams.

Over the boundary-line into the fifth segment and you are in what most country lovers claim to be the most beautiful area of all these beechwood-clad Chilterns. Hauntingly beautiful villages proliferate, too many to be named. Penn, for instance, has part-brick half-timbered seventeenth-century cottages; its Church of the Holy Trinity has one of the finest fifteenth-century roofs of any small country church in England, and brasses here commemorate William Penn and many of his descendants. At Penn the inn, church, and village green are all close together, integrating the whole. A mile or so to the north is Penn Street, with its oddly-named Hit or Miss Inn, wistaria-clad, once just a pair of linked cottages (as were so many inns); it is worth entering, even if you are not thirsty, for its imaginative display of typical Chiltern chair-making craftsmanship. Much of this is the work of the traditional Chiltern 'bodgers' – a community now virtually defunct since High Wycombe, three miles distant, has taken over the former woodland 'industry' and truly industrialised it in factory style.

It is on the outskirts of High Wycombe that you will come upon Hughenden Manor, once the home of Benjamin Disraeli, Earl of

Stocks and Manor House, Aldbury

Milton's Cottage, Chalfont St Giles

Beaconsfield and former Prime Minister. He spent the last thirty-five years of his life, and died, here; his study has been preserved as nearly as possible as it was when he worked in it, with countless relics such as manuscripts of his novels and his correspondence with Queen Victoria. Hughenden is open to the public most days of the week from (unusually) February to November.

A few miles to the west is the village of West Wycombe, famous for the way in which its medieval buildings have been preserved; famous, too, for West Wycombe Park, a Palladian-style mansion open to the public from June to the end of August. It is notorious, rather than famous, perhaps, for its association with that scandalous character Sir Francis Dashwood, who was both Chancellor of the Exchequer and Founder of the infamous Hell Fire Club. The village is dominated by a 600-foot hill topped by the Church of St Lawrence, its golden ball a landmark for miles around. In the church tower, traditionally, the Hell Fire Club used to practise their black magic rites when they were not doing so at Medmenham in the Thames Valley.

In the sixth segment, towards the north-west-facing slope of the Chilterns, is another Prime Minister's country house – Chequers. The map does not show it, but it is to be found in the parish of Ellesborough, near the Kimbles. Of more interest to most visitors is the fact that the recently-opened through-route for walkers runs south-westwards here from Ivinghoe Beacon, to pass within 400 yards of Chequers; the fact disturbs the authorities responsible for the safeguarding of the Prime Ministers when in residence. It was as recently as 9 September 1973 that this 'Nature Freeway' – in effect an extension of the ancient Ridge Way that we have already seen running north-eastwards from Silbury Hill – was officially opened with a ceremony on Coombe Hill, close by. From start to finish it is some eighty-five miles long. If the south-western end is the more spectacular, with its Iron Age forts and Whitehorse Hill, certainly the north-eastern end is the more beautiful.

On the perimeter of this sixth segment, a mile over the Oxfordshire border, is Thame, a minor township that well merits exploration. You will at once be struck by the extraordinary width of its High Street, in which the annual Thame Show is still held, as it has been ever since Thame received its Charter when it was still part of the Kingdom of Mercia. At one end of the street there is a group of sixteenth-century almshouses and, just beyond these, the Old

Grammar School, also sixteenth-century, at which for a time John Milton was an industrious pupil.

Two or three miles to the north, and again right on the perimeter, though now we are back in Buckinghamshire, is Long Crendon. The fifteenth-century Court House, now National Trust property, was a gift to Catherine of Aragon from Henry VIII, and is only one of a number of historic buildings that you will perhaps be surprised to find in so small a village. Small – but once very important: four centuries ago this was the only place where the all-important housewife's needle was made. This was a cottage industry; when industrialisation threatened, the cottagers laid down their files and abrasives and the town of Redditch took over where they had left off. Close to Long Crendon is Haddenham, with its satisfying triangular green and cottages of character, many of them with what are known as 'wichert' walls to their gardens – a variant of the thatched cob walls so characteristic of Berkshire and Wiltshire.

Over the boundary-line into the seventh segment is Waddesdon Manor, another National Trust property. With its pepperpot turrets and variegated roof styles it suggests French origin or inspiration. It was built for Baron Ferdinand de Rothschild exactly a century ago and, appropriately, houses a magnificent collection of French furniture. It is surrounded with outstandingly beautiful woodlands, which in part explain why, though only just a century old, it gives the impression of having been there for so very much longer. It is open on five days a week from late March to the end of October.

This seventh segment seems curiously empty. Once again, the place of greatest interest is to be found close to the perimeter: Claydon House, five or six miles north of Waddesdon Manor. This National Trust property dates mainly from the middle of the eighteenth century, though part of the fabric is much earlier. It lies at the heart of four hamlets: the East, Middle, Steeple and Botolph Claydons. The interior of Claydon House will appeal more to the visitor than its exterior. Quite apart from the ornate and mainly rococo rooms, large and small, there is a suite that was for a time occupied by Florence Nightingale, whose sister, Parthenope, was married to the owner, Sir Harry Verney. After her memorable work at Scutari in the Crimean War of 1854, Florence returned to England, to die in 1910 at the astonishing age of ninety. She had long taken to her bed, either in her own home or in that of her sister, here at Claydon; the bedroom here is now a museum dedicated to her memory. In the garden overlooked by these windows are some cypresses allegedly grown from seeds that she brought back with her as simple souvenirs of Scutari (now Uskudar).

The Grand Union Canal cuts across this segment and enters the final one close to the village of Ivinghoe, which tends to be ignored because those visiting this area are almost certainly bound for the Beacon that dominates it. The village is undeservedly neglected, for it is among the most pleasant spots in Buckinghamshire. It has a church of particular beauty, both as a whole and in small details. The connoisseur will admire the carving on the stonework that supports the impressive roof; he will also, no doubt, appreciate the 'poppy-head' pew ends which are, many of them, grotesquely and also amusingly carved, giving the impression that the wood-carver was given *carte blanche* to produce whatever stirred in his imagination.

It is in this final segment that the Grand Union Canal becomes increasingly serpentine; its meanders offer the leisurely walker, the seeker after silence and peace, endless hours of simple pleasure. Here and there is a canal-side inn, such as The Globe just north of Leighton Buzzard and Linslade; the two oddly-named hamlets of Heath and Reach lie just beyond; near by there runs the three-and-a-half-mile stretch of narrow-gauge railway between Page's Park and Munday's Hill, reminiscent of the little Hythe and Dymchurch Railway, open to the public on Sundays from the end of March to the end of October.

Farther north lies Bletchley, 'halfway-house' between Oxford and Cambridge. Hereabouts are limitless acres of clay used for the inescapable brickworks – the 'mud', perhaps, of which its detractors declared the county of Bedfordshire to be composed, even though it was adorned with steeples! Better, therefore, to cut your losses and ignore the perimeter of this segment, and turn inwards. You cannot miss the signposts drawing your attention to the fact that you are now within hail of one of England's three best-known great houses. Woburn Abbey. It is listed in the annual publication *Historic Houses, Castles and Gardens* as 'Woburn Abbey and Wild Animal Kingdom'; nor is this really an exaggeration. Indeed, it could be said to be but a half-truth.

Here, inside and out, there is 'just about everything'. Certainly you could visit, revisit, and visit again and again this country seat of the Dukes of Bedford, and never exhaust the riches to be found on display there. It contains a collection of masterpieces by the world's

Florence Nightingale's bedroom, Claydon House

Globe Inn, Grand Union Canal

greatest painters whose value cannot begin to be assessed; the furniture and furnishings and *objets d'art* are hardly to be matched in any other great house in this country or abroad. There are more than a dozen State Apartments, in more than one of which Royalty as well as the nobility have been entertained over the centuries.

The village of Woburn, redolent of the great house near by, lies between the M1 and the A5. So vast is the estate of Woburn that the motorway had to be diverted eastwards to avoid encroaching upon it; the park surrounding Woburn Abbey extends to some 3,000 acres, containing the largest privately-owned game reserve in all Britain. Woburn Abbey – no abbey at all, of course, but a secular treasure-house – lies at the heart of it. From its vast, open parkland you can look due south along the foothills of the Dunstable Downs. Raising your eyes, you can look towards the summit of this fine undulating ridge of smooth, pale-green turf so thinly overlying the chalk beneath, to the viewpoint so aptly termed Ivinghoe Beacon, exactly ten miles distant. It offers a perfect contrast between man-accumulated riches and the simple natural beauty of chalklands sculpted unobtrusively, inexorably, throughout aeons of time that cannot be measured either by calendar or by clock.

Queen Victoria's State Bedroom, Woburn Abbey

Glynde Place, near Lewes

Ditchling Beacon

The northernmost point on this circle is about twenty-five miles from central London. The viewpoint is close to the eastern end of the long-distance South Downs Way that runs westwards to Butser Hill and beyond; indeed like Silbury Hill and Ivinghoe Beacon, Ditchling Beacon and Butser Hill are linked by a walkers' through-way, and the enthusiast can visit them both, and the linking stretches of East Sussex, West Sussex, and Hampshire, in the course of one long-distance walk, as the present writer did some thirty years ago, long before the South Downs Way was officially open. This is as fine a long-distance walk as any in England, and substantially less arduous than the Pennine Way northwards from Edale.

The dominant feature of this, and the next, circle is, of course, the line of the South Downs. Until some seven thousand years ago, when the Atlantic broke through to join the North Sea, a huge domed whaleback of chalk arched over what is now the English Channel, linking us physically with the Continent; the South Downs are the relic of that whaleback, extending from Beachy Head (a couple of miles outside this circle) westwards beyond Butser and into Hampshire. From Ditchling Beacon to Butser Hill in a straight line it is just forty miles; but the Way meanders so much that the distance walked could be half as much again.

To the south, the coastline carries Seaford, Newhaven, Brighton and Hove, Shoreham-by-Sea, Worthing, and Goring-by-Sea; Angmering like Eastbourne, just escapes the circle. The A27 coast road spans the four southern segments; the A23 London-to-Brighton road runs due south from Gatwick to the coast; the A272

Croydon 16 miles
N
Croydon 16 miles
Dorking 9 miles
NW
W
SW
S
Portsmouth 29 miles
Lowfield Heath
Langley Green
Shipley Bridge
Copthorne
Felbridge
Three Bridges
Pound Hill
Crawley Down
Worth
Ifield
Rusper
Lambs Green
Crawley
Tilgate
M23
Turner's Hill
Faygate
Pease Pottage
Selsfield Common
West Hoathly
Sharpthorne
Warnham
Colgate
Roffey
Broadbridge Heath
Horsham
St. Leonard's Forest
Balcombe
Highbrook
Tower Hill
Handcross
Ardingly
Itchingfield
Five Oaks
Mannings Heath
Monk's Gate
Slaugham
Staplefield
Lower Beeding
Brook Street
Billingshurst
Barns Green
Southwater
Nuthurst
Warninglid
Whitemans Green
Lindfield
Copsale
Cuckfield
Coneyhurst Common
Dragons Green
Maplehurst
Crabtree
Bolney
Ansty
Haywards Heath
Scayne's Hill
North Heath
Broadford Bridge
Coolham
Shipley
Cowfold
Crosspost
Littleworth
Broomer's Corner
West Grinstead
Wineham
Hickstead
Wivelsfield
Wivelsfield Green
Dial Post
Twineham
Sayers Common
Burgess Hill
Nutbourne
WEST SUSSEX
Partridge Green
West Chiltington
Thakeham
West Chiltington Common
Hurst Wickham
Henfield
Blackstone
Albourne
Hurstpierpoint
Plumpton Green
Ashington
Ashurst
Hassocks
Ditchling
Streat
Cootham
Storrington
Keymer
East Chiltington
Clayton
Westmeston
Rock
Sullington
Kithurst Hill 700
Washington
Small Dole
Pyecombe
Ditchling Beacon 813
Plumpton
Mount Harry 639
Steyning
Fulking
Poynings
Edburton
Harrow Hill 549
North End
Bramber
Truleigh Hill 708
Devil's Dyke 711
Upper Beeding
Stanmer
Findon
Botolphs
Patcham
Coldean
Falmer
Coombes
West Blatchington
Kingston near Lewes
Patching
Clapham
North Lancing
Portslade
Preston
Salvington
Sompting
Shoreham-by-Sea
Southwick
Woodingdean
Angmering
Durrington
Broadwater
Lower Cokeham
Kingston by Sea
South Lancing
Hove
BRIGHTON
Ovingdean
Telscombe
Kemp Town
Rottingdean
Ferring
Kingston
Goring-by-Sea
Worthing
Peacehaven
Scale : 5 miles to 1 inch
17½
15
10
5
0
MILES

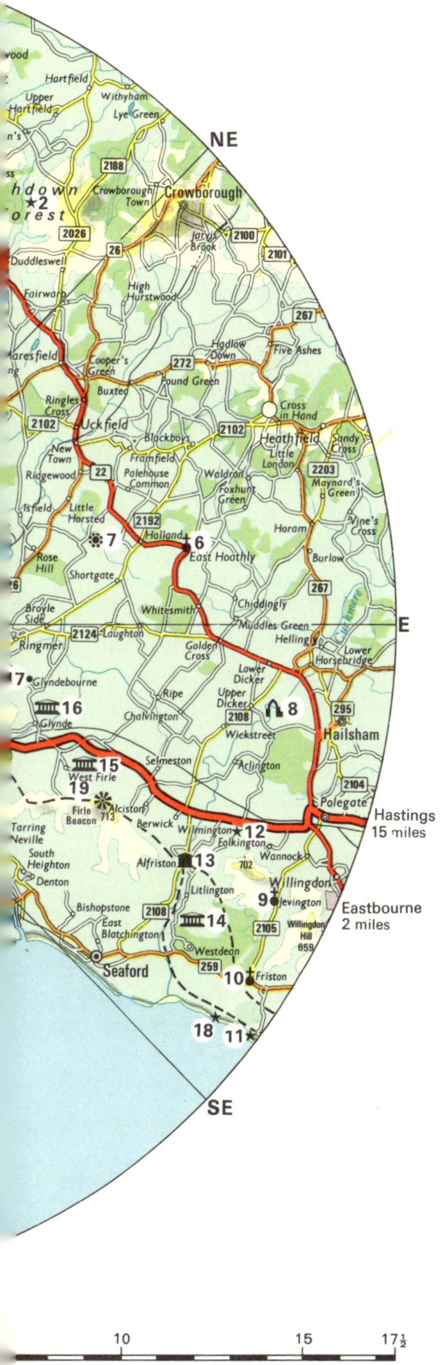

Ditchling Beacon

1 Ditchling Beacon
2 Ashdown Forest
3 Sheffield Park Gardens
4 Bluebell Railway
5 West Hoathly
6 East Hoathly
7 Bentley Wildfowl Gardens
8 Michelham Priory
9 Jevington
10 Friston
11 Birling Gap
12 Long Man of Wilmington
13 Alfriston
14 Charleston Manor
15 Firle Place
16 Glynde Place
17 Glyndebourne
18 Seven Sisters
19 Firle Beacon
20 Devil's Dyke
21 Clayton
22 Pyecombe
23 Poynings
24 Fulking
25 Edburton
26 'Jack & Jill' windmills
27 Truleigh Hill
28 Cissbury Ring
29 Parham Park
30 Shipley Windmill
31 Newtimber Place
32 Danny
33 South Lodge
34 Nymans Gardens
35 Borde Gardens
36 Heaselands

spans the four northern segments; a network of good roads links these, and a plethora of minor roads wriggle amongst them, tempting you on to the downs, which form a magnificent backcloth wherever you happen to be. Most of this circle is set in the counties of East and West Sussex.

The wider part of the first segment is filled by the vast empty acreage of Ashdown Forest. This was originally part of the Saxons' Andreadsweald – the extensive, near-impenetrable forest that filled much of Kent and Sussex, 'thick and inaccessible, a retrete for deer and swine, wolves and wild boars'. Six centuries ago Edward III gave it to his son, John of Gaunt; as in Wychwood Forest, monarchs hunted here, and village names such as Buckhurst, Hartfield, and Hindleap are reminders of the fact. In later centuries the great trees were felled for ships' timbers and for the smelting of iron and making of charcoal: apart from thickets here and there you will find little true forest land hereabouts, though there are warnings of the presence of deer, and you may occasionally spot one when driving over Ashdown Forest at night. But it offers fine walking country, much of it above the 700-foot level.

As you approach the downs the landscape changes fundamentally. Watered by the Ouse and its tributaries, it is lower-lying, more intimate. Near Fletching, where Simon de Montfort's army camped before the Battle of Lewes in 1264, a place known, as its name suggests, for its manufacturing of arrow-heads (*flèches*) you will find the Sheffield Park Gardens, partly laid out by 'Capability' Brown. At the station there you are at the southern terminus of a 5-mile section of the old London, Brighton and South Coast Railway, a line constructed in 1882. The northern terminus is also in this segment, at Horsted Keynes. This Bluebell Railway is a Mecca for all steam-locomotive enthusiasts and lovers of vintage rolling-stock. The work of restoring a section of this line began as long ago as 1960 and still continues. The stations as well as the rolling-stock have been restored to their nineteenth-century 'style', with oil-burning lamps, 'period' advertisements and equipment, all nostalgically reminiscent of Victorian and Edwardian times. One locomotive, the 'Fenchurch', is a hundred years old but still in service. A ten-mile journey out and back in one of these vintage trains – full-gauge – hauled by a steam engine offers a chance to step back in time to the days our grandfathers, even great-grandfathers, knew. This railway operates all the year round, at weekends in the winter months, daily during the

Vintage train on the Bluebell Line

summer, the timetable being available on request from Sheffield Park Station.

Five miles north of the northern terminus is West Hoathly, a Wealden village with a beautiful half-timbered cottage, originally belonging to the Cluniac priory at Lewes, and still known as 'The Priest's House', though it is now a small museum of rural Sussex interest. Twelve centuries ago, here in Andreadsweald, vast herds of swine grazed beneath the oaks and beeches allocated to the people by the Mercian king. Just over the boundary-line into the second segment you will come to Beeches Farm. If not comparable with great houses such as Glynde, Firle, or Parham, it is still a beautiful example of a sixteenth-century farmhouse, notable for its tile-hung exterior, a feature often to be noted in East Sussex and in Kent. Its gardens, velvet lawns, yews, and flower-beds, are open to the public all the year round; the house by appointment only. To many, its unpretentiousness will appeal more strongly than the great houses.

There is something of interest to be found in almost every one of the countless villages in this segment, the tight little lanes that link each with the next: a picturesque tile-hung cottage here, mellow brickwork there, as in and around Hadlow Down, for example. East Hoathly has a church with an ancient tower and a Norman piscina, happily replaced in position when restoration was in progress. Just beyond is Chiddingly, with the remains of an Elizabethan manor from which, allegedly, there is an underground tunnel leading to the church which is one of only four in Sussex with a stone spire. You set out to explore it (almost certainly in vain!) at your peril. These villages, ending in 'ly', must be heavily accented as 'lie'.

Not far to the west are the Bentley Wildfowl Gardens, a remarkable Nature Reserve less well known than, say, Slimbridge, but very well worth a prolonged visit. The Bentley Wildfowl Collection rightly claims to be among the most important in the whole country. Started by the late Gerald Askew in 1962, it is now lovingly and skilfully tended and developed by his widow. Open from the end of March until the end of September on three days a week, it offers the chance to study at close quarters some hundred different species of wildfowl, living in surroundings which are not only beautiful in themselves but, so far as is practicable, natural to the birds. These include not merely ornamental species such as peacocks but, to mention only a few, Siberian Geese, Ross's Snow Geese from the arctic coast of Canada, Patagonian Crested Duck, Carolina and Cinnamon Teal, West African Crested Cranes, Silver Bahama Pintails, Chilean Flamingos, Red Crested Pochards, and Bewick Swans and their cygnets. This brief catalogue barely touches on the rich resources of this collection, the result of so many years of search, skilful breeding, and dedicated cherishing. In itself the setting is memorable: though it has been modernised, the building stands on a site once owned by the Tudor ancestors of the Gage family who now live at Firle Place, to be visited in the next segment of this circle.

It is perhaps now that we come to the richest area – and the term is not used in the monetary sense. Where to start? It may be best to do so from the perimeter of this third segment, moving in towards the viewpoint itself, Ditchling Beacon. Two miles west of Hailsham, and fortunately sequestered from the busy A22, is the Augustinian Priory of Michelham, preserved by the Sussex Archaeological Trust. You enter its exquisitely-tended precincts by way of a formidable

Mandarin drake, Bentley

gatehouse. Michelham was founded in 1229, to be occupied by twelve canons and a prior (representing Christ and his Apostles). Among their guests was Edward I, who is known to have lodged there in 1302. Though it is small in comparison with many other priories and abbeys, it is surrounded by one of the largest moats to be found anywhere in England. Moat and grim gatehouse give the impression that it was built as a fortified house rather than as a priory. What you see today (it is open to the public from April to October) is a mansion built in Tudor times, at the south end of the west range of the original priory buildings; their outlines have been carefully preserved, and stand out clearly in white stone footings set off perfectly by the greensward. The mansion is beautiful in itself, and contains period furniture and fittings that enhance its overall effect.

Overleaf, *Michelham Priory, south elevation*

Due south of Michelham, in the hamlet of Jevington, is St Andrew's Church, in whose graveyard is a nameless tomb, without headstone, that consists of a granite slab on which 'floats' eternally a copper model of a square-rigged, three-masted schooner; beneath her stern there also 'floats' the vessel's boat at the end of a miniature chain. All that seems to be known about this grave is that beneath the schooner lies the coffin of a merchant whose fleet of vessels traded with distant China.

This is indeed a richly-rewarding segment. Friston has its small church, that served for centuries as a landmark both for honest mariners plying the Channel and for the innumerable smugglers who made such good (or nefarious) use of this stretch of coastline. Eastdean, a mile away, has its Tiger Inn at the foot of the sloping green which has a flagpole – or is it the maypole? – and a row of cottages and small shops overlooking it. Two miles distant is Birling Gap, for centuries a landing-place for smugglers, but known perhaps two thousand years ago by the men who carried tin from Cornwall along the downs to off-load it for shipment across the Channel. Climb the gentle downland slope between Jevington and Alfriston and you can look northwards over the chalk-cut figure of the Long Man of Wilmington, staves in his outstretched hands, holding the secret of his age and purpose from archaeologists to this day.

A footpath serpentines westwards by way of the allegedly 'smallest church in England' (rivalled by Culbone in Somerset) and down by way of The Clergy House, dating from 1350 and interesting incidentally as being the first building to be acquired by the National Trust, to Alfriston, where The Star Inn awaits you, among the half-dozen most beautiful medieval timber-built inns in England. It was designed five centuries ago as a Guest House for pilgrims making their way to the shrine of St Richard at Winchester and as a Rest House for the monks from Battle Abbey, but it has long supplied more secular needs. The quality of its timber, and of course even more the quality of the workmanship, is clear evidence of the purpose for which it was built.

Before going farther along the A27 in the direction of Lewes, the county town of East Sussex, pause at Charleston Manor, a private house in which Norman, Tudor, and Georgian architecture may be seen and, curiously, without conflicting one with the other. The gardens are opened from mid-May to September, but the house only by appointment and on one day a week. Now westwards bound on the A27, you come first to Firle Place. The original house here was built in the fifteenth century, but was almost entirely demolished in the eighteenth century. Happily, however, when it was rebuilt most of the beautiful Caen stone from Normandy that had been used for the original house was re-used; with it you will find also some of the finest stone that exists in the south-east, Horsham stone. The house is rich in treasures: paintings by English, Italian, and Dutch artists, Sèvres china and porcelain, furniture by designers and craftsmen such as Chippendale, and *objets d'art* of the Louis XV period. Firle Place is open to the public on three days a week from June to September.

On the opposite side of the A27, and also reached by only a very minor road, is Glynde Place. This was first built a hundred years later than Firle; then part-demolished and largely rebuilt, as its neighbour was, in the eighteenth century. It too is a treasure-house of paintings, notably in its famous Long Gallery, by artists such as Lely, Rubens, Kneller, Zoffany, and their peers; and of bronzes by artist-craftsmen such as Soldani. The house itself is particularly attractive in that it was built round a courtyard, and the chief materials consist of a judicious admixture of brick and local flint as well as stone. It is open to the public from early May to early October, on three days a week. The house stands midway between Glynde and Glyndebourne, and it is of course here that the annual season of music festivals was inaugurated in 1934, and has continued ever since. Glyndebourne Opera House, brain-child of the late John Christie, holds its festival of music – concerts as well as opera – between May and August. In addition to the beauty and dignity of the house and the serenity of the gardens, there is an air of panache – or at least a sense of style; none of the Last-Night-of-the-Proms delirium here; instead, evening-dress and the appropriate decorum, even reverence.

Because, essentially, this is walking country, we must, before taking a close-up look at our viewpoint, back-track for fifteen or twenty miles. The South Downs Way to all intents and purposes may be said to commence on Beachy Head, a couple of miles outside this segment. You may take one of two tracks westwards which unite just short of Alfriston. One of them runs along the coast immediately above the chalk cliffs always known as the Seven Sisters; the other passes a few miles inland, by way of Jevington, over the brow of the Long Man of Wilmington, skirting (as this Way does for most of its length) the northern, and steeper, escarpment of the downs. If this were a book designed solely for the determined walker, this would be the point at which to establish grid-references and other data. Those who want such detailed information should read Edward C. Pyatt's recent *Chalkways of South and South-east England*, which gives it all with admirable lucidity.

You may walk as little or as much of it as you choose. The Way passes across Firle Beacon (713 feet) and you can come close to this from Firle Place itself. It continues, looping boldly northwards to by-pass the outskirts of Brighton, and takes us back to Ditchling Beacon (813 feet), a distance of nine miles as the crow flies but considerably more on foot! If you are not disposed to walk, you can arrive within a hundred yards or so of Ditchling Beacon (as you can of Ivinghoe Beacon) on a well-made road, either from the coast or from the village of Ditchling to the north. The view in all directions is breathtaking; here is one of those sites at which you feel impelled to cry: 'Here I'm on top of the world and monarch of all I survey!'

Given a clear day, without the heat-haze so prevalent in summer, you can see north-eastwards thirteen miles to Wych Cross, sixteen miles to Crowborough Beacon on Ashdown Forest, and twenty-three miles to Brightling Beacon. To the south-east you can see thirteen miles to the chalk mass of Seaford Head, beyond Newhaven harbour and its busy little yacht marina. South-westwards, you can see the Devil's Dyke, a mere five miles distant, and the best-known of all South Downs landmarks, Chanctonbury Ring, twelve miles distant. To the north-west – but you must have an ultra-bright day for this – you can see Leith Hill, twenty-three miles distant; Reigate Hill, two miles farther on; Box Hill, at twenty-six miles; and the Hog's Back, at thirty-one miles. In what other part of all England can so many named hilltops be seen from any one viewpoint at distances comparable with these? Not even in the Lake District.

If you are not walking you can still get the feel of intimacy with the downs from this point onwards, for a very minor road creeps close beneath the north-facing slopes westwards by way of Clayton, Pyecombe, Poynings, Fulking, Edburton, and Upper Beeding to Bramber, Steyning and Storrington, and points west, out of the present circle and into the succeeding one based on Butser Hill, where West Sussex comes close to Hampshire. The first of this string of hamlets, Clayton (in the seventh segment), has its folly-type entrance to the tunnel that takes trains to and from London and

Walkers approaching Ditchling Beacon

Yacht marina, Newhaven

Brighton. It also has 'Jack and Jill' – its pair of windmills high on the downs, dominating the skyline.

Pyecombe village (in the sixth segment) lies just off the A23, up a narrow lane. It appears to consist solely of a church and a smithy. Much of the church's fabric is Norman, though it has been largely restored; the triple chancel arch is perhaps its most noteworthy feature, though some may think that the Norman lead font, one of only three in the county, is of even greater interest. Like so many churches in the region, it is built largely of the local flint. Standing in the churchyard, you look over a low wall straight into the front of the smithy on the opposite side of the lane. Here, 'since time was', shepherds' crooks have been made – crooks that have no equals; and they are made here still, though flocks are beginning to disappear from the downs. The smith will tell you that 'no sheep once caught in a Pyecombe crook will ever escape'. The curve is cunningly designed so that it equally well catches a ewe by the hind leg or a lamb by its neck. The present smith, Sean Black, makes not only shepherds' crooks (and bishops' crosiers) but wrought-ironwork that is evidence of true creative artistry as well as pure blacksmith's know-how.

A narrow, zigzagging road leads us from Pyecombe up the north slope of the downs to the Devil's Dyke (711 feet), over which the South Downs Way passes. Traditionally, Old Nick attempted to carve a large nick through the downs so that the sea would flood in. He failed, but is commemorated by this landmark. From it you look due north over Poynings, a hamlet whose history goes back to Saxon times. Unlike most of these hamlets, it has a very large church, built on a Saxon mound and out of all proportion to the population it serves. Just beyond is the equally modest hamlet of Fulking, with its Shepherd and Dog Inn at the foot of the tree-embowered hill, and a perpetually-flowing spring close by where the flocks were watered while the flock-master, Pyecombe-made crook across his knee, slaked his own thirst.

It is here that we pass into West Sussex. The Way runs along on the skyline over Truleigh Hill (708 feet), high above little Edburton, with its privately-owned pottery and (curiously) its salmon-smoking establishment. It dips down to the River Adur between Upper Beeding and Bramber, with the remains of its flint-built castle overlooking the valley. From here either of two roads will take you towards the coast, where you will find at Shoreham-by-Sea Ye Olde Red Lion, with its grim story of the gallows that once stood behind it.

Sean Black, Pyecombe crook-maker

Windmill residence at Salvington

Now the northern fringe of Worthing reaches outwards and the Way curves north-westwards to avoid it, heading for Chanctonbury Ring; there is a diversion to near-by Cissbury Ring, an Iron Age fort that commended itself to the Romans some two thousand years ago. Before leaving this sixth segment you may care to enter the outskirts of Worthing, if only to see how skilfully a windmill at Salvington has been converted into a private dwelling.

Just over the boundary-line into the seventh segment, close to the perimeter, is Parham, certainly the most distinguished great house in this region, and one of the finest of Tudor mansions. It is superbly sited in its great park, overlooked by the line of the South Downs; it possesses the longest Long Gallery of any great house that is still privately owned; from its windows you look out over beautiful gardens and parkland that appears to be limitless. You may find that the single most memorable feature inside is the elaborately embroidered bed which is traditionally believed to have belonged at one time to Mary, Queen of Scots. Parham is open to the public on three days a week from Easter until October.

The A272 somewhat dominates this segment. A few miles to the north of Parham, and just off this main road, is the white-painted smock-mill at Shipley where Hilaire Belloc spent so many years; it is still visited by those of us who revere him as a fine writer, whether we are of his faith or not. Farther in towards the viewpoint are two more houses that are well worth visiting, though they may not be in the same class as Parham. One of these is Newtimber Place, just north of Pyecombe, a moated house that lies snug beneath the downland slope; its gardens are beautiful and offer a splendidly intimate view of the downs. House and gardens are open to the public on one day a week from May until August. The other is the oddly-named Danny, close to Hurstpierpoint and its famous college. This is an Elizabethan house shaped, as was customary in those days, like a vast letter E – in honour of the reigning monarch. The place is open to the public on two days a week from May until September.

There is less of note for the sightseer in the final segment than in those that have preceded it. The vast urban sprawl of Crawley New Town dominates the outward end of it, with Gatwick Airport right on the perimeter. Horsham, once an old market town, seems now to be growing so fast that you have to look with some persistence to find what remains that is truly old. Fortunately, however, it possesses its own museum, embodied in the sixteenth-century Causeway

Sussex farmhouse kitchen, Horsham Museum

Corner of Nymans Gardens

House, a beautiful building in itself. The museum is primarily of Sussex interest. Having crossed its threshold, you pass out of the present century into remote times. Here you will find the Sussex of the Iron Age – in the last centuries BC; Sussex in Roman times, in Saxon times, in medieval times, down the years, down the long centuries. Not the least interesting of its exhibits are the reconstructed Sussex farmhouse kitchen and the Iron Display Room.

South Lodge, five miles to the east, has gardens open to the public on only a few days in the summer months and will be enjoyed by all garden lovers. Nymans Gardens, to the east again, are National Trust property and open most days of the week from April to October, the 'walled garden' being a particular attraction. Borde Hill Garden, a few miles east by south, is on a somewhat larger scale and contains rare trees, shrubs, and woodland walks. They are open on three days a week from April to August. Finally we come close to the boundary-line between this eighth segment and the first, and to Heaselands. Here are some twenty acres of gardens, including water-gardens, aviaries, and a variety of waterfowl. Unfortunately these gardens are open to the public only on a very limited number of days in the summer.

The proliferation of gardens in this area – the two northernmost segments of the circle – is evidence of the quality of the land and the good use made of it by those fortunate enough both to own properties here, and to be public-spirited enough to share their good fortune. But even at that, probably the most lasting impression left on those who have explored this circle based on Ditchling Beacon is the whale-back of chalk, turf-clad, that parallels the coastline and offers such continuously superb views from a thousand and one viewpoints along its undulating length.

Royal Pavilion, Brighton

Butser Hill

The South Downs Way, which begins a few miles to the east of Ditchling Beacon (813 feet), ends, to all intents and purposes, at Butser Hill, just beyond the border between West Sussex and Hampshire; a gap of barely five miles separates the two perimeters drawn round these viewpoints, and the Way of course spans this. At 888 feet, Butser is easily the highest point on the South Downs, topping its nearest rival, Teglease, by more than fifty feet. Among the seventy-odd 800-foot-and-over chalk summits of East and West Sussex, Hampshire, Wiltshire, Buckinghamshire, Berkshire, Surrey, and Dorset it ranks as number fourteen.

It is not only its height but its shape that tempts one to rank it among the most impressive of these summits. A writer who is a specialist on our 'chalk ways' quotes an anonymous topographer who described Butser Hill as having 'no fewer than eight spurs, with almost headlong combes tapering down from the circular plateau, so making it the "starfish" of the southern hills'. The description is apt; but to obtain the overall picture it would be necessary – as on Berkshire's Whitehorse Hill – to have a bird's-eye view, and preferably towards late afternoon, when shadows fill the combes and light falls only on the intervening ribs or shoulders.

There is another reason why this viewpoint itself is of particular interest. The Hampshire County Council have as it were taken it under their wing, for it is in fact a site of quite exceptional interest. Prehistoric man lived here: not merely Neolithic Man, who flourished in southern England four thousand years ago, but Palaeolithic (or Old Stone Age) Man, his remote ancestor. A flint axe-head, or

Bayleaf House, Weald and Downland Open Air Museum

N
NW
W
SW
S
Basingstoke
8 miles
Newbury
22 miles
Romsey
6 miles
Southampton
5 miles
Southampton
4 miles
HAMPSHIRE
Winchester
Weeke
Winnall
Kings Worthy
Martyr Worthy
Itchen Abbas
Itchen Stoke
Avington
Ovington
Easton
Chilcomb
Stanmore
Oliver's Battery
Compton
Shawford
Otterbourne
Twyford
Morestead
Owslebury
Colden Common
Allbrook
Bishopstoke
Eastleigh
Fisher's Pond
Fair Oak
Horton Heath
SWAYTHLING
Moorgreen
West End
BITTERNE
THORNHILL
SHOLING
SOUTHAMPTON
Old Netley
Bursledon
Hamble
Lower Swanwick
Sarisbury
Park Gate
Lock's Heath
Warsash
Hook
Titchfield
Fareham
Funtley
Stubbington
Bridgemary
Peel Common
Hill Head
Lee-on-the-Solent
Gosport
Brockhurst
Alverstoke
Stokes Bay
Gilkicker Point
Spithead
Portchester
Wallington
Wymering
Cosham
Hilsea
Horsea I.
Whale I.
Portsmouth Harbour
North End
Portsea
Portsea Island
Southsea
Milton
PORTSMOUTH
Langstone Harbour
Drayton
Bedhampton
Havant
Warblington
Emsworth
Hermitage
Langstone
Northney
North Hayling
Thorney Island
Stoke
Fleet
Hayling Island
South Hayling
West Town
Eastoke
Hayling Bay
Chichester Harbour
Purbrook
Waterlooville
Cowplain
Leigh Park
Stockheath
Forest of Bere
Southwick
Boarhunt
North Boarhunt
Wickham
Curbridge
Burridge
Hedge End
Botley
Curdridge
Shedfield
Waltham Chase
Bishop's Waltham
Durley
Durley Street
Long Common
Lower Upham
Upham
Dean
Newtown
Hoe
Swanmore
Hillpound
Shirrell Heath
Droxford
Soberton
Soberton Heath
Hoe Gate
Hundred Acres
Meon Valley
Meon
Anthill Common
Worlds End
Denmead
Lovedean
Hambledon
Horndean
Catherington
Chalton
Blendworth
Clanfield
Chidden
Brockbridge
Meonstoke
Corhampton
Old Winchester Hill
Exton
Warnford
West Meon
East Meon
Ramsdean
Langrish
Butser Hill
888
Coombe
768
648
659
Buriton
Weston
Stroud
Petersfield
Sheet
Steep
Froxfield Green
High Cross
Privett
East End
West Tisted
Bramdean
Hinton Ampner
Brockwood
Kilmeston
Beauworth
Lane End
Langwood Warren
Baybridge
Hinton Marsh
Cheriton
Tichborne
New Alresford
Old Alresford
Gundleton
Bishops Sutton
Bighton
Ropley
Ropley Dean
Ropley Soke
North Street
Kitwood
Charlwood
Monkwood
East Tisted
Four Marks
Soldridge
Medstead
South Town
Wivelrod
Hattingley
Chawton
Alton
Beech
Anstey
Bentworth
Holt End
Lower Wield
Wield
Bradley
Shalden
Lasham
Southrope
Herriard
Ellisfield
Wallop
Weston Patrick
Nutley
Axford
Preston Candover
Chilton Candover
Brown Candover
Micheldever Forest
Popham
Woodmancott
East Stratton
Northington
Swarraton
Itchen Stoke
Long Sutton
South Warnborough
Well
Lower Froyle
Froyle
Golden Pot
738
Binsted
Holybourne
Wyck
East Worldham
West Worldham
Oak
Farringdon
Lower Farringdon
Newton Valence
Selborne
Blackmoor
Colemore
Empshott
Hawkley
West Liss
Liss
723
571
707
West Marden
Finchdean
Forestside
Rowland's Castle
Lordington
Westbourne
West Wittering
Hartings
Horndean
1
3
4
22
23
26
27
28
29
30
31
32
33
34
35
36
M27
Scale : 5 miles to 1 inch
17½
15
10
5
0
MILES

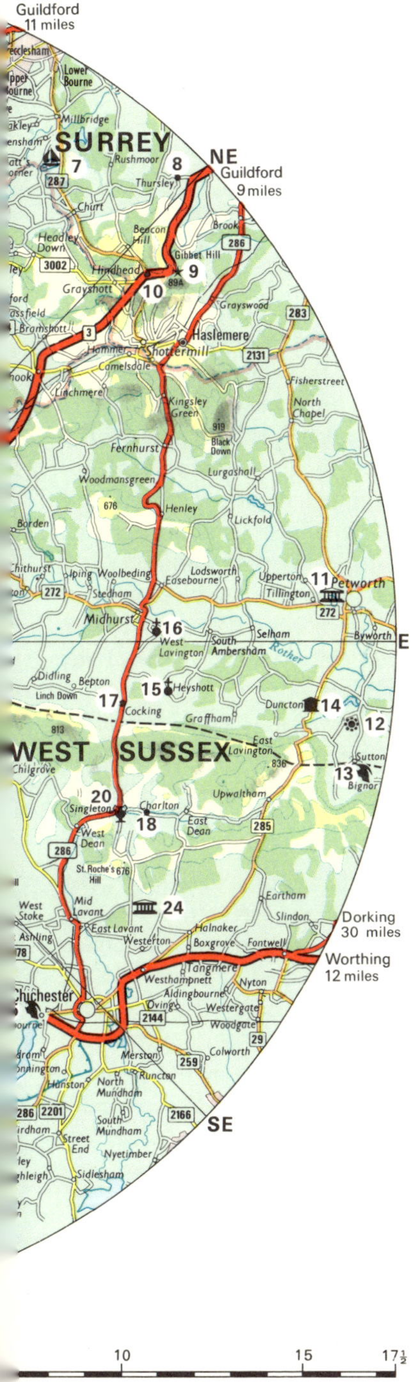

Butser Hill

1 Butser Hill
2 Farnham
3 Selborne
4 East and West Worldham
5 Kingsley
6 Oakhanger
7 Frensham Ponds
8 Thursley
9 Gibbet Hill
10 Hindhead
11 Petworth House
12 Sutton End Gardens
13 Bignor
14 Duncton
15 Heyshott
16 West Lavington
17 Cocking
18 Charlton
19 Elsted
20 Singleton
21 South Harting
22 Buriton
23 Uppark
24 Goodwood House
25 Roman palace
26 Sailing area
27 Portchester Castle
28 Portsmouth
29 Titchfield Abbey
30 Netley Abbey ruins
31 Soberton
32 Broadhalfpenny Down
33 Old Winchester Hill
34 Tichborne
35 Avington Park
36 Chawton

possibly skinning-knife, has been found on Butser, and experts suggest that it could date back some 250,000 years. Appropriately enough it has been adopted as a symbol, and when you reach the summit you will find neat finger-posts each inscribed with this symbol and pointing to one of the ten or more 'Butser Trails'. Free illustrated leaflets are available on the site, indicating what is to be seen on each of these trails.

For example, one leads to a system of earthworks carved on the north-east slope of Butser by Neolithic tribes; another, on the south-east face, consists of a network of tracks used by the Saxons a mere thirteen centuries or so ago and, curiously enough, developed by French prisoners during the Napoleonic Wars who were given the task of collecting flintstones to form the foundations of what is now the A3 London to Portsmouth road, which passes immediately beneath Butser's east face. Others of the trails will appeal to the naturalist, the botanist, and the tree lover, for the chalk and subsoil as a result of erosion over the years have led to the appearance of unexpected flowers, plants, shrubs, and trees; there are more than a hundred species to be found here. The Forestry Commission has made good use of these changes in subsoil content: on the downland slope on the side facing the eastern slope of Butser Hill, separated from it by the A3, there is one of the great orderly stands of the Commission's conifers, also numerous beechwood stands.

As you stand on the rounded summit, the ground falls away in all directions. The A3 slashes its way north-eastwards to Petersfield and the North Downs beyond the Surrey border, and southwards to Portsmouth harbour and the deep, tortuous inlets that characterise this coastline from Chichester to Fareham; you can see the Isle of Wight with ease on a clear day. To the north-west lies the historic city of Winchester, just within the perimeter and beyond the South Downs. Due east the downs begin (or approach their end if you have been following them westwards).

Butser is a superb vantage-point, one of a succession of south-coastal signalling points known to the Saxons as such, and part of the strategic link by which, in 1588, the approach of the Spanish Armada was made known from Devon to Kent by beacons. A GPO radio mast stands where the beacons used to flare and smoke, but somehow is acceptable – perhaps because it is the contemporary version of an old tradition. You may climb to this 888-foot summit the hard way, on foot, from any direction; but thanks to the GPO there

Radio-controlled aircraft on Butser Hill

is now a good road curving round Butser's south-west flank and a free car park on the summit. A whole day spent within the mile-long circuit of this hill alone would not be too long to exhaust its potential; model airplane enthusiasts use its western face for launching their radio-controlled craft.

A small wedge of Surrey penetrates the circle in its first two segments, with the old market town of Farnham right on the perimeter. True, it is something of a 'dormitory town', but it exists in its own right, too. It is a former 'wool' town and, according to Defoe, 'the greatest corn market in England, London excepted'. It has a twelfth-century castle with a fine Norman shell-keep; interestingly, this has served as a resting-place for a long succession of Bishops of Winchester and Guildford, and monarchs from Edward I to Victoria have slept within its ancient walls. The town is filled with picturesque corners: the Old Almshouses; eighteenth-century Willmer House, now a museum; the Lion and Lamb Courtyard; and the church, where you may see one of the comparatively rare 'vinegar' Bibles.

If William Cobbett, author of *Rural Rides,* was Farnham's most notable son, it is the parson-naturalist-writer Gilbert White whose name will be for ever associated with the village of Selborne, some ten miles into this segment. He was born there in 1720, and in his middle seventies died there at The Wakes, his home, now a museum. Every naturalist knows his *Natural History of Selborne*, the outcome of a lifetime of dedicated exploring of a relatively small but abundantly varied district, published only a few years before his death. To appreciate the book to the full you must visit Selborne; to appreciate Selborne fully you must have read the book. The National Trust owns some 250 acres, virtually the whole of Selborne and district.

Between Farnham and Selborne there lie 'lost hamlets' such as East and West Worldham, Kingsley, Oakhanger, and Frensham, with its open stretches of water oddly designated 'ponds'. Near the boundary-line with the next segment is the charming village of Thursley. In the churchyard of St Michael and All Angels is the tomb of a young sailor murdered at a spot near the Devil's Punchbowl, right on the edge of the A3. The road parallels the boundary-line and you can see, a few miles south of Thursley, a memorial stone that marks the murder site and names the three villains, 'Edw. Lonegan, Michael Gancy and Jas. Marshal' who, 'Taken That Day Were Hung in Chains' for their crime; Gibbet Hill (894 feet), in the second segment, is the spot where they were hanged.

All this region, north of the laterally-running A272, is beautifully forested, noted for beechwoods rivalled only, perhaps, by those of the southern Chilterns and the glorious expanse of Savernake Forest. Haslemere and Hindhead are of course the 'show places' in this small neck of Surrey that probes into Hampshire; but they are only the two best-known of the many tree-encircled rural townships, villages, and hamlets that here abound, each lovelier than the last. Petersfield, just over the West Sussex–Hampshire border, is another delightful small town, somewhat handicapped by lying astride the A3; it is to be hoped that it will soon be by-passed so that its many fine Georgian houses, which remind one of Farnham, may be saved and the town be permitted to relapse into deserved serenity. Like Farnham it was once a 'wool' town; it was also an important staging-post in the era of the long-distance coaches.

Another township that at present suffers from through traffic is to be found on the A272 near the perimeter of this segment: Petworth. It is best known for Petworth House, a seventeenth-century mansion built for the Duke of Somerset but occupying a site that originally belonged to the Earl of Northumberland in Norman times. The estate is bounded by a wall thirteen miles long, which gives some idea of its size; the house's west façade is over 300 feet in length – surely the longest façade of any great house? In its 750 acres of parkland deer roam, browsing among the splendid stands of trees. In the wealth of its treasures, its paintings, carvings, ceilings, panelling, sculptures, and staircases it is a match for any save a handful of the greatest houses in the land. The whole is now the property of the National Trust, open to the public on three days a week from April to October.

South of the A272 we are very soon on the lower slopes of the West Sussex Downs. Close to the perimeter of the third segment are the Sutton End Gardens. While garden-lovers linger among its beauties, those to whom the period of the Roman occupation of Britain appeals more strongly will make their way southwards along minor roads to the astonishing Roman Villa of Bignor. This was not a Roman settlement in the sense of those adjacent to Hadrian's Wall, but the home of an obviously wealthy and well-connected Roman citizen who established here a country seat during the Romano-British era towards the end of the second century AD. Discovered during ploughing in 1811, it has been systematically excavated over the years, to reveal a completely engrossing picture of how an affluent citizen-by-adoption lived in those remote days. Here are details of his central-heating system (not bettered until this century), the mosaics he had made for his artistic satisfaction, his farm and granary buildings, his waste-disposal system; all these, and much more, have been revealed, recorded, and either covered over for their protection or preserved for inspection by those who care to visit.

There is hardly a village or hamlet hereabouts that lacks a claim to interest. Duncton has its Cricketers' Arms, a Mecca for lovers of the game as it was once owned by John Wisden, whose name the cricketer's 'bible' bears to this day. Here, too, was born 'Jemmy' Dean, the first man to establish round-arm bowling, which was to succeed the old-style under-arm. There is much use here of the local flint, often combined with stone or, in stronger contrast, with mellow brick. Heyshott, where the free trader Richard Cobden was

Buriton, Hampshire

born, has its flint-built church; his memorial is here, though he was buried at neighbouring West Lavington. Just to the south, Cocking has a notable display of this local building material, nowhere better seen than in these Wealden villages overlooked by the northern slopes of the West Sussex Downs. The Fox, at Charlton, as typical a country inn as any you may ever see, demonstrates a nice admixture of this flint and brick, the former inset in irregularly-sized but well-proportioned panels of the latter. Elsted has its tiny church, largely restored but still showing the notable Saxon herringbone stonework at its western end.

Perhaps the most picturesque of all these scattered hamlets is Singleton, just beyond Charlton. It lies close to, but fortunately is just by-passed by, the A286 Chichester road. The church is a fine example of ecclesiastical flintwork, with a Saxon tower. It also possesses an unusual feature in its 'Priests' Room', designed for visiting clergy and equipped in such a way that the visitors could look down on the worshippers below. To see the most interesting feature of Singleton, however, you must leave the village by the main road southwards, turning off almost immediately along a minor road on the left. This will take you to the Weald and Downland Open Air Museum, a few hundred yards distant.

This is a comparatively new venture, inspired to some extent by the open air museums of Scandinavia and deserving of support from all who love traditional things of a truly rural flavour, whether sawpits or tread-wheels, charcoal-burners' camps or wattle-inset timberwork from medieval times. Here, in open meadowland extending to some thirty acres and almost completely surrounded by woodlands, half-timbered buildings such as Bayleaf House, barns, toll-cottages, and other relics of former days are being installed. They have been salvaged from various corners of Sussex, Hampshire, and even Kent; then they have been skilfully re-assembled and, where necessary, restored in period with contemporary timbers and other materials. Not the least interesting exhibit here is what remains of a Saxon hut believed to have been occupied by weavers for many centuries. To wander untrammelled about an open site such as this is to step back in time and truly savour what life must have been like in rural England in medieval times. It is open daily from Easter to the end of September.

To the north-west of Singleton, only a few miles short of Butser Hill, are the three Hartings – South, East, and West; hardly a mile

H.M.S. Victory *at Portsmouth*

separates all of them and each is individually attractive. The largest of them is South Harting, dominated by its church built on rising ground in the twelfth century, though most of what you see today is of later date. Did its congregations as they filed into and out of it before and after the services pay any attention to the stocks and whipping-post (the latter with iron wrist-cuffs designed to hold juvenile offenders) which are set hard up against the gateway? Midway between the Hartings and Butser is the village of Buriton, in this writer's opinion at least prettier than any of them. Its twelfth-century Church of St Mary, like that of South Harting, stands on high ground; but its massive tower looks down upon a large pond with ducks lazily paddling on it or going ashore on the little island with its weeping willow in the centre. The pond is part-surrounded by white wooden rails, backed by more, and larger weeping willows and other trees which almost enclose it. There are trim, snug, well-kept cottages and a Georgian house or two; but above all, a sense of undisturbed peace pervades the whole.

From South Harting southwards a mile or so brings you to Uppark, a National Trust property open to the public three days a week from Easter until the end of September. Incidentally, it was here that H. G. Wells spent his childhood, his mother being housekeeper. The approach is through a fine avenue of noble beeches, but the interior is more impressive than the exterior. In the drawing-room is the original red flock wallpaper, and the original silk curtains still hang in the salon, whose theme is white and gold. Since its building, in the eighteenth century, furniture, paintings, china, porcelain, and *objets d'art* have been steadily accumulated in this 'gentleman's mansion'.

South and east of Uppark, a network of minor roads lead to Goodwood House, near the perimeter, associated in everyone's mind with racing. This great house belongs to the Earl of March, and has been the country seat of all nine Earls of Richmond. Its origin is Jacobean, but it has been altered over the centuries, and greatly restored in recent years. Here are paintings by Van Dyck, and Canaletto, among others and, as you might expect from its connection with the racecourse, the inimitable Stubbs. Here visitors may book themselves what are significantly called 'Luncheon Tours': the price is naturally steep, but many will feel that to lunch as well as to sightsee here is worth a good deal. The house is open intermittently, 'according to events'.

Over the boundary-line into the fourth segment we come immediately to Chichester, the Romans' Noviomagus and later named the *castra* of Cissa, son of the first of the Saxon kings – hence the name. Its layout, four roads running straight north, east, south, and west from the medieval cross, whose only rival is the one at Malmesbury, is evidence of the town's Roman origin. There is more to see here than can be described adequately in so small a compass, so we will turn to the Roman Palace shown on the map near Fishbourne immediately to the west, the most remarkable relic of its kind in the country.

It is in fact the largest Roman building so far discovered in this country, and one of the largest in Europe. 'Palace' rather than 'villa' because it was so obviously the property of one of the highest-ranking Romans, or possibly a British chieftain favoured by them in Romano-British times. The remains of the extensive buildings that have been excavated have been roofed over, so that you may wander at will over most of the site in any weather; museum exhibits,

Gatehouse at Titchfield Abbey

diagrams, 'artists' impressions', models, and so on all help the visitor to understand how life was lived at the time.

South of the A27 coast road, almost the whole of this fourth segment and the next consists of water and intruding promontories, tongues of land interspersed among natural harbours. A dozen or so sailing symbols on the map draw attention to the chief amenities; small-boat sailors, yachtsmen, and those who enjoy seeing others 'messing about in boats' will be in their element here. In the fifth segment, however, there is something of more classic interest: on the tip of the small promontory between Fareham and Cosham is Portchester Castle. This was one of a string of fortresses built by the Romans during the third century AD, others being at Pevensey, Richborough, and Reculver, and is the only Roman fortress in northern Europe whose walls are still intact. Some nine acres are enclosed within four 200-yard-long walls, two of them on the water's edge, access being gained through a Water Gate on the east side. So well did the Romans build that nine centuries later the fortress could be adapted as an Augustinian priory, while other parts of it were elaborated by Henry I into a fortress in his own idiom. The keep has walls thirteen feet thick at the base, and the curtain-walls are hardly less massive: a reminder of how well both Roman and medieval builders did their work. The site is open to the public from April till September.

From here you look across the harbour to Portsmouth. For most visitors the outstanding exhibit in the Royal Naval Museum is Nelson's flagship, H.M.S. *Victory*. She stands in a new berth at No. 2 Dock, dressed overall. But she is only one (if the greatest) of the many exhibits here, which include Charles II's state barge, a gown worn by Emma, Lady Hamilton, Nelson's silver snuff-box and personal quadrant, and a letter written by Captain Hardy, in whose arms the victor of Trafalgar died.

Just over the boundary-line with the sixth segment and clear of the outskirts of Fareham is Titchfield Abbey, a Premonstratensian foundation that dates from 1232. It was of course a victim of the Dissolution, but such of the ruins as remain are immensely impressive. Three years after its abandonment one Thomas Wriothesley, utilising much of the material, built for himself 'a right stately house, embatled and having a goodlye gate'. There can be few more interesting examples of the conversion of an ecclesiastical building to secular use than this. And incidentally, the little town from which

Netley Abbey, Hampshire

the abbey takes its name is worth more than a passing glance for its seventeenth- and eighteenth-century buildings; it was formerly a smallish seaport on the west bank of the River Meon, a few miles before its point of entry into the Solent.

Five miles to the west, close to the perimeter of this sixth segment, are the tree-embowered ruins of another abbey, that of Netley, a Cistercian foundation of the same century. Only its shell now remains, for after the Dissolution most of the stonework was cannibalised for building purposes by the Marquess of Winchester, who actually incorporated part of the abbey church in his mansion. Some two centuries later it was further cannibalised and much of the stonework removed wholesale to a new site; the north transept was re-erected as a sham ruin, or 'folly', in Cranbury Park some miles away. But Netley is well worth visiting even though so little of the original building can still be seen, for there is a great sense of peace resulting from the tree-filled site, all so close to Southampton Water.

Southampton and Eastleigh sprawl astride the perimeter; if you are in search of rurality you will now do well to follow the course of the Meon north-eastwards through this segment. Its wide, shallow valley will take you through a string of charming hamlets, each with its individual feature of interest, and for the most part unspoiled, even though many of them are linked by the comparatively busy A32. Soberton has its finely-sited church and 'centurion's coffin' by the South Porch; Hambledon has Broadhalfpenny Down a coin's toss away, where the Bat and Ball inn overlooks the site of the Hambledon Cricket Club's ground on which, in 1770, the village team defeated an all-England team by an innings and 168 runs. Droxford, Brockbridge, and Meonstoke all lie on this serpentining stream; as does Corhampton, right on the boundary-line with the seventh segment: all are hamlets of charm, even minor distinction – but how could it be otherwise in a setting so delectable?

On this boundary-line, too, stands – or rather soars above the valley of the Meon – Old Winchester Hill. Its summit, at 648 feet, offers a spacious view eastwards to Butser Hill and the South Downs beyond, and westwards across the valley, and northwards over West Meon village, and southwards to the Solent and its shipping; it is worth the easy climb for these views alone, and though you must do the climb on foot, the summit is 240 feet lower than that of Butser Hill.

We have crossed now into the penultimate segment. The A272 spans it, to terminate at Winchester. Here are yet more scattered villages, no less appealing than those in the previous segment: Bramdean and Beauworth, East Meon and Coombe, Brockwood ('Badger's Wood'?) and Hinton Ampner, Cheriton and Tichborne. It is in this last-named place that the ceremony of the Tichborne Dole is enacted annually on 25 March, Lady Day, as it has been for eight hundred years past. The 'dole' used to consist of 1,400 twenty-six-ounce loaves; today the traditional thirty hundredweight of flour is distributed among the 200 villagers of Tichborne and neighbouring Cheriton. The story behind this ancient and impressive ceremony is well worth reading in detail.

Compared with the eastern part of this circle, there are surprisingly few great houses open to the public. One such, however, is Avington Park, between Winchester and Alresford (it must be pronounced 'Awlsford'). It is one of the lesser examples, built in red brick and consisting of both seventeenth- and eighteenth-century work.

Jane Austen's Home, Chawton

Thatched cottage, East Tisted

In the older portion Charles II once sojourned for a while with his mistress, Nell Gwyn, probably the house's chief claim to fame. It is open twice weekly from May to September.

A network of minor roads criss-cross one another in this final segment between the perimeter and the busy A31 and A32. Close to the junction of these two roads, fortunately by-passed by both of them, is the very picturesque hamlet of Chawton, a place of pilgrimage for devotees of Jane Austen. Here is Jane Austen's Home, sponsored by the Memorial Trust named after her. In this red brick house she lived from 1809 until 1817 and wrote *Mansfield Park*, *Emma*, and *Persuasion*. The house's exterior is not impressive; indeed, it is probably the least interesting-looking of all Chawton's houses and cottages, many of them half-timbered and thatched. But it was Jane's home for eight years, and is carefully preserved as a very personal museum. A tablet on the outer wall, erected by 'her admirers in this country and in America', declares: 'Such Art as Hers Can Never Grow Old'. Admirers of this Hampshire-born writer, whose body lies buried in Winchester Cathedral, will echo the sentiment. But it is inside this house, among her personal and well-loved possessions and her many relics, rather than in the cold grey stone cathedral, that one is most conscious of her presence. It is open every day of the week, and all the year round.

She was fortunate in her place of work. From Chawton southwards to Butser Hill there is tree-clad country, sloping gently upwards all the time; there is abundant thatch as, for example, in the minuscule hamlet of East Tisted, with half-timbering, and an old-world atmosphere prevailing among the lanes and in the hamlets all the way, until you cross the A272 once more for a final look far and wide to the horizon in every direction from the viewpoint of Butser Hill.

Portchester Castle, Hampshire

Athelhampton

The Cerne Giant

Some thirty miles separate the western limit of the chalk country of the South Downs, at Butser Hill, from the Dorset Downs that occupy about half the circle whose focal point is the Giant of Cerne; between these lie the New Forest and the hinterland of Bournemouth. You will not find the Cerne Giant actually marked on any but large-scale maps. He is a hill-figure, carved like the White Horses of Wiltshire and Berkshire, out of chalk and spread-eagled – all 180 foot of him, with the gigantic symbol of his masculinity (offensive to Victorian and Edwardian eyes) erect for all to see – across the summit of a hill that rises immediately to the north of Cerne Abbas. This village once possessed a Benedictine abbey, wholly dominated during its centuries of existence by this figure of essentially pagan origin.

Almost the whole of this circle lies in Dorset; Somerset occupies part of the northern segments near their perimeter, the border entering the first segment at Blackmoor Vale and zigzagging south-westwards by way of Yeovil to make its exit south-west of Crewkerne. About half the circle – its central and most of its southern portion – is chalk land; it is in essence a continuation of the South Downs after that interruption. The similarity is remarkable. There are half a dozen or so heights along the South Downs that top the 800-foot mark; in Dorset there are more than twice that number, while Bulbarrow and Pilsdon Pen actually top 900 feet. There is as yet no through-route for walkers, as such; but the enthusiast for chalkland walking will find all that he needs to satisfy him in this, the least spoiled (apart from much of its coastline) of all our counties.

As in Wiltshire, to the north-east, this territory was occupied by

N
NW
W
SW
S
Basingstoke 65 miles
Shepton Mallet 13 miles
Exeter 38 miles
Exeter 35 miles
Exeter 34 miles
SOMERSET
Wincanton
Holton
Sparkford
North Cadbury
Compton Pauncefoot
Downhead
Podimore
Northover
Ilchester
Bridgehampton
Yeovilton
Chilton Cantelo
Limington
Ashington
Tintinhull
Chilthorne Domer
Yeovil Marsh
Mudford
Yeovil
Preston Plucknett
Montacute
Stoke sub Hamdon
Norton sub Hamdon
Odcombe
Chiselborough
Brympton
West Coker
East Coker
North Coker
Barwick
Stoford
West Camel
Queen Camel
Marston Magna
Corton Denham
Rimpton
Adber
Sandford Orcas
Trent
Nether Compton
Over Compton
Sherborne
Poyntington
Oborne
Milborne Port
Milborne Wick
Henstridge
Stalbridge Weston
Stalbridge
Purse Caundle
Stourton Caundle
Bishop's Caundle
Caundle Marsh
Haydon
North Wootton
Allweston
Folke
Long Burton
Bradford Abbas
Thornford
Beer Hackett
Lillington
Knighton
Ryme Intrinseca
Yetminster
Holnest
Totnell
Leigh
Chetnole
Three Gates
Middlemarsh
Hermitage
Crouch Hill
Boys Hill
Glanvilles Wootton
Pulham
Buckland Newton
Duntish
Lyon's Gate
Minterne Magna
Hilfield
Up Cerne
Henley
Alton Pancras
Plush
Cerne Abbas
Sydling St. Nicholas
Up Sydling
Nether Cerne
Godmanston
Piddletrenthide
Charminster
Dorchester
Stratton
Bradford Peverell
Burton
Frampton
Grimstone
Muckleford
Forston
Compton Valence
Winterbourne Abbas
Kingston Russell
Martinstown
Winterbourne Steepleton
Winterborne Monkton
Winterborne Herringston
Black Down
Portesham
Friar Waddon
Upwey
Coryates
Shilvinghampton
Broadwey
Bincombe
Preston
Osmington
Osmington Mills
Rodden
Langton Herring
Chickerell
Fleet
Charlestown
Radipole
Westham
Melcombe Regis
Weymouth
Weymouth Bay
Rodwell
Wyke Regis
Portland Harbour
Castletown
Fortuneswell
West Bay
Chesil Beach
Abbotsbury
West Bexington
Little Bredy
Long Bredy
Litton Cheney
Puncknoll
Swyre
Berwick
Burton Bradstock
Shipton Gorge
Chilcombe
Askerswell
Uploders
Loders
Bradpole
Walditch
Bridport
Bothenhampton
Eype
Seatown
Chideock
North Chideock
Symondsbury
Whitchurch Canonicorum
Ryall
Dottery
Broad Oak
Salway Ash
Shave Cross
Pilsdon
Bettiscombe
Birdsmoor Gate
Netherbury
Melplash
Waytown
Beaminster
Stoke Abbott
Broadwindsor
Burstock
Drimpton
Mosterton
Seaborough
Clapton
Misterton
Hewish
Crewkerne
Roundham
Haselbury Plucknett
North Perrott
South Perrott
Merriott
Hinton St. George
Lopen
West Chinnock
Middle Chinnock
East Chinnock
Over Stratton
Bower Hinton
Hurst
Ash
Hardington Mandeville
Hardington Marsh
Pendomer
Closworth
Halstock
Chedington
Corscombe
West Chelborough
East Chelborough
Melbury Osmond
Melbury Sampford
Melbury Bubb
Evershot
Holywell
Batcombe
Frome St. Quintin
Rampisham
Hooke
Wraxall
Lower Kingcombe
Chilfrome
Cattistock
Maiden Newton
Mapperton
North Poorton
Toller Porcorum
Toller Fratrum
Wynford Eagle
West Milton
Powerstock
Nettlecombe
West Compton
NORTH DORSET DOWNS
SOUTH DORSET
Res.
Scale : 5 miles to 1 inch
17½
15
10
5
0
MILES

Cerne Giant

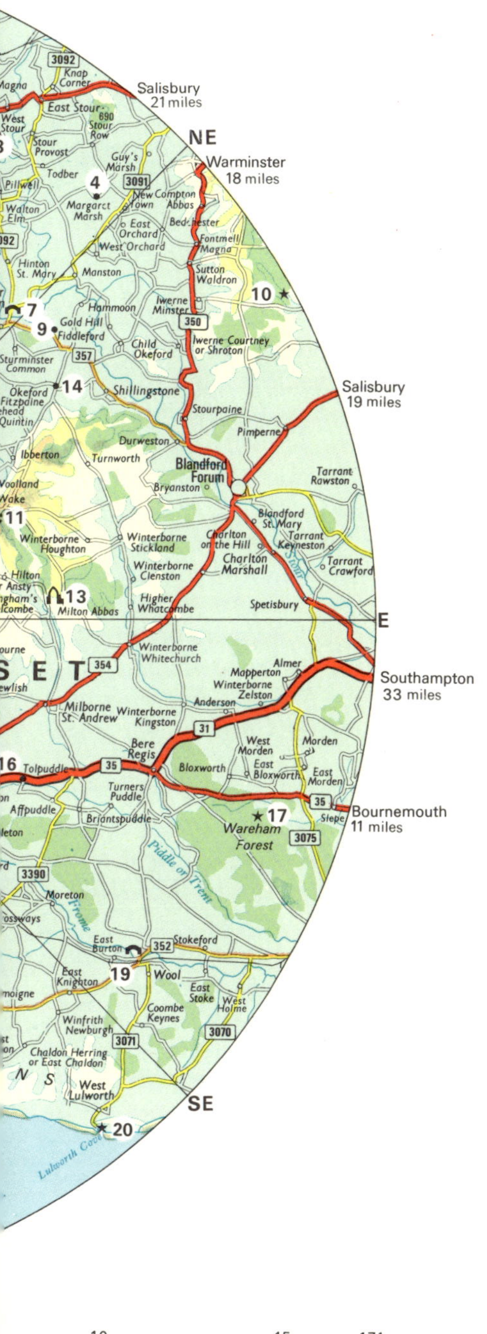

I ❋ Cerne Giant
2 ★ Blackmoor Vale
3 • Fifehead Magdalen
4 • Margaret Marsh
5 • Purse Caundle
6 • Stalbridge
7 ⌒ Sturminster Newton
8 ⌒ Fifehead Neville
9 • Fiddleford
10 ★ Cranborne Chase
11 ❋ Bulbarrow Hill
12 ★ Rawlsbury Hill
13 ∩ Milton Abbas
14 • Okeford Fitzpaine
15 • Plush
16 • Tolpuddle
17 ★ Wareham Forest
18 🏛 Athelhampton
19 ⌒ Wool
20 ★ Lulworth Cove
21 ⌂ Thomas Hardy's cottage
22 • West Stafford
23 ♜ Maiden Castle
24 ★ Hardy Monument
25 ★ Chesil Beach (or Bank)
26 ★ Abbotsbury Swannery
27 ∩ Abbotsbury Abbey ruins
28 ▲ Burton Bradstock
29 • Whitchurch Canonicorum
30 • Toller Fratrum
31 ❋ Pilsdon Pen
32 🏛 Brympton d'Evercy
33 ♁ Melbury Bubb
34 🏛 Montacute House
35 ♁ Yetminster
36 • Sherborne

the earliest settlers in England. Their hill-forts, earthworks, burial-places, and other relics of cultures that flourished from Neolithic times through the Bronze and Iron Ages well into the Romano-British era abound here. The greatest of them all, of course, is Maiden Castle to the south-west of Dorchester, the county town, to which we shall come exactly at the half-way mark round this circle. There are many others, lesser in extent but in fact more nobly sited, so enthusiasts here in Dorset may take their large-scale maps and seek the innumerable hill-top earthworks and the burial-sites, criss-crossing the North and South Dorset Downs in any direction that pleases their fancy.

Alone among the fifteen viewpoint circles in this book, those drawn round the Cerne Giant and round Glastonbury Tor actually intersect, on the border between Dorset and Somerset, some of the material therefore inevitably overlapping. In general, places of interest that lie in both circles, but belong to Somerset, will be dealt with in the Glastonbury Tor viewpoint, though mention may also be made of them, if need arises, in the present viewpoint.

The chief feature of the first segment is Blackmoor Vale, which roughly parallels the county border and is watered by gently-flowing streams such as the Stour, the Lydden, and their tributaries. The name suggests moorland, but it is in fact a shallow, widespread valley, 'a landscape rich and discreetly wooded,' as the artist Paul Nash once described it, 'mapped out to a large design giving a sense of ease, plenty and, above all, of detachment and dignity. An aristocratic country, well cared for and seeming conscious only of its own world.' This area is far removed from what is generally regarded as the 'true' Dorset scene; but at least it has the merit of throwing into greater relief the chalk uplands so well known to the occupants four thousand years and more ago and still keenly relished by downland walkers today.

In this segment you will find a proliferation of small villages, each of real character; they may be taken at random, scattered about a network of delightful twisting lanes. Fifehead Magdalen, for instance, has a church with a thirteenth-century tower; the hamlet largely set about with trees on gentle hill-slopes. Margaret Marsh (it sounds like a schoolgirl's name!) is a cluster of small dwellings lying so low that, like many neighbouring hamlets, it is frequently cut off from the rest of the vale by flood-waters. Purse Caundle has a manor house that dates from the fifteenth century and, with its steep roof,

Medieval market cross, Stalbridge

Sturminster Newton bridge

gables, and mullioned windows, is a reminder of the Cotswolds, forty miles to the north-east. It is allegedly haunted by the ghost of a huntsman said to have been killed on the orders of Henry III because he set his hounds on the monarch's White Hart; this rash act led not only to the man's execution but the imposition on Blackmoor Vale of a tax 'in perpetuity'.

Two other of the many possible places may be mentioned before we pass into the next segment. Stalbridge, a market township, is unusual in that its fourteenth-century market cross stands, not in its centre, but by the roadside near its outskirts. It is a beautifully-ornamented cross-shaft rising to perhaps twelve or fifteen feet from pedestal and three-tiered plinth. Tall and slender, carved out of mellow stone, its outlines have been softened, blurred, by some six centuries of weathering. It does not need an expert's eye to discern that the uppermost section is considerably less old than the main, medieval portion. On this the scene of the crucifixion is ably carved, and it will be agreed that the relatively new blends well with the old.

The Stour has given its name to a cluster of villages, the best known of which is Sturminster Newton. Though it lies all too close to a main road, it retains much of the charm it has always possessed. It has long had a regular market; it has a seventeenth-century mill that was working at least until very recently, and may still have its uses; and it has one of the finest bridges in a county noted for such features. Built some five hundred years ago of pale grey stone that is in strong contrast to, for instance, the ochre sandstone of Stalbridge's market cross, it has six pointed arches, elegantly proportioned, with chiselled cornices and moulded coping-stones. By contrast, there is the plaque (similar to those to be found on Wool bridge and elsewhere) grimly warning users that if they damage it they will be sentenced to transportation for life. It was not today's type of common vandal who was being warned, but carriers who might cross it with unduly heavy loads. The old mill stands close by, and wagon loads of corn and flour must have been passing over the bridge to and from the mill for centuries.

Over in the second segment the villages continue to proliferate. Fifehead Magdalen is twinned now with Fifehead Neville, where there is one of Dorset's most attractive packhorse bridges, set alongside a ford on a twist of the lane and embowered in trees so that it is difficult to find a moment in the day when the sun shines

Milton Abbas

fairly enough on it for a photograph. Fiddleford's name is unpromising, but the place is worth seeking out for the history that lies behind it. The mill and adjoining farm are of medieval origin, parts of them Tudor; the wall of the mill, operated by the Stour, carries an inscription carved in the mid-sixteenth century; two hundred years later, surprising as it may seem in so serene a spot, this was a base for the distribution of contraband by packhorse trains far and wide. It is pure chance that the first part of the place-name suggests nefarious practice!

Cranborne Chase, which flows across the perimeter of this segment from Wiltshire, was once good hunting country, jealously preserved for monarchs from King John to King James I. It is no longer as heavily wooded as it used to be, though extensive beech and hazel will be found climbing the chalk slopes of the hills beyond which, to the north, lies Blackmoor Vale. So excellent was the game here until the last century that there was constant warfare between bands of would-be poachers and strong forces of keepers. Such local names as 'Bloody Coppice' are reminders hereabouts of pitched battles fought between them, and there is a display of mantraps and other vicious deterrents to be seen in the Farnham Museum.

Most of Cranborne Chase is good farmland today; but in the middle of last century it could be described (rather as Ashdown Forest could) thus: 'Nothing can be more wild than this leafy labyrinth. On the bordering downs no object meets the eye except here and there at a distance a small, round clump of trees called by the people of the country "a hat of trees".' Do not be put off by this: Cranborne Chase is now largely open country, gently wooded, mellowed by time, 'tamed' where this was necessary and, like the uplands beyond, relatively sparsely inhabited. You can be isolated here, if you wish so to be, but never unduly far from the amenities of towns such as Blandford Forum. Its name suggests Roman origin; in fact it is a remarkably modern town, for on 4 July 1731 it was virtually destroyed by fire, to be almost wholly rebuilt, largely in Georgian style, of red brick and stone; it is the 'Shottesford Forum' of Hardy's Wessex novels, the only 'Forum' among English place-names in fact. It still has, however, a few pre-destruction seventeenth-century buildings.

In towards the viewpoint the chalk hills slope upwards to Bulbarrow Hill (901 feet). Unlike most of Dorset's chalk summits, this can be reached by road. There is no Iron Age camp here, but it offers magnificent views in most directions: north-eastwards up Blackmoor Vale to Salisbury Plain; north-westwards to the Mendips and the Quantocks. Ten minutes' walk along the northern escarpment will bring you to the Iron Age camp on Rawlsbury where, emphatically, there is no car park.

Southwards, close to the boundary-line with the third segment, is Milton Abbey, an eighteenth-century house built on the remains of a fifteenth-century abbey and, because it is now a school, open to the public only in the Easter and summer holidays. It stands in parkland only a mile from the village of Milton Abbas, the site of a monastery founded in 938 AD by King Athelstan, though nothing of this remains today. There is a curious sense of 'newness' about this village, for all its medieval and earlier associations; the explanation is no less curious. The village consists of one sloping street lined by trim, identical thatched cottages, each with its unfenced lawn slanting down to the road; and a tree or two between each cottage and its neighbour.

It is a 'model village', though not in the sense of the scale-model villages at Bourton, Wimborne Minster, and elsewhere: it is 'model' because when the Earl of Dorchester bought the eighteenth-century mansion he decided that the old village was an eyesore, and too close to his grand residence for comfort. He therefore had it razed to the ground, and entirely rebuilt where it could not obtrude on his line of vision, and in a style 'right and proper' – by his standards. It would be hard to find in all Dorset a village in stronger contrast to the truly rural ones such as, for example, Okeford Fitzpaine, Mappowder, Folly, Plush, Hazelbury Bryan, Turnworth, or a score of others within a short radius of Milton Abbas.

The A31 and A35 unite in the third segment. They run between the South and North Dorset Downs, in low-lying terrain watered by the Frome and the Piddle. The latter has given its name to a group of villages along its length: Puddletown, Affpuddle, Briantspuddle, Turners Puddle, Tolpuddle, and Piddletrenthide, in which the river's alternative name, Trent, is oddly incorporated. The map shows the comparative emptiness of the area through which the river flows south-eastwards to Wareham and Poole Harbour – the area called Wareham Forest. This is no forest, but a vast expanse of furze-covered, wild and lonely heathland, now almost wholly taken over by the Army and so much more 'occupied' than it was when it was the 'Egdon Heath' of Hardy's *Return of the Native*. It is hardly exaggerating to state that the finest piece of atmospheric-descriptive writing in the whole corpus of Hardy's novels is that which evokes this brooding, menacing expanse:

> 'The heath wore the appearance of an instalment of night which had taken up its place before its astronomical hour was come . . .. The sombre stretch of rounds and hollows seemed to rise and meet the evening gloom in pure sympathy, the heath exhaling darkness as rapidly as the heavens precipitated it. The obscurity in the air and the obscurity in the land closed together in a black fraternisation towards which each advanced half-way.'

As strong a contrast with this heathland as could well be imagined is the serenity of Athelhampton, without question the most beautiful Tudor dwelling in Dorset. It lies just off the A35, midway between Tolpuddle (of the 'Tolpuddle Martyrs' fame) and Puddletown, set amid some ten acres of gardens. Built in the latter part of the fifteenth century, it has been owned and occupied by a succession of families, every one of which, to this day, has cherished it; this accounts for the very strong impression you have, as you enter its portal in the

L-shaped façade and find yourself immediately in the Great Hall, that this is a home, not a mere museum-piece. Splendid as Woburn, Longleat, and Blenheim Palace are, Athelhampton appeals as a great-house-in-miniature, everything within and without appealing to the eye and lingering long in the memory. With its Great Hall, its Long Gallery, secret rooms and lovely gardens, it is open to the public three days a week from mid-April until early October.

Before the ground begins to rise and shape itself into the South Dorset Downs you will come to Wool, on the Frome, with its famous bridge, comparable with that at Sturminster Newton, plaque and all. It is overlooked by one of Dorset's most notable lesser manor houses, Elizabethan in date like the bridge itself, Woolbridge Manor. It was, incidentally, once the home of the Turberville family, and Hardy used it as the setting for the unhappy honeymoon of the central figure in *Tess of the D'Urbervilles*. From hereabouts the chalk downs melt into the Purbeck Hills, from which is quarried the famous Purbeck marble; they run south-eastwards from East Lulworth, just inside the perimeter, to Corfe Castle, which dominates the misnamed Isle of Purbeck – for it is no island, or even peninsula. Westwards, the chalk downs flow across the fourth segment between the A352 on their northern escarpment and the coastline. Here is that geologist's delight, Lulworth Cove, with its violently contorted strata, that has an explicit tale to tell of remote architectonic activities.

The choice now awaits you: follow the downs along the coast to Weymouth Bay, and its sailing amenities, and thence southwards to the near-island of Portland, or turn north-westwards to the viewpoint itself. Portland is one of the strangest and, let us admit it, most forbidding spots in all England: one vast mass of Portland stone pitted with quarries formerly worked by convicts and dominated by their prison, now a Borstal. The place-name Fortuneswell, just within the perimeter, seems inappropriate. But Portland Bill, just south of the actual perimeter, is well worth a visit if only for the impressive view seawards in all directions, including the well-named 'Pulpit Rock' and, beyond, the Shambles Lightship that stands sentinel over the warring tides that make this one of the most dangerous areas of coastal waters anywhere east of Cornwall.

You climb gently over the South Dorset Downs by any one of several roads from Weymouth in the general direction of Dorchester. One will bring you to the hamlet of Stinsford and, immediately beyond, among the close-pressing woods, to Thomas Hardy's

Thomas Hardy statue, Dorchester

Cottage, National Trust property. Hardy was born in the neighbouring hamlet of Higher Bockhampton; he loved Stinsford so well that he brought it into his novels (as Mellstock) more often than any one other place in Wessex, and asked that his heart might be buried in the churchyard. The grounds are open to the public from March until October, but permission must be sought in advance if you wish to go inside the cottage itself. The devotee will not begrudge the effort of tramping along the rough and narrow lane that ends among the trees that keep the thatched cottage in permanent shadow.

Another road from Weymouth will take you by way of the unspoiled village of West Stafford, with its interesting Wise Man Inn, to Dorchester – Hardy's 'Casterbridge'. At the upper end of High West Street, at Top o' Town, Eric Kennington's statue of Hardy broods beneath a tree in a pose that seems wholly appropriate to the character of the man as we know him through his novels and poems.

He faces the gateway of the barracks that contain the Military Museum. Of more general interest, however, is the Court Room at the rear of the Antelope Hotel where the infamous Judge Jeffreys held his 'Bloody Assizes' in 1685 and condemned no fewer than 292 prisoners to death. On a gentler note, there is the County Museum, in which you will find a reconstruction of Hardy's study at Max Gate, the home he designed for himself on the southern outskirts of the town; here you may see his desk and, displayed on it, his pocket-book, writing materials, penknife, magnifying-glass, letter-balance, blotting-paper, and inkwell and – perhaps most personal of his possessions – his small pince-nez.

From his stance at Top o' Town, over the brow of the western-running A35, or at the end of a short, narrow road branching south-westwards off it, you come soon to the most famous Iron Age camp in all England, Maiden Castle; it has been declared the largest and most perfectly-designed earthwork in the world. Its complex of turf-clad walls and intervening ditches, oval in shape, more than half a mile on the longer axis and almost a quarter of a mile broad, is two miles in circumference and encloses an area of 130 acres; but such bare figures fail entirely to enable one to grasp the picture; only an aerial photograph can achieve this.

No one can say who constructed this, or just when, though archaeologists have been at work there for years. It certainly dates back beyond 2000 BC; it was occupied, enlarged, and elaborated by a succession of cultures, one at least of which had crossed the English Channel from Brittany during the Iron Age and brought unique know-how to the design of the eastward-facing entrance, which has no parallel elsewhere. Forty years ago a mass grave containing an untold number of skeletons, some with axe-heads still in their skulls or between their ribs, was unearthed; near by was an 'ammunition pit' containing some 20,000 sling-stones.

Maiden Castle spreads its elliptical length across into the fifth segment. From here you can make your way across the open downland south-westwards, by-passing Weymouth to your left, and with the Hardy Monument as your landmark all the way. This is not a memorial to the Wessex novelist and poet but to the flag-captain (later appointed admiral) in whose arms Nelson died at Trafalgar. From there – indeed from almost any one of the numerous vantage-points along this westwards-running whaleback ridge – you look seawards over the unique Chesil Beach, or Bank. This runs in a

Abbotsbury Swannery and Chesil Beach

Tithe barn, Abbotsbury

delicate curve for sixteen unbroken miles westwards from Portland: a giant wall of graduated pebbles 170 yards at its widest and twenty-three feet high at its westward end, just to the south of Abbotsbury. It encloses a narrow, lagoon-like strip of water for the greater part of its length, and has puzzled geologists for generations past.

It is at its western extremity that you come to the famous Swannery, which is open to the public daily from May to mid-September, while the Sub-tropical Gardens here are open from mid-March until the end of September. The Swannery is much older than you might suppose. It existed in the late-fourteenth century, when it was established and 'farmed' by the monks of the Benedictine monastery a mile inland from the end of the lagoon where some two thousand descendants of their swans thrive today. The ruins of the abbey are few; outstanding among them is the enormous tithe barn, 272 feet long and over thirty feet wide, buttressed heavily to support its huge span of roof.

Westwards from Abbotsbury and over into the sixth segment the coastline becomes increasingly dramatic, for the great cliffs consist of alternating strata of hard and less-hard sandstone, undercut by the tides that eternally surge against their feet. They are to be seen at their most spectacular near Burton Bradstock. So outstanding is this length of coastline that, as the map shows, much of it has been taken into the protection of the National Trust. It is to be hoped that more and more stretches of our coastline will be similarly taken over, and so be spared the ugliness that all too often arises from unsuitable development.

It is in this segment that the place-names of Dorset are perhaps seen at their most varied: Toller Porcorum, Toller Fratrum, Wynford Eagle, Dottery, Uploders, Askerswell, and Whitchurch Canonicorum, for example; the last has a strong ecclesiastical flavour. Toller Fratrum, again, refers to the Knights Hospitallers of St John of Jerusalem who had close ties with Forde Abbey, a twelfth-century Cistercian foundation lying just over the perimeter of the seventh segment. To find Toller Fratrum you must take a minor road that has no exit, southwards off the A356 just beyond Maiden Newton; even though it is now no more than a complex of farm buildings, the old refectory now converted into stabling, it amply repays the effort expended in tracking it down.

Nearer to the perimeter in this sixth segment is Pilsdon, lying low in Marshwood Vale and notable for its Tudor manor house (which is

Burton Bradstock cliffs

not open to the public). North of it, right on the boundary-line with the seventh segment, is Pilsdon Pen which, at 908 feet, is the highest point on all the chalk downs of southern England, after the 937 feet of Pilot Hill; as to the Dorset Downs, it is the 'daddy of them all'. To achieve the summit you must go on foot a steep climb from the road below; on it, Iron Age Man established one of his smaller earthworks, but the highest by far of those he constructed. He probably did not appreciate the immense view, especially westwards and southwards, that it afforded him, for he was concerned before all else with security against attack. You, on the other hand, should feel, as you did on Ditchling Beacon, monarch of all you survey.

To the north, you look from Pilsdon Pen across the seventh segment and over the Somerset border. The choice of places to visit is as wide as ever. Shall it be Beaminster – 'Be'm'ster', as it is known locally? It has a glorious early-sixteenth-century church, that of St Mary, built of the beautiful Ham Hill stone of the region; its pinnacled tower is not only one of the finest in Dorset, but comparable with those in neighbouring Somerset. Shall it be, just over the county boundary, Brympton d'Evercy, a mansion with a late-seventeenth-century south front and Tudor west front that claims to possess the longest *straight* staircase in England? It is open to the public from the beginning of July to the end of October. Or, back in Dorset, shall it be Melbury Bubb, whose church contains a pre-Norman font on which stone lions, horses, wolves, and stags are carved *upside-down*, signifying, according to tradition, 'that all cruelty shall cease through the influence of Christ'? The choice is as wide as ever.

Montacute House lies in this seventh segment, but will be left until the next viewpoint as it belongs to Somerset. So we remain in Dorset, to take in what many consider to be the most beautiful town the county has to offer – Sherborne (in the eighth segment). It was a cathedral town in Norman times; it had a monastery from 864 AD until the Dissolution; King Alfred – the 'Scholar King' – was educated at the school adjoining the abbey. Sherborne possesses a wealth of medieval stone buildings unsurpassed in the county, hardly surpassed elsewhere. So it is fitting that we come to a halt here; for enshrined in stone of a peculiarly beautiful ochre hue is all that is finest architecturally and traditionally in this, the present writer's best-loved county. He begs the reader to take his stance on the Cerne Giant, just ten miles to the south; and look about him; and to note that wherever he may start his peregrination among the infinite resources of this county, Sherborne is the magnet towards which he must be irresistibly, and most rewardingly, drawn.

Maiden Castle

Nunney Castle

Glastonbury Tor

It may seem odd to select this as a viewpoint, for Glastonbury Tor is less than 200 feet above sea level, whereas the Mendip Hills, which run for more than twenty miles north-west to south-east across the three northern segments of this circle, are a whaleback ridge seven, eight, even nine hundred feet on average, and topping the 1,000-foot mark at Blackdown. Topographically speaking, they are without question the dominant feature, and Cheddar Gorge, which slices through them at their western end, the most spectacular of all. Composed of carboniferous limestone, they offer the finest pot-holing area in all England, after Derbyshire and the Yorkshire Pennines. Here, too, lead mining was carried on in the days of the Romans. The Mendips present a landscape singularly reminiscent of the open, or occasionally drystone-walled, stretches of the Pennines; they are lofty, bare, windswept, reaching for the sky.

So, you may well ask: 'Why not pick one of the Mendip summits – 1,068-foot Blackdown, for example?' A reasonable enough question. The answer is this: Glastonbury, alone among our viewpoints, is a hallowed spot, indeed, a sacred spot; coincidentally it thus offers as nice a contrast as could be found to the viewpoint overlooking Cerne Abbas, with its huge sprawling pagan figure of the Cerne Giant.

The Tor rises a mile or so south-east of Glastonbury. It is regarded, with Walsingham in Norfolk, as one of the two most hallowed sites in all England. The tower is the sole relic of the fourteenth-century church that once stood here. Close by, on the steeply-falling slope, beneath a spring, it is still believed that Joseph of Arimathea buried the Holy Grail, the chalice from which Christ bade his disciples drink

N
NW
W
SW
S
Bristol
10 miles
Bristol
5 miles
Bristol
22 miles
Taunton
2 miles
Exeter
34 miles
Taunton
3 miles
Chard
9 miles
Exeter
34 miles
Exeter
40 miles
AVON
SOMERSET
MENDIP HILLS
BRISTOL (LULSGATE)
Lulsgate Bottom
Upper Town
Felton
Winford
Cleeve
Downside
Congresbury
West Hay
Redhill
Wrington
Puxton
Brinsea
Lower Langford
Upper Langford
Lye Cross
Ridgehill
Butcombe
Chew Stoke
Chew Magna
Chew Valley Lake
Nempnett Thrubwell
Blagdon
Blagdon Lake
Burrington
Ubley
West Harptree
Compton Martin
East Harptree
Sutton Wick
West Wick
Locking
Weston-super-Mare
Hutton
Sandford
Banwell
Churchill
Star
Winscombe
Shipham
Christon
Bleadon
Brean
Barton
Loxton
Compton Bishop
Cross
Axbridge
Charterhouse
Cheddar Gorge
Mendip Forest
Cheddar
Cheddar Res.
Eastertown
Biddisham
Lower Weare
Weare
Lympsham
Edingworth
Rooks Bridge
Badgworth
Hythe
Clewer
East Brent
Brent Knoll
Stone Allerton
Chapel Allerton
Battleborough
Berrow
Burnham-on-Sea
Edithmead
Highbridge
Watchfield
Mark
Mark Causeway
West Stoughton
Blackford
Wedmore
Cocklake
Draycott
Rodney Stoke
Priddy
Townsend
Greendown
Green Ore
Westbury-sub-Mendip
Wookey Hole
West Horrington
Easton
Theale
Panborough
Wookey
Henton
Wells
Dulcote
Woodford
Coxley
Polsham
Southway
Godney
Meare
Westhay
Mudgley
Heath House
Westham
Bason Bridge
Alstone
Steart
Huntspill
West Huntspill
Huntspill Level
East Huntspill
Stockland Bristol
Stretcholt
Otterhampton
Combwich
Pawlett
Woolavington
Edington Burtle
Catcott Burtle
Dunball
Puriton
Knowle
Cossington
Rodway
Cannington
Chilton Trinity
Charlinch
Wembdon
Bridgwater
Bradney
Bawdrip
Stawell
Chilton Polden
Edington
Catcott
Shapwick
Glastonbury
West Pennard
Edgarley
North Wootton
Northover
Street
Ashcott
Walton
Overleigh
Butleigh Wootton
Baltonsborough
Butleigh
West Bradley
Parbrook
Chedzoy
1865
Sutton Mallet
Moorlinch
Polden Hills
Greinton
Pedwell
Four Forks
Durleigh
Enmore
Rhode
Goathurst
Huntworth
Weston zoyland
Nythe
Moor
King's Sedge
Henley
Compton Dundon
Middlezoy
Thorngrove
North Petherton
Northmoor Green or Moorland
North Newton
Othery
Pathe
Beer
High Ham
Cary
Littleton
Barton St. David
Kingweston
Keinton Mandeville
Ham Street
Southwood
West Lydford
Babcary
Thurloxton
Adsborough
West Monkton
Hedging
Lyng
Burrow Bridge
Athelney
Stathe
Aller
Low Ham
Pitney
Somerton
Charlton Mackrell
Charlton Adam
West Lyng
Durston
Creech Heathfield
North End
Mare Green
Stoke St. Gregory
West Sedge Moor
Wick
Langport
Huish Episcopi
Upton
South Hill
Kingsdon
Cary Fitzpaine
Downhead
Podimore
Creech St. Michael
Knapp
North Curry
Curry Rivel
Drayton
Muchelney
Long Sutton
Knole
Thornfalcon
Wrantage
Meare Green
Fivehead
Isle
Thorney
Hambridge
Long Load
Milton
Northover
Ilchester
Bridgehampton
Yeovilton
Chilton Cantelo
Limington
Ashington
Curry Mallet
Beercrocombe
Isle Brewers
Isle Abbotts
Kingsbury Episcopi
Coat
Stapleton
Ash
Martock
Tintinhull
Chilthorne Domer
Yeovil Marsh
Mudford
Westport
East Lambrook
Lambrook
Barrington
Bower Hinton
Hurst
Stoke sub Hamdon
Montacute
Preston Plucknett
Ilton
Puckington
Stocklinch
Shepton Beauchamp
South Petherton
Norton sub Hamdon
Odcombe
Chiselborough
Brympton
Whitelackington
Hurcott
Seavington St. Michael
Seavington St. Mary
Dinnington
Lopen
Over Stratton
West Chinnock
Middle Chinnock
East Chinnock
West Coker
Barwick
North Coker
East Coker
Hardington Mandeville
Merriott
Yeo
Parrett
Brue
Axe
Tone
M5
Scale : 5 miles to 1 inch
17½
15
10
5
0
MILES

Glastonbury Tor

1 Glastonbury Tor

2 Isle of Avalon

3 Stanton Drew

4 Chew Magna

5 Toll-house

6 Chew Valley Lake

7 Blagdon Lake

8 East Harptree

9 West Harptree

10 Castle of Comfort Inn

11 Miner's Arms Inn

12 Priddy

13 Wookey Hole

14 Wells

15 Nunney Castle

16 Shepton Mallet

17 Castle Cary

18 Bruton

19 Stourhead

20 Cadbury Castle

21 Lytes Cary

22 East Coker

23 Barwick

24 Montacute House

25 East Lambrook Manor

26 Kingsbury Episcopi

27 Martock

28 Muchelney

29 River Parrett

30 King's Sedge Moor

31 Sedgemoor battlefield

32 Westonzovland

33 Chedzoy

34 Meare

35 Cheddar

36 Cheddar Gorge

on the occasion of the Last Supper. It was near here, but lower down, that this same Joseph thrust into the soil his thorn staff, which miraculously took root and thereafter flourished as the now-legendary winter-flowering 'Glastonbury Thorn'. Here, tradition has it, he built a simple church, hardly more than a cell, in which to convert the people to Christianity. In 688 AD a monastery was established that was to become one of England's greatest abbeys.

Again, if firmly-held tradition is to be accepted, the legendary King Arthur and Queen Guinevere were re-buried here, their bodies having been reverently transported from their original burial-place. Immediately to the north of the Tor on the map are the words 'Isle of Avalon', strange words to appear so close to a town; Avalon, of course, is irrevocably associated in our minds with the immortal legends of King Arthur and his Knights of the Round Table. So then: a hallowed place, identified with the earliest stirrings of Christianity in this country and, later, with a monarch who, whether he lived in full fact or part-myth, is always associated with virtue and knightliness.

Glastonbury Tor has much, therefore, to commend it as a viewpoint. Though it lacks absolute height relative to much of the terrain that extends about it, it affords some remarkable views in all directions. To the immediate north and west the ground is only thirty or forty feet above sea-level; farther away, Burnham-on-Sea and Weston-super-Mare are at sea-level; to the south and south-west, though a low ridge here and there may intervene, much of the ground lies below the 40-foot mark; names such as Sedge Moor, and the map symbols for marshland, abound; almost immediately to the west-north-west is the strange, empty region in which the terrain lies so low that the people who occupied it in remote times built themselves 'lake villages' on stilts and faggots of brushwood, linking one hut with another.

Near the perimeter of the first segment, beyond the Mendips and only some five miles short of Bristol and Bath, lies the hamlet of Stanton Drew. Up a twisting lane, behind a farm, is a trio of prehistoric Stone Circles, much smaller than Oxfordshire's Rollright Stones, but thought to date back to the same period and culture as Avebury. Few of the stones are much taller than a man, and none of them compare in bulk with the Avebury megaliths; but they are well worth a visit, not least for their unexpected appearance within the confines of so small a hamlet. Not far away are three much larger

Mendip Hills, from the south

stones, set in such a fashion as to suggest that they were the framework of a cromlech. Archaeologists have still not finally established their origin or purpose; they bear the odd local name 'The Cove', but are more officially referred to as Hautville's Quoit, and that last word is found also in Cornwall: Trethevy Quoit and Lanyon Quoit, famous and recognised megalithic burial-places, or cromlechs.

Between Stanton Drew and neighbouring Chew Magna, at a T-junction, stands one of the most delightful small tollhouses remaining in England. It is five-sided, with a Gothic window or two, a diminutive pillar-box let into the side that contains the door, a wrought-iron bracket over the porch that once held an oil lamp by which the toll-keeper could check the moneys paid to him, and a neat roof of thatch.

Inwards from Stanton Drew, before the ground begins to form the foothills of the Mendips, you come to the shapely expanses of

Chew Valley Lake and Blagdon Lake, reservoirs in which there is good trout fishing to be had; they are best seen from the upper slopes immediately to the south. It is on these slopes that you will come to East and West Harptree. In the churchyard of the latter's Church of St Mary the Virgin, beneath a yew tree, lies John Wright, who died just as he reached his century – a ripe age indeed for a countryman in his day or indeed ours. Near East Harptree, from which there is a glorious view over the lakes, there is a mellow stone-built cottage whose owner has been a dedicated topiarist throughout his occupation.

Beyond these villages you climb to close on the 1,000-foot mark; a road flows along the length of the Mendips past the Castle of Comfort Inn (and where could you find a more reassuring inn name than that?) and the Miner's Arms. It was in the region of Priddy, a couple of miles away, that lead mining was carried on actively from the Middle Ages onwards, and it was not until the turn of last century that St Cuthbert's lead mines, near here, ceased to be commercially worth exploiting any more.

It is in this region, too, that the sign so familiar in the Rogan's Seat circle – the red circle with 'Pot' alongside it – is to be seen again; this is good pot-holing terrain, and the most famous of all the Mendip pot-holes is Wookey Hole. This is very much more than the name suggests. It is in fact a vast labyrinth of caverns, many of them with stalagmites and stalactites, known to the Iron Age inhabitants of the region and to some extent exploited later by the Romans. But the Wookey Hole complex was known very much earlier than that, as was revealed when scientific exploration began seriously in the early part of this century. In the remotest, least accessible caverns the bones of hyena and mammoth and other beasts were found, victims of hunters who had occupied these sheltered spots during the last part of the latest Ice Age, thousands of years ago. Human bones, too, were found among them; there are relics of all this in museums at Glastonbury, Shepton Mallet, and elsewhere.

Only three miles to the south is Wells, one of the most beautiful of all our cathedral cities. Though smaller by far than many of our cathedrals, many connoisseurs rank it among the most beautiful and impressive. The building commenced in the final decades of the twelfth century and continued through to the fifteenth. The glorious West Front, seen at its best when the late-afternoon sun is just beginning to slant across it, accentuating the depth of the niches occupied

Glastonbury Tor

by the stone-carved figures between the ornamental window-lights, dates from some fifty years after the laying of the foundations; the great central tower dates from a century later. It is in the moat, part-surrounding the Bishop's Palace in the cathedral precincts which dates from the thirteenth century, that the swans come to pluck at a bell-pull just within their reach when they wish to be fed. Inside the cathedral there is the famous fourteenth-century astronomical clock over which, on the hour, medieval mounted figures ride out to meet in knightly combat.

Over the boundary-line into the second segment we find less that is noteworthy. Radstock cannot be commended: a small town in which, perhaps surprisingly, coal was mined on a small scale six hundred years ago, and is still being mined. But seven miles to the south, just beyond the eastern fringe of the Mendips, lies the village of Nunney. It possesses a small gem of a castle, albeit sorely dilapidated. It is a castle-in-miniature, symmetrical, compact, unlike Raby or Richmond, vast and overwhelming. It was built in 1373: a massive stone rectangle consisting of four corner drum-towers and their linking walls rising to some fifty feet or so. Sections of the original moat are still to be seen, and there is evidence that this was contained within a massive exterior wall; but much of this has been removed, stone by stone, for farm and other buildings in the village, as was the case with Hadrian's Wall. The damage to the fabric was caused by Cromwell's men, who reduced the castle to a shell.

Farther in towards the viewpoint is the old market town of Shepton Mallet, the centre of which, unfortunately for traditionalists, is being largely rebuilt. But it still has its market cross, though the expert eye will spot that, beautiful as it is with its crockets and pinnacles, much of it has been restored within the last century or so. It does not begin to compare with the crosses at Chichester and Malmesbury. The fifteenth-century church, however, with its remarkable carved barrel-ceiling, is worth looking at closely; remembering the Cotswold 'wool' churches, you will not be surprised to know that in its day Shepton Mallet was a wool town too – 'wool-wealthy'.

Over the boundary-line into the third segment, Castle Cary lies astride the A371 which runs south from Shepton Mallet. Many of its older houses are built of the fine Ham Hill stone of the region, but the most interesting single building is the lock-up, built in 1779 at a cost of £23 'provided by the local charities' (*sic*) – no small

Topiary near East Harptree

Wells Cathedral: West Front

sum in those days when labour was so cheap and stone lay ready to hand. It is circular, with a domed top and a nail-studded door approached by three stone steps up which one can imagine the vagrant or felon being unceremoniously thrust, to crack his skull against the low lintel. There must have been a castle in the vicinity for the village to bear this name; it would have been on the low hill overlooking the village, but you will look in vain today for even the scantiest remains of it.

Five miles to the north-east is the township of Bruton. Its fifteenth-century church has one of the best towers in the county; more interesting, if more lowly, however, is the packhorse bridge spanning the River Brue; it is so narrow that it would seem only the most spindly-shanked of quadrupeds, and with the slenderest of loads, could have negotiated it. Other beasts must perforce have made use of the adjacent ford.

Close to the perimeter of this segment is Stourhead, a National Trust property, close to the village of Stourton. The house is among the first, and certainly one of the finest, to have been built in this country in what is known as the Palladian style, in the early eighteenth century. It is rich in furnishings and paintings and other treasures, but many visitors may feel that the greatest attraction of the place lies in its extensive gardens and grounds. Set about the beautifully-shaped lake are a number of charming and sometimes imposing smaller buildings; these include a Temple of Flora, a temple modelled on the famous Temple of the Sun at Baalbek, and the so-called Pantheon of Rome; it is all very memorably classical.

Immediately south of the A303, and in the fourth segment, is one of Somerset's relatively few hill-forts that can compare with the many in Dorset. The site is the rounded summit of a hill rising from relatively low-lying ground, on which Cadbury Castle stands. Careful excavation has revealed that it was occupied by a succession of cultures, starting with Neolithic Man and ranging through at least to the Anglo-Saxons, a period covering something like three thousand years in all. This is established fact; tradition – accepted as fact by very many people, essentially romantics at heart – has it that this is the 'Camelot' of the Arthurian cycle; King Arthur is believed by all save hardened sceptics to have reigned during the fifth century AD.

Less old by years that can can be measured in thousands is the manor house of Lytes Cary, on the opposite side of the A303 and nearer to the next boundary-line. This dates from the fourteenth and

Messiter's Folly, Barwick

fifteenth centuries, and is relatively unusual for so modestly proportioned a manor house in having its own chapel. It is National Trust property and open to the public on two afternoons a week only, from March to October.

Seven or eight miles to the south is the industrial town of Yeovil, and just to the south of this again what might be termed the 'lost' hamlet of Barwick; it lies within furlongs of the border with Dorset and the much better known hamlet of East Coker. Here the poet T. S. Eliot, born American but a naturalised Briton, lies buried, for it was from here that his seventeenth-century ancestors emigrated, and he had always expressed the wish to lie in ground which had been familiar to them. Barwick itself – 'Barrick' to the locals – is less well known; pilgrims to the grave of T. S. Eliot rarely bother to linger there, perhaps because they do not know what they are missing. For here, in open parkland, is a quartet of very oddly-shaped and improbable constructions known generally as the 'Barrick', or Messiter's, Follies.

Messiter was a local philanthropist who set this work in hand to give paid employment to men who were out of a job. The four 'follies' bear odd names: 'Jack-the-Treacle-Eater' is one of them; another is the 'Fish Tower'; a third is 'The Needle'; the fourth (which surely ought to have been called 'The Needle') simply bears Messiter's name. It is a steeple-like structure some seventy-five feet in height, supported on Gothic-style arches and tapering elegantly all the way to the small stone globe on its tip. Standing well removed from the others, it has a dignity and poise that give it predominance over its fellows. Legends, of course, have grown up about them.

A few miles over the boundary-line with the fifth segment is one of our finest great houses, Montacute House, one of the best-regarded Elizabethan houses in the country. It is built of stone from the neighbouring Ham Hill quarries, its foundations laid in the year of the Armada, and stands amid gardens meticulously cared for, peaceful, spacious, and wholly matching its unassailable dignity. It was built for the Phelips family, and the second owner, Sir Edward Phelips, became Speaker of the House of Commons and in due course Chief Prosecutor in the trial of Guy Fawkes. The place has been National Trust property for the past forty years, and is open to the public on five days a week from April until September. Not the least interesting of its contents is the notable display of heraldic glass, a joy to those

Glastonbury Abbey

whose interest lies in this relatively esoteric type of art.

On a much smaller scale, but having the character that will endear it to those who prefer the homelier type of old building, is East Lambrook Manor, midway across this segment to the west of Montacute. The manor house dates from the fifteenth century, which makes it nearly a hundred years older than its more splendid neighbour; but additions were made to it in the sixteenth century, though happily no attempt was made to imitate the scale of Montacute. It is not National Trust property but is privately owned, and there is evidence at every turn (as at Athelhampton in Dorset) that its successive owners have cherished it as a home rather than as a mere show-piece. The house is open on one afternoon a week from March until October; the 'cottage-style' gardens and nursery-gardens, lovingly tended, are open on six days a week from as early as February until as late as November.

A couple of miles north of this manor house is a hamlet that bears a name out of all proportion to its size: Kingsbury Episcopi. Here the monarchic and ecclesiastical would seem to have combined to give the 'bury' (or 'burgh') a dual dignity and significance. As at Castle Cary, however, the chief interest here is the village lock-up. Instead of being round, this one is octagonal, and it possesses a particularly impressive conical roof of well-jointed stone. Its designers seem not to have borne in mind the fact that it might sometimes have to contain a sturdily-built or even corpulent felon, for the nail-studded door fills an unusually narrow doorway. Perhaps squeezing through was regarded as part of the punishment awaiting him when the assize court determined his full sentence? Two very narrow vertical air-vents have mitigated the darkness within and allowed him sufficent air to breathe – none were provided at the more austere Castle Cary lock-up.

Kingsbury Episcopi is but one of the many hamlets in this segment that are worth seeking out for such small treasures as they may possess: a church brass or two here, some well-moulded stonework there, a cottage with a mullioned window of unusual quality somewhere else. Martock, larger than most, has a late-fifteenth-century church in whose fabric stonework from a much older period may be discerned; a really unusual feature of this church may be seen near the north porch, where in the eighteenth century a buttress enabled enthusiasts to utilise an adjacent wall as a fives court. Ham Hill stone, already seen at Montacute and elsewhere, is much in evidence here, notably in the church and in a building still known as the Treasurer's House which dates from the thirteenth century and was formerly occupied by the Treasurer of Wells Cathedral.

Muchelney (the 'ey' always stands for an islet), set amid the low-lying terrain watered by the Parret a few miles to the north, was once virtually an island-site standing only just clear of the treacherous marshland all about it. Here may be seen the remains of a monastery founded in the late seventh century and once second only to Glastonbury itself. The Abbot's House may still be seen, and the remains of the washroom used by the twenty monks who originally occupied this isolated, indeed desolate, site; but these, and the few other surviving buildings here, are all of later date than the Anglo-Saxon period

Abbot's Fish House, Meare

when the monastery was founded, allegedly by the king of Wessex.

This low-lying ground spreads over into the sixth segment. King's Sedge Moor occupies part of it, and the Battle of Sedgemoor took place in 1685 just to the north of Westonzoyland. Immediately north of the battlefield is Chedzoy. Here, on the corner of a buttress against the south transept of the church, you can see, and feel, the deep vertical grooves (known technically as *polissoirs*) cut when Monmouth's rebel army, equipped largely with makeshift weapons such as billhooks and sickles as well as spears, gave these an additionally fine cutting-edge before going out to do battle.

And so to Glastonbury itself. The town lies at the narrowest point of this segment, and the remains of the monastery, founded in 688 AD, constitute its focal point. Few abbey remains are more beautifully sited – not forgetting Fountains and Byland in North Yorkshire; and there are few whose lofty, windowless walls – even Guisborough, Wenlock, and Tintern – make a more powerful and lasting impression. Among the most interesting ancillary buildings is the near-unique Abbot's Kitchen, an octagonal structure with a conical tiled roof and lantern-chimney designed to contain the flues and carry upwards the smoke from the hearths while preserving the appearance of a monastic rather than a purely utilitarian building. It forms a striking contrast to the lofty walls and piers, and to the foundations and crypt marked out so clearly in the greensward, revealing that the abbey church was no less than 600 feet long and nearly 100 feet wide – larger, in fact, than any English church of today.

Other buildings of note in Glastonbury include the George and Pilgrims Inn, built five centuries ago specifically to accommodate honoured visitors to the abbey. It is said that Henry VIII, who was later to order the Dissolution of the Monasteries, spent a night here on a state visit to Glastonbury. The Church of St John, with its fine fifteenth-century tower, is believed by many to contain the tomb of Joseph of Arimathea, who buried the Holy Grail on the slopes of the Tor only a mile distant to the south. Another building from the same century, the Abbey Court House, now a museum, contains a collection of local relics that have been revealed during years of excavating in the region of Meare, to the north-west in the seventh segment. It is at Meare, some five miles distant, that you will find the fourteenth-century manor house, formerly a small monastery; it stands on a slight rise, and in the hollow below is an isolated building approached by a stone-flagged causeway and known as the Abbot's Fish House. The title is self-explanatory: here fish caught locally was salted and stored for the use of the monks either at Glastonbury or, more probably, at Meare, on Fridays throughout the year.

This whole region is strange, slightly sinister, even in sunshine. The relics of the lake villages built on stilts and brushwood in remote times have largely been obliterated; some were recovered and are preserved in various museums, notably at Taunton, the county town of Somerset. From this region, generally so featureless, you obtain a notable view northwards to the Mendips, some five miles distant. Cheddar, with the famous gorge climbing dramatically away from

Motor and Transport Museum, Cheddar

the actual village, is within sight, midway across the final segment. The gorge, inevitably, has been commercialised, chiefly at its south-western end where the famous Gough and Cox Caverns, with their stalagmites and stalactites, are a Mecca for millions. In this labyrinth of caverns and linking passages, as at Wookey Hole, the remains of prehistoric man and beast have been found; the gorge was well known to Iron Age Man and to the inhabitants of the Romano-British period. It is beyond the caves, where the steep sides of grey limestone crowd in upon you, the road climbing steadily all the time, that the gorge becomes most impressive, even menacing; you emerge from it on to high ground: a vast, virtually empty region of grey-green turf, stone walls, and limitless views.

The old part of Cheddar village retains its charm. There is a market cross where genuine Cheddar cheese (so much now comes from Canada and New Zealand!) used to be sold; the church dates from the late fourteenth and early fifteenth centuries; behind farm buildings are the remains of a medieval chapel. And in strong contrast, there is the Cheddar Motor and Transport Museum, where the oldest exhibits date, not from medieval, Romano-British, or Neolithic times, but from the earliest days of the car, little more than three-quarters of a century ago. It is less well known, less high-powered, than the one at Beaulieu, but is well worth a visit if you are a fanatic about vintage and veteran cars, and also steam-driven vehicles, traction engines, and so forth. This museum has the great merit that the exhibits are constantly being changed, so that on each visit you will find something you have not seen before.

But when all is said, Glastonbury Tor is the essence of this circle. You may have commenced your perambulations beneath the shadow of the ancient church tower which stands on the Tor itself. At Cheddar you are some ten miles from the viewpoint. Take, therefore, the winding Mendip roads and lanes south-eastwards one more time at least, and stand once again on this hallowed spot and look about you. Choose an evening, if you can, when most visitors have departed. The present writer was most recently there at just such a time. There were not half a dozen people present on the site. One of them was a teenage girl. She was sitting alone, in almost yogi-like introspection, wholly withdrawn from the world about her. There was a look, one might say, of beatification on her young, serene countenance. She was absolutely still, oblivious. She may or may not have been a religious person in the orthodox sense; but it was manifest that she was drawing from the smooth turf on which she was sitting so motionless something which was spiritually satisfying, sustaining – that she had surrendered herself absolutely to those powerful influences which belong here more than to any other site in all England.

Montacute House

Crowcombe church

Dunkery Beacon

Roughly one-third of the circle drawn round this viewpoint is occupied by the Bristol Channel. The coastline, allowing for hollows and headlands, runs for some forty miles from east of the Quantocks to just short of Combe Martin Bay, some five miles north of a line drawn laterally through the Beacon. Of the land mass itself, rather more than half is designated an Area of Outstanding Natural Beauty; the Exmoor National Park covers an area of about 250 square miles. Its average height above sea level is about 1,000 feet, its many summits rounded rather than, as on Dartmoor, rocky and pointed. Not a few top this average by several hundred feet. Winsford Hill (1,404 feet), five miles south of Dunkery, offers almost as fine an all-round view as the Beacon does, though not a view northwards to the sea; Span Hill (1,618 feet), on the Somerset–Devon border, offers a fine view westwards to Barnstaple, twelve miles distant – unlike Dunkery, however, it cannot be approached closely by road, and you must cover two strenuous moorland miles, doing it the hard (but rewarding) way.

Less exacting, but still accessible only on foot from a minor road a mile or two to the south, is Haddon Hill, which offers a satisfying view over the lower ground that separates Exmoor from Dartmoor. There are other good summits, none of them too exacting, the routes to many of them often neatly signposted. Each offers us a rewarding experience of long-distance views attained by leaving the car by the roadside and going off to feel the heather-clad turf beneath our feet and exercise our muscles.

Dunkery is without question the best of them all. A minor road

N
NW
W
SW
S
BRISTOL CHANNEL
Foreland Point
Lynmouth Bay
Woody Bay
Lynton
Lynmouth
Countisbury
Trentishoe
Martinhoe
Heale
Dean
Ilfracombe 7 miles
Kentisbury
Blackmoor Gate
Kentisburyford
Arlington Beccott
Barnstaple 7 miles
Barton Town
Knightacott
Bratton Fleming
Lower Loxhore
Benton
Stoke Rivers
Gunn
Stone Cross
Accott
Stoodleigh
Charles
East Buckland
West Buckland
Riverton
Barnstaple 6 miles
Heddon
Filleigh
South Molton
Hill
George Nympton
Alswear
Parracombe
East Ilkerton
Martinhoe Cross
Shallowford
Barbrook
Cheriton
Furzehill
Brendon
Malmsmead
Tippacott
Shilstone Hill
Brendon Common
Oare
Oareford
EXMOOR
Challacombe
Shoulsbarrow Common
Leworthy
Fullaford
Bray
Brayford
High Bray
Molland Cross
Yard Gate
North Radworthy
Bentwitchen
South Radworthy
Heasley Mill
Flitton Barton
Rabscott
North Molton
Millbrook
Twitchen
Molland Common
Bickingcott
Molland
Sheepwash
Bish Mill
Mole
Yeo
Bottreaux Mill
Newtown
Bishop's Nympton
Ash Mill
Mariansleigh
Rose Ash
Yard
Meshaw
Knowstone
Creacombe
Rackenford
Queen Dart
Bradford Mill
Little Dart
Templeton Bridge
DEVON
SOMERSET
Simonsbath
Exe
Newland
Landacre
Withypool
Withypool Common
Sandway
Edgcott
Exford
Luckwell Bridge
Winsford Hill
Liscombe
Hawkridge
Dane's Brook
West Anstey
East Anstey
Nightcott
Yeo Mill
Oldways End
East Knowstone
Roachill
North Esworthy
Worthy
Porlock Weir
West Porlock
Porlock
Porlock Bay
Hurlstone Point
Selworthy Beacon
Bossington
Lynch
Allerford
Selworthy
Woodcombe
West Luccombe
Horner
Luccombe
Stoke Pero
Huntscott
Wootton Courtenay
Tivington
Dunkery Beacon
Dunkery Hill
Burrow
Cutcombe
Wheddon Cross
North Quarme
Lype Hill
Heath Poult Cross
Winsford
Exton
Bridgetown
Higher Combe
Battleton
Dulverton
Brushford
Upcott
Exebridge
Morebath
Bampton
Oakfordbridge
Oakford
Broadmead
Stoodleigh
Ford Barton
Loxbeare
Washfield
Tiverton 1 mile
1 2 3 4 5 6 7 15 16 17 18 19 20 21 22 23 24 25 26 27 28 29 30
39
3358
3226
3223
3224
3222
361
3227
3221
396
1036 1104 1574 1599 1079 868 1329 1284 1040 1527 1456 1705 1043 1013 1618 1454 1427 1238 1265 1404 518 929
Scale : 5 miles to 1 inch
17½ 15 10 5 0
MILES

Dunkery Beacon

1 Dunkery Beacon

2 Selworthy Beacon

3 Selworthy

4 Allerford

5 Horner

6 Luccombe

7 Timberscombe

8 Dunster

9 Cleeve Abbey (part-ruined)

10 Brendon Hills

11 Monksilver

12 Bicknoller

13 Crowcombe

14 Cothay Manor

15 Bampton

16 Dulverton

17 Winsford

18 Exton

19 Tarr Steps

20 Winsford Hill

21 Withypool

22 Parracombe

23 Shallowford

24 Watersmeet

25 Brendon Common

26 Shilstone Hill

27 Malmsmead

28 Oare

29 Lynmouth

30 Porlock

zigzags southwards over its eastern flanks from near Porlock; from the road there is an easy track over firm, springy turf, to be measured in furlongs rather than in miles. From the summit you can look due north to Porlock Bay and, on a clear day, across the thirty-mile width of the Bristol Channel to the south coast of Wales near Porthcawl. In every other direction the combes and valleys, the rounded contours, the occasional sparkle of water emerging from among trees, and the spider's-web of tiny roads of Exmoor call you to explore. One of these roads runs almost due south-east along the Brendon Hills towards the Quantocks, which break into this circle on its eastern perimeter. Many lovers of the West Country's hinterland prefer Exmoor to Dartmoor and Bodmin Moor because of the intimacy that characterises it; they do not, however, ignore the fact that, like those other moors, it can take on a less homely character, even a dangerous one, when the weather turns against you.

The initials 'NT' appear three times on the map in the very small land area of the initial segment. Immediately to the north of the A39 coastal road, running for the most part in low-lying terrain in the eastern half of the circle, the ground slopes steeply upwards to Selworthy Beacon (1,013 feet). The hillside on which Selworthy village lies is thickly wooded, and inviting. Opinions are divided as to whether this village or the neighbouring Allerford is the most beautiful in this whole region; claims are made also for Timberscombe, Luccombe, Crowcombe, and several others: you take your choice.

None of those, however, has the advantage of a site such as Selworthy's. With its white-painted chimneys topping the thatched cottages, no two of them in line or at the same level, each with a well-stocked garden contained within a creeper-clad wall, essentially individualistic, Selworthy has for back-drop close-set trees that climb to the horizon – a hanging wood such as that about which Gilbert White wrote so well during his long life at Selborne, Hampshire. One feature alone possibly mars the idyllic scene: the church. It is not easy to explain why. The church is of the sixteenth century, its castellated tower two centuries older. Perhaps it is just that the whole is too square-cut, a little too obtrusive, dominating a hamlet whose every other building seems to have had its corners, and even its chimneys, rounded, and all roof angles blurred and softened by the thick, overlying thatch.

A lane curves appropriately through the village; to reach Selworthy Beacon, a bare mile to the north, you must take a track up through the

Exmoor's rounded summits

trees beyond the church. There is, however, an alternative line of approach by a minor road that runs westwards from Minehead, five miles to the east and in the next segment. It will lead you right to the Beacon; but you will not have the same sense of achievement that would have been yours had you gone there on foot from the heart of the village.

Travelling westwards along the A39, you could easily miss Allerford altogether, for it lies a few hundred yards off the road, midway between the branch lane to Selworthy, and Porlock, some three miles to the west. It is on a 'blind' right-angle left turn, potentially hazardous. The focal point here is the exceptionally attractive packhorse bridge. It has two shapely arches rising steeply, one from each bank, to meet above a massive central buttress with a cutwater jutting out into the ford on the upstream side. The footway is cobbled, the parapets low enough for a pack-pony to cross even if he carried a bulky load on each side. Immediately behind the bridge is a pair of pantile-roofed cottages of russet stone with a tall, cylindrical chimney, not, as at Selworthy, painted white but continuing the mellow stonework of the wall. A porch with a small room above it overlooks the far end of the bridge, and a walnut tree leans at an improbable angle over the parapet. This must surely be one of the most idyllic standing-stone-and-running-water sites in the whole of the West Country.

This part of Somerset is veined with streamlets such as the one spanned by this bridge, all flowing northwards off the moors. Only two miles to the south-west of Allerford is the village of Horner, again with a packhorse bridge, though this is not quite in the same class. Near the boundary-line with the second segment there is another cluster of hamlets, each a delight in itself, and not least for the rough warm-russet stone of which cottages and farms alike are built hereabouts. Luccombe (in the first segment) is one such, with its homely, inviting little church, and cottages overflowing all the year round, it would seem, with flowers; more than one of them has in evidence the great bread-oven that used to be so common a feature of the end wall, a reminder of the departed days when bread indeed was bread. Among the many 'combe' place-names of the region, Wootton Courtenay, in the second segment, falls oddly on the ear, reminiscent of the Thames Valley; but there are also Ranscombe, and Alcombe, and Woodcombe, all homely names for homely places, and Timberscombe, with its little church on a steepish slope overlooking the village.

Selworthy

The best-known town in this second segment is of course Minehead. The holiday-makers' part of it may be ignored as too obvious for comment: ever since the coming of the railway, just a hundred years ago, this has been increasingly a seaside resort. But there is also 'Old Minehead', at its western end. Here are russet and ochre-coloured cottages, most of them with thatched roofs and many with the tall stone chimneys so characteristic of the region. They front on to what is more a leisurely flight of cobbled steps than a street as such, leading to a church, parts of which date back to the fifteenth century. Within, you may see an illuminated manuscript dating back a hundred years earlier. The cottages were once lived in by the herring-fishers, and the small Chapel of St Peter, set among them, began its long life as a store for salt. Alas, the harbour silted up, and the herring shoals went elsewhere for food; other 'shoals' took their place – the tourists – and the town's economy was assured.

Older by many centuries than anything to be found in Minehead is the castle that dominates from its natural eminence to the south the feudal village and erstwhile market town of Dunster. The castle was built four years after the Norman Conquest, and has been continuously occupied to this day, for the last five centuries by the Luttrell family, who gave their name to what was built as a 'town

Allerford packhorse bridge

Dunster Castle

residence for the Abbot of Cleeve', though it is now an outstandingly beautiful hostelry, The Luttrell Arms. It overlooks the sixteenth-century Yarn Market which dominates the upper end of the sloping main street. The lower end of this street, and its side streets, have a curiously medieval feel about them that lingers long.

Eastwards of Dunster a thin length of coastline runs to the perimeter, with Blue Anchor, a tiny village overhung by cliffs, and beyond this the old seaport of Watchet in Bridgwater Bay. Over the boundary-line in the third segment, a couple of miles south-west of Watchet, are the remains of Cleeve Abbey (whose abbot had the 'town residence' in Dunster). This was a small Cistercian foundation, with only thirty monks in its heyday, and but half that number when the Dissolution came. As the property of the Department of the Environment, it may be visited (as may Dunster Castle itself) by the public; but not until you are close to it, at the end of the narrow lane that branches off the A39, will you find it easy to distinguish between the farm buildings that now form so much of the complex, and the original abbey. Parts of the monks' living quarters, however, are still to be seen – notably their dormitory, which dates from the thirteenth century, and their refectory, which was built two centuries later to replace the original one. It has a very fine timbered roof.

This whole segment, with the Vale of Taunton Deane crossing the perimeter from the east, is full of surprises and delights. The Brendon Hills run south-eastwards along it, resembling the Mendips in miniature – homelier, less bare. Clatworthy Reservoir, at their eastern end, has something of the shape of a sea-horse, though this can only be appreciated from the map or a bird's-eye view. Monksilver (what an evocative name!) has a small church with some remarkable bench-ends (a feature of this county) of fifteenth-century craftsmanship. Williton unfortunately lies on the junction of the A39 and the A358, but is close enough to the Quantocks to absorb some of their memorable beauty; historians may remember that it was the home of Reginald Fitzurse, one of those who murdered Thomas à Becket. Bicknoller (another claimant to be the prettiest village hereabouts) is a little poem in russet stone and white paint, bedecked with flowers; its little church, in the Perpendicular style, dominates it from a knoll and is worth entering if only for more carved bench-ends and its beautifully carved screens.

Still on the south-west flanks of the Quantocks, there is Crowcombe. Its church stands on a slight eminence, in a sloping graveyard – another poem in russet sandstone. The fine tower dates from the fourteenth century and once carried an eighty-foot spire, but

Dunster Yarn Market

this was blown down in a great gale just before Evensong one Sunday in 1725; the roof was destroyed, but miraculously not one of the worshippers was harmed. Immediately outside the south porch stands the original church cross, the work of some medieval sculptor using the local sandstone. The softness of the stone has led to a blurring of the outlines, but still to be discerned on the twelve-foot shaft are John the Baptist, a mitred bishop with staff in one hand, the other raised in blessing, and the figure of a woman traditionally believed to be the abbess of a Benedictine nunnery in the district. The uppermost portion of this cross-shaft (for there is no actual crosspiece) is puzzling: it could almost be a stylised flower-head. Facing the gateway is the Church House, dating from 1515. It was built as a place of assembly and also as a small hostelry for itinerant vendors; later it was given an upper floor which was utilised as the village school, while the lower floor served as accommodation for the homeless wanderer until he (or she) could be passed on to the next parish.

Milverton is about the largest of the townships in this segment, mainly interesting for the sixteenth-century bench-ends in its church. There is less of medievalism here, but a Georgian flavour wholly acceptable as a contrast. From here a sequence of intertwining lanes, narrow and often high-hedged, will lead you over the boundary-line into the fourth segment, and on to a point actually on the perimeter, and just short of the Devon border. Here is a most entrancing small manor house. Cothay Manor has been called an 'architectural sleeping beauty', and the phrase is apt, especially when you look at its fifteenth-century gatehouse mirrored in the small lake that it overlooks. Just inside, on the right, is the chapel, as simple as that of any small convent. Cothay has been the cherished home of three West Country families, spread over some four centuries. Until very recently it was open on one day a week; then its ownership changed, and at the time of writing it is no longer open, but it is hoped that it will be once again some day, to delight those who love the smaller medieval manor houses.

Turning in from the perimeter towards the viewpoint we very soon cross the Devon border and come to the township of Bampton, through which the A361 wriggles awkwardly on its way from Taunton to Barnstaple. Its small parish church, set about with yews, stands on top of the steep hill, its main fabric dating back, like that of so many of these churches, to the early fifteenth century. The name will

St Petrock's Church, Parracombe

be familiar to all lovers of Exmoor, and of ponies too, for this is the setting for the annual Exmoor Pony Fair held always in October, a venue for bidders, buyers, and sightseers from miles around.

Northwards the A396, one of Exmoor's most beautiful roads, climbs gently, by-passing Dulverton with its thirteenth-century church tower, to Wheddon Cross; on either side branch roads, often no more than lanes, will lead you well off the beaten track to hamlets such as Winsford. Beyond this you will come to the clapper-bridge, Tarr Steps (in the fifth segment) a parapetless packhorse bridge with a causeway that gives it 180 feet of overall length, unique in England. Exton (in the fourth segment), with its miniature church at the end of a steep track, is not far away; nor is the hamlet of North Quarme. There are fewer villages and hamlets here than in some other segments, for it was only in the tight little valleys that settlements could ever become established and survive.

In the fifth segment Winsford Hill (1,404 feet), National Trust property, dominates. The River Barle flows past at its foot, southwards-bound for Tarr Steps and spectacular when in spate. The Exe has its source some miles to the north-west, across in the seventh segment and almost on the Somerset–Devon border. Villages are thinner on the ground than even in the fourth segment, at least on the north side of the A361 Barnstaple road, where Exmoor in all its glory and challenge makes itself once more truly felt. Before leaving this segment it is worth a diversion to Withypool, as pretty as its name suggests; of greater interest, however, is Landacre Bridge, in the sixth segment, spanning the Barle to the north of Withypool Common.

Perhaps, though, the best of Exmoor lies over the boundary-line in the seventh segment. Here are to be found the sources of the East and West Lyn, Farley Water, and Hoaroak Water. These, and their tributaries, divide the high, rolling landscape into shoulders, deep combes, and linking valleys, almost chasms sometimes, their steep sides so thickly clad with stunted, close-set trees as to impart to them a veritable air of secrecy.

In the outer part of this segment, within some three miles of the perimeter, is the moorland hamlet of Parracombe. It is chiefly notable for its very ancient Church of St Petrock – a saint whose name appears thirteen times in Devon and Cornwall. It is believed that he established a cell here early in the sixth century, and set about converting the moorlanders. The church you see today, however, dates from the eleventh century, its tower from a century later. Inside you will find an unusual three-decker pulpit, a Clerk's Seat, very old oak benches, and some unusually high pews. It is thought that this was the last church in the county to have musicians to support the singing, and evidence of this lies in the curious recess cut in one of the main pews, apparently to accommodate the bow of the man who played the bass-viol. It is tiny details such as this that can make visits to unlikely sites so unexpectedly rewarding. The two cottages standing partly in the churchyard are survivors of the Church Ale House, where thirsty worshippers could take refreshment before setting off on their long trek across the moor to their scattered and isolated homes.

Only one road of any size runs north-eastwards from Parracombe. It twists and turns until it approaches Lynton, when it drops with dramatic suddenness into Lynmouth, on the coast far beneath its lofty-sited twin. Branch roads lead off on either side, running themselves to a standstill within a mile or two, as the map clearly shows: to East Ilkerton and Shallowford; Furzehill, Cheriton, Martinhoe, and Heale. Where the main road makes a violent left-

Approach to Watersmeet

hand turn just short of Lynmouth you can branch off, leave your car, and take a track that leads, shadowed by trees for most of the way, to perhaps the most beautiful spot on all Exmoor – Watersmeet. Here the East Lyn and its tributaries unite before flowing on to Lynmouth and into the bay. There are other ways of approaching this delectable spot, notably by a descending track through a succession of combes running southwards from Countisbury Hill, one of the trio of challenging hills on this coastline – the others are Beggarsroost and Porlock Hill.

The whole of this region is more than memorable; turn in from the coastline, and you cannot go wrong. The emptiness of Brendon Common, spanning the county boundary, awaits you. You can climb on to Shilstone Hill at 1,329 feet. A network of narrow lanes will allow you to visit in short space Tippacott and Brendon; Malmsmead, with its old packhorse bridge and ford spanning Badgworthy ('Badgery') Water; Oare, with its minuscule church high on a steep mound; and Oareford, a mile or two beyond. All this is *Lorna Doone* country; you travel it preferably on foot – or in the saddle if possible: this is first-class and deservedly popular pony-trekking country.

Lynmouth is the goal of those who prefer the pretty little seaside resort to the finer hinterland. In 1952 disaster on a major scale befell the place. As a result of a cloudburst over the moors, the East and West Lyn rose in wrath and swept down upon the village, destroying everything in their furious path. Much of the place had to be rebuilt from scratch; only houses, cottages, and inns fortunate enough to stand high above the level of the floodwaters – the Rising Sun, for example – survived.

Eastwards from Lynmouth, once you have climbed Countisbury Hill, the coastal road skirts the northern fringe of Exmoor, at many points topping the 1,200-foot mark, to descend in due course by one of the steepest and most treacherous roads in the country from nearly 1,500 feet to near sea-level. A more gently graded toll-road offers an alternative route, which should be taken unashamedly by the less-experienced driver. And at Porlock (in the eighth segment), with its famous Ship Inn, its white- and pink-washed plasterwork and its cylindrical chimneys, we have come full circle. The village would be even more attractive if only the traffic on the main road could be diverted away from it. But here we are only three miles removed from our viewpoint, Dunkery Beacon, soaring to its 1,707 feet above the rest of Exmoor to the immediate south.

Rising Sun, Lynmouth

Cathay Manor

Dartmoor

Cumbria, which contained the first circle considered in this book, offered nearly 200 viewpoints that topped the 2,000-foot mark and several that topped the 3,000-foot mark. Dartmoor, the last of our circles, cannot compete with such figures. Though it has more than 150 tors, few of them come anywhere near the 2,000-foot mark, and only Yes Tor (2,030 feet) and High Willhays (2,038 feet) exceed it. The majority are lower by several hundred feet; and in fact this viewpoint is not even a tor. There is a good reason for the choice decided upon: to approach the finest of the tors usually means a journey on foot that is not only strenuous but potentially dangerous. Dartmoor – England's largest expanse of granite – is overlaid by deep bogland that can be treacherous in the extreme. No visitor should ever set off across the moor without ascertaining where (or indeed whether) that stretch is safe; and as on the Pennine moors, he should always carry with him, if he contemplates a journey out of sight of a road, a compass (which he should know how to read), and a whistle for emergency.

The viewpoint on Dartmoor is a point on the B3212 at 1,420 feet, a few hundred yards north-east of Warren House Inn, where an ancient roadside cross marks the junction of two age-old moorland tracks known to professional Dartmoor pack-pony men. Such trails have certainly been used since early medieval times. But even with this knowledge, the stranger will be well advised not to follow them without ascertaining conditions in advance from some local source, including weather prospects, and without leaving information as to his intended route if it is of any length. No area in all England is more

Haldon Belvedere

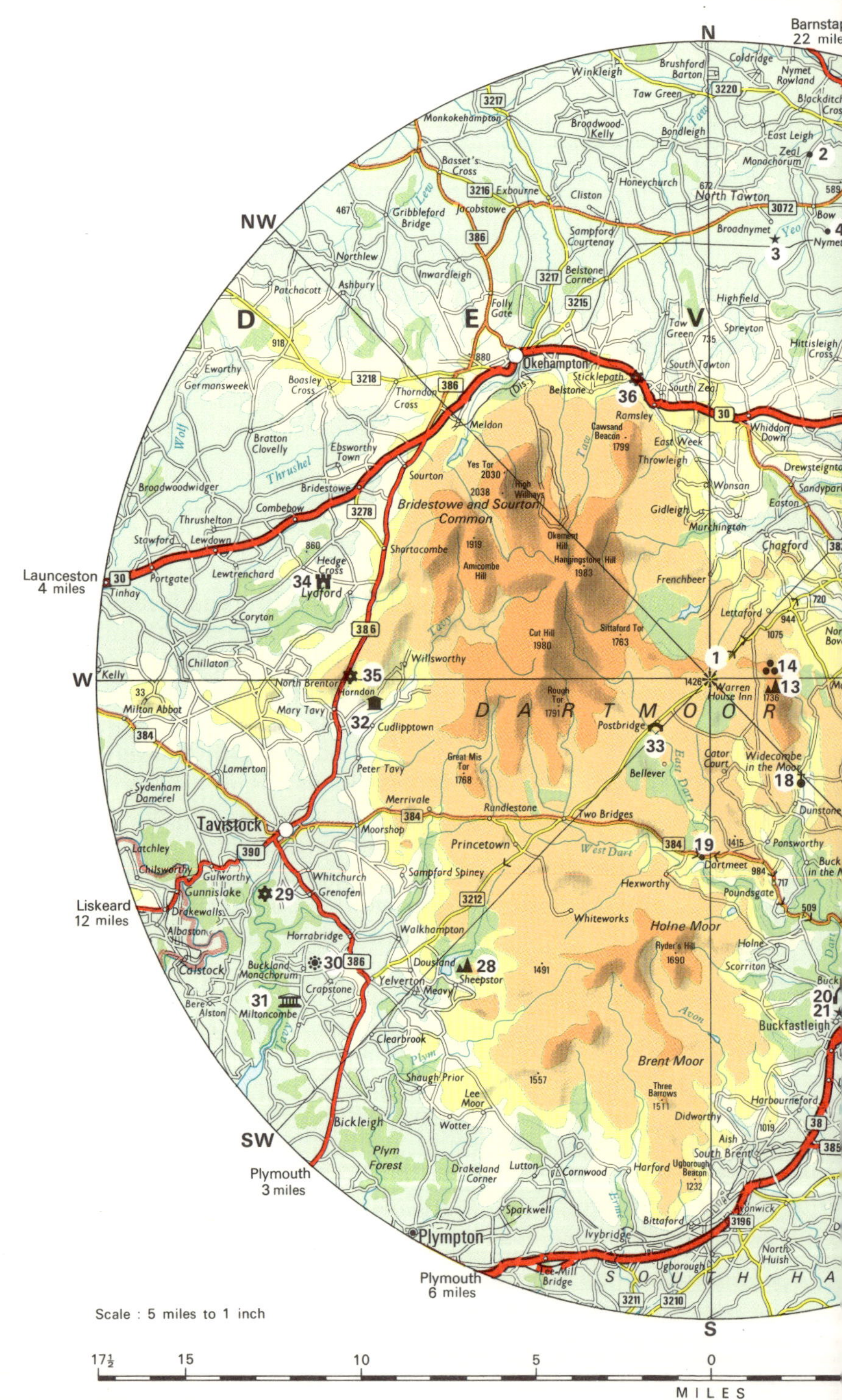

N
NW
W
SW
S
Barnstaple 22 miles
Launceston 4 miles
Liskeard 12 miles
Plymouth 3 miles
Plymouth 6 miles
D E V
D A R T M O O R
S O U T H H A
Winkleigh
Brushford Barton
Coldridge
Nymet Rowland
Blackditch Cross
Taw Green
3220
3217
Monkokehampton
Broadwood-Kelly
Bondleigh
East Leigh
Zeal Monachorum
2
Basset's Cross
Honeychurch
North Tawton
3216
Exbourne
Cliston
3072
Bow
Broadnymet
Yeo
Nymet
3
4
467
Gribbleford Bridge
Jacobstowe
386
Sampford Courtenay
Northlew
Inwardleigh
3217
Belstone Corner
Patchacott
Ashbury
Highfield
Folly Gate
3215
Taw Green
Spreyton
918
Hittisleigh Cross
880
Okehampton
South Tawton
Eworthy
Germansweek
Boasley Cross
3218
Thorndon Cross
386
Sticklepath
Belstone
South Zeal
36
30
Whiddon Down
Ramsley
Meldon
Cawsand Beacon 1799
East Week
Bratton Clovelly
Ebsworthy Town
Throwleigh
Drewsteignton
Thrushel
Yes Tor 2030
Sourton
High Willhays
Wonsan
Sandypark
Broadwoodwidger
Bridestowe
2038
Bridestowe and Sourton Common
Gidleigh
Easton
Combebow
3278
Murchington
Thrushelton
Stowford
Lewdown
860
Okement Hill
Chagford
Shortacombe
1919
Hanging Stone Hill
Hedge Cross
Amicombe Hill
1983
Frenchbeer
Portgate
Lewtrenchard
34
Lydford
30
Tinhay
Coryton
Lettaford
720
386
Sittaford Tor 1763
944
1075
Cut Hill 1980
Tavy
Willsworthy
1
14
13
Chillaton
Kelly
35
North Brentor
Horndon
Rough Tor 1791
1426
Warren House Inn
1736
33
Milton Abbot
Mary Tavy
32
Cudlipptown
Postbridge
33
384
Cator Court
Widecombe in the Moor
Lamerton
Peter Tavy
Great Mis Tor 1768
Bellever
East Dart
18
Sydenham Damerel
Merrivale
Rundlestone
Two Bridges
Dunstone
384
Tavistock
Moorshop
Princetown
West Dart
384
19
1415
Ponsworthy
Latchley
390
Dartmeet
984
717
Buckland in the Moor
Chilsworthy
Gulworthy
Whitchurch
Sampford Spiney
Hexworthy
Poundsgate
Gunnislake
29
Grenofen
3212
509
Drakewalls
Whiteworks
Holne Moor
Albaston
Horrabridge
Walkhampton
Holne
Ryder's Hill 1690
Dart
Calstock
Buckland Monachorum
30
386
Dousland
28
1491
Scorriton
Sheepstor
Yelverton
Crapstone
Meavy
20
Bere Alston
31
Miltoncombe
21
Avon
Buckfastleigh
Clearbrook
Tavy
Plym
Brent Moor
Shaugh Prior
1557
Lee Moor
Three Barrows 1511
Harbourneford
Didworthy
Bickleigh
Wotter
1019
38
Plym Forest
Aish
South Brent
385
Drakeland Corner
Lutton
Cornwood
Harford
Ugborough Beacon 1232
Erme
Sparkwell
Avonwick
Bittaford
3196
Plympton
Ivybridge
North Huish
Lee Mill Bridge
Ugborough
3211
3210
Scale : 5 miles to 1 inch
17½
15
10
5
0
MILES

Dartmoor

1 Dartmoor
2 Zeal Monachorum
3 River Yeo
4 Nymet Tracey
5 Fingle Bridge
6 Dunchideock
7 Haldon Belvedere
8 Doddiscombsleigh
9 North Bovey
10 Lustleigh
11 Hay Tor
12 Rippon Tor
13 Hameldown Tor
14 Grimspound
15 Ilsington
16 Bradley Manor
17 Compton Castle
18 Widecombe in the Moor
19 Dartmeet
20 Buckfast Abbey
21 Buckfastleigh railway station
22 Dart Valley Railway
23 Berry Pomeroy
24 Dartington Hall
25 Harberton
26 Torbryan
27 Littlehempston
28 Sheepstor
29 Morwellham Quay
30 The Garden House
31 Buckland Abbey
32 Horndon
33 Postbridge
34 Lydford
35 Wheal Betsy/Gibbet Hill
36 Sticklepath

unpredictable in regard to weather – especially the onset of mist. On the credit side, however, there is probably no other area in England where one can get a stronger impression of isolation and of the haunting presence of those who have gone before. It is a known fact – testified to by such prehistoric sites as Grimspound – that in prehistoric times 'wild' Dartmoor was more thickly populated than it has been for many years past or will ever be again.

The circle passes through Exeter on its north-east perimeter; through the Torbay complex on its south-east perimeter; and through the expanding outskirts of Plymouth on its south-west perimeter. Newton Abbot, Tavistock, and Okehampton are the only towns of any size within the circle, the whole central portion of which is occupied by the 300-odd square miles of Dartmoor, which averages over 1,000 feet above sea-level. Apart from the main roads that skirt it, roads even of modest size are scarce; true Dartmoor is not road-bearing terrain. Nevertheless, in so circumscribed an area the motorist can come within easy reach of almost any objective that appeals.

It is in the first segment that we come to the curious word 'zeal' in place-names in the West Country. Zeal Monachorum does not imply that certain monks pursued their calling more actively than their fellows; the word is simply a corruption of *sele*, an establishment. The alluringly-named hamlet lies on the River Yeo, which waters much of this low-lying area, prelude to the slopes of Dartmoor to the south of the A30. Near by is the hamlet of Nymet Tracey; it has a link with Williton, noted in the Dunkery Beacon circle, for here

Yes Tor and High Willhays

Nobody Inn, Doddiscombsleigh

is one of several churches in the area allegedly built by William de Tracey, one of the murderers of Thomas à Becket, in expiation of the crime he shared with Reginald Fitzurse.

It is in this region that the great visual glory of the Devonian red sandstone is best seen: in the large cruciform church at Crediton, for example, the county's cathedral city for 150 years until the mid-eleventh century when the see was moved to Exeter. This was, incidentally, a 'wool' town, reaching its heyday in the fifteenth century; there is evidence of its prosperity and affluence on every hand to this day.

Nearer to the viewpoint and easily reached along a network of minor roads is Drewsteignton, one of many Devon villages that vie for the term 'prettiest of all'. It has no village green, but a square, with thatched cottages and an inn set about it, and a fifteenth-century church near the inn at one corner. The Upper Teign (which gives its name to so many places) flows near by and is spanned by the magical Fingle Bridge a mile from the village. Larger, and better known, and actually inside the periphery of the Dartmoor National Park is Chagford. Again the village is built round a square. Massive (though not over-large) houses, including the Three Crowns Inn, a former manor house built in a style to match the standards of its original owners, a fine fifteenth-century church, and a comparable Church House: these make up what is memorable about Chagford. As a bonus, the Teign flows past, practically on its doorstep. Any one of a number of very narrow lanes will take you viewpoint-wards from here; on every hand there is something of simple beauty, while ahead and to either side of you the northern flanks of the moor rise with their infinite promise.

The outer part of the second segment will be ignored, for it is wholly dominated by the city of Exeter (a treasure-house in itself) and by the monumental development (deplorable but doubtless essential) of the motorway spreading south-westwards across it towards Plymouth. This makes it difficult to track down the many small and so far happily unspoiled villages that lie to the west of it. Dunchideock is one of these. Its modest red sandstone church lies, not in its centre but on its northern outskirts, largely surrounded by farm buildings. It is of fourteenth-century origin and contains a memorial to General Stringer Lawrence; but a far more remarkable memorial to him exists in the spectacular Haldon Belvedere not far away. It stands on an eminence some 830 feet above sea level, triangular, with a drum-tower at each corner rising to crenellations some seventy feet above ground, from which an enormously wide view can be obtained, especially to the east across the estuary of the Exe. The windows are Gothic-arched and vary greatly in size. From

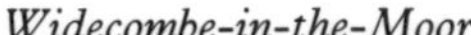

Widecombe-in-the-Moor

Church House Inn, Torbryan

the track leading steeply up to it the belvedere appears ruinous, but in fact it is occupied and contains such features as mahogany floors, rose-centred ceilings, and an unusually beautiful staircase. Unfortunately it is open to visitors only on very rare occasions, and only by prior arrangement.

So close set about with trees is this belvedere or folly – known also as Lawrence Castle – that even though you spot it from a distance, you may have difficulty in tracking it down. Another approach to it is by way of a yet more enchanting hamlet with the 'Enid Blyton-type' name of Doddiscombsleigh. Here the post office and the Nobody Inn are in fact two adjoining cottages, for most of the year virtually obliterated by a riot of climbing plants and creepers. It is hard to think of any village, even in South Devon, where you find yourself more truly 'out of this world', yet within so few miles of a roaring motorway, than at Doddiscombsleigh.

A potential rival both to Drewsteignton and the last-named village for beauty and serenity is North Bovey, one of a cluster of villages on the little River Bovey. Unlike Chagford and Drewsteignton, it is built round a sloping, tree-clad green. Many of its cottages are thatched, and there is a fifteenth-century church at one end, with a quite outstanding (for so small a place) carved screen and wagon-roof. The Ring o' Bells inn is so unobtrusive that you may mistake it for a farmhouse; it lies on the opposite side of the green to the highly-photogenic post office, behind the stand of trees.

In the third segment familiar names crowd the scene, most of them all too close to the motorway. At Lustleigh, though thatch happily persists, the red sandstone is now giving place to moorland granite. Here is another rival in the stakes for the county's finest village: 'finest', not 'prettiest', for there is nothing pretty about granite. Here, though, is a fifteenth-century church; another outstanding building is the fourteenth-century Court House, converted into a manor house 300 years later.

In this segment you come to one of the best-known of the tors: Hay Tor (1,491 feet); it is perhaps the most readily accessible from the road of the major tors – a rewarding, quite safe, and not too strenuous walk of nearly a mile from a minor road to the south, ending in a vast accumulation of tumbled granite boulders. Two miles distant is Rippon Tor (1,563 feet), also easily accessible from a minor road to the south; Hameldown Tor (1,736 feet) rises on the other side of a network of minor roads, close to the viewpoint and again accessible from the road without undue effort. But it is not only the heights in this segment that are notable; there are lowlier, unsung points of interest. In the hamlet of Ilsington, for instance, take a look at the lych-gate-cum-gatehouse of the Church of St Michael: it has an exterior granite staircase that gives access to a small, self-contained room, complete with fireplace and chimney – built, in all probability, for one of the earlier priest-incumbents. On the other side of the motorway, beyond Newton Abbot, there is the National Trust property of Bradley Manor, a small, fifteenth-century manor house complete with Great Hall and its own chapel; it is open on Wednesday afternoons from June to September. Nearer to the Torbay complex is another National Trust property, open to the public on three days a week from April to October. This is Compton Castle, which is in fact a fortified manor house, also with a Great Hall, though this has been much restored.

Close to the viewpoint and just over the boundary-line into the fourth segment is perhaps the best-known, most 'loudly-sung' of all Devon villages – Widecombe-in-the-Moor. Though it lies on high ground, the moor slopes so steeply upwards from it on all sides that it appears to be at the bottom of a cup. It possesses a late-fifteenth-

Buckland Abbey

century church, among the finest in Devon, with a tower that soars 120 feet into the sky. The church overlooks a sloping village green, with its Church House, of the same massive granite blocks but a century later, close by the gateway. To the north-west of Widecombe (but in the second segment) is the most important of the moor's prehistoric sites, Grimspound; Dartmeet, where East and West Dart meet in a medley of boulders, lies some three miles to the south-west; beyond is Holne Moor, rising to just short of 1,700 feet at Ryder's Hill (fifth segment). This is as dramatic a portion of Dartmoor as you will encounter, but inaccessible by road and to be treated with circumspection.

But we are not done with our fourth segment, despite this advance reference to Holne Moor. All too close to the new motorway lies Buckfast Abbey, not to be overlooked. It is unique among our abbeys for having been built, in the early decades of this century, by a band of French Benedictine monks supervised by an architect and one professional mason – an astonishing achievement as well as a noble building. As a complete contrast, it is from Buckfastleigh station, just south of the abbey, that the newly-revived Dart Valley Railway runs the eight meandering miles down to Totnes, through unmatched, unspoiled woodland scenery. No 'miniature railway' this, but standard-gauge, even if the rolling-stock is vintage and hauled by a steam engine.

There is much to be seen in this segment even between the motorway and the perimeter: Totnes, for example, situated at the highest navigable point on the Dart, with its narrow Fore Street climbing steeply to the remains of the twelfth-century castle by way of East Gate. On the left-hand side is a medieval merchant's half-timbered house that now contains a museum of exceptional interest. In Totnes, Tuesday evenings are 'Elizabethan': the inhabitants don true period costumes and indulge in musical and other entertainments for their own pleasure, not as a 'show' laid on for visitors. It is in this town, too, that you will find the age-old Pannier Market.

Two miles away, at Berry Pomeroy, is the newly-established Torbay Aircraft Museum, whose ex-RAF owner displays both in the open air and in cleverly-designed galleries vintage civil and military aircraft and relics of historic importance of interest to old and young alike. Near by, too, is Dartington Hall, an ever-expanding and highly progressive cultural centre in which many kinds of crafts are practised.

It is in this segment that you will find the many small villages possessing great church towers, as at Harberton and Torbryan, and, close to them, the many Church House inns. The inn at Harberton is perhaps the most famous of them all, remarkable for its noble timberwork. Like all these inns, it was originally designed to house the masons working on the church adjoining it; this one was later adapted for use as a Chantry House, with a Great Chamber and chapel and a workshop for the artisan-monks. More picturesque, if lowlier, is the Church House inn at neighbouring Torbryan. Here, as at Parracombe on Exmoor, parishioners could partake of the 'Church House Ales' to fortify them for their long homewards trek after service. Each inn has some distinctive feature: medieval glass here, a screen retrieved from some abandoned church in another parish there, or some other unusual piece of furnishing. A ceiling beam at Torbryan is inscribed with the date 1485, showing that the inn was built to accommodate the masons who built the second church to stand on this site.

Near here, too, is the Tally Ho at Littlehempston, a wholly

Princetown church

different style of inn: no cob walls here, but solid granite. Though built as a Church House inn a few yards from the church, it was granted an ale licence in the fourteenth century and later served, like the Church House Inn at Torver and so many others, as Court House for the magistracy; an exterior granite staircase leads up to the actual Court Room.

Over the boundary-line into the fifth segment roads become fewer. This is the emptiest of all the segments: only the A384 spans it, close to the viewpoint, and the A38 as it approaches Plymouth. A number of streams flow down off Holne Moor; there is rock-climbing between Sheepstor and (just over the next boundary-line) Meavy. In the sixth segment the neighbouring county of Cornwall zigzags across the perimeter for a few miles just west of Tavistock, a granite-built town which holds an annual Goose Fair in October. It achieved high status as a stannary town in 1305 and remained important for many centuries in respect both of tin and of wool. It is from this base that you can explore widely in this segment, and every journey will prove rewarding.

A few miles down the River Tavy (from which the town, and many hamlets, take their names) is Morwellham Quay, where an intensely interesting experiment in the rehabilitation of an ancient, traditional industry is in full swing, and open to visitors. There is enough to see here to fill a long day and more: industrial archaeology again, and at its best. Buckland Monachorum (the name is self-explanatory) offers The Garden House. The gardens will appeal strongly to all horticulturists, as well as to garden-lovers: with their rich display of plants, flowers, shrubs and trees, expertly tended and skilfully landscaped, they are open to the public on Wednesday afternoons throughout the summer in support of the National Gardens Scheme.

A mile or two beyond there is Buckland Abbey, not only beautiful in itself and beautifully sited but of particular interest because of its unusual history. It was founded by the Cistercians in 1278. After the Dissolution it was converted by Sir Richard Grenville (of Spanish Armada fame) into a private dwelling. Subsequently it became the property of an even greater seaman, Sir Francis Drake. Not surprisingly, it is rich in naval treasures, personal possessions of Sir Francis, and museum exhibits of primarily Devonian interest, especially domestic and farm implements and equipment.

Along the western fringe of Dartmoor in the sixth and seventh segments the Tavy flows southwards from its source at over 1,900

Moorland road near Princetown

feet on Bridestowe Common. Tucked away and often hard to find are delightful hamlets such as Mary Tavy, Peter Tavy, and Cudlipptown. Horndon is another, with its inn bearing the improbable name, Elephant's Nest. Both the B3212 and the A384 lead indirectly to Princetown, with its grim prison built by French and American prisoners-of-war taken during the Napoleonic Wars, and enlarged thereafter to hold greater numbers of English prisoners (once known as convicts) to whom, as to the underworld at large, this prison is always known simply as 'The Moor'.

Ugly as its associations must always be to the rest of us also, Princetown should be visited for one truly interesting feature, its Church of St Mary and All Angels. Standing higher than any other church in the land, it was built by the same men who built the prison, and of the same grey Dartmoor granite. Only one thing about it is more than about a century and a half old, and that is the Jacobean pulpit transferred to it from an Exeter church. It is the immediate precincts that leave the dominant impression. Near the west end are two long and two short rows of eighteen-inch headstones, some seventy-five in all. Each bears just initials, and a date. They record the burial of prisoners who died within 'The Moor'. The latest date is 1962. Two deaths have taken place since – both suicides. One corpse was cremated, the other compassionately handed over to the family for burial elsewhere. There is a memorial plaque on an outer wall to '3 valiant soldiers of the 7th Fusiliers who died in a snowdrift on 12th Feb. 1853, aged 20, 23 and 27'. This was some fifty years after the church was built, and is a reminder (if such is needed) that weather has always been a hazard here.

The A384 and the B3212 cross just beyond, at Two Bridges. Here the views in all directions are spacious and impressive: Great Mis Tor rises to 1,768 feet a little to the north of west, and Rough Tor (1,791 feet) is some four miles due north. Postbridge, a few miles along the road, has its medieval clapper bridge and tracks which tempt the enterprising but, like all Dartmoor tracks, should be followed with caution at all times.

Over the boundary-line into the seventh segment only the A30 and the A386 offer themselves, though a network of minor roads lies between them. One will take you to Lydford, no more than a hamlet but, according to the map, possessing a castle. It is not truly a castle, or even castle ruins, but historic nevertheless. Lydford was held by the Saxons against the Danes thirteen centuries ago; it was then deemed important enough to be the site of a mint – one of only four in all Devon. For centuries it was the headquarters of the all-powerful tin-mining fraternity which dominated this side of the

Lydford Stannary Castle

Wheal Betsy engine-house

moor; the so-called castle, the property of the Department of the Environment, was built in 1195 as a prison for those who offended against the official stannary laws which controlled the assessing and pricing of tin. But here the very powerful miners could also exercise the powers of what today we call a 'kangaroo court' and throw into prison any outsider – be he an MP or any other individual – who got in their way. Eight centuries ago this was the richest source of tin in Europe, and the miners had enormous power, which records show they used unscrupulously and to their own benefit.

The ruins of the gaol rise against St Petrock's Church. This saint (who gave his name to Parracombe, on Exmoor) had a dozen other West Country churches dedicated to him. He established a chapel here in the sixth century; this was destroyed by the Danes in 997 AD, and later replaced by a Norman church, which was in turn replaced by the thirteenth-century church you see on its mound today. Close to the small south porch is the tomb of a local watchmaker, one 'Geo. Routleigh', inscribed with what must surely be one of the most elaborate and apt epitaphs ever devised. It ends: 'Wound up in hopes of being taken in hand by his Maker and of being thoroughly cleaned, repaired and set a-going in the world to come.' An ancient 'lych-way' leading off the moor from old-established settlements to the north of Two Bridges may be picked out on large-scale maps such as the one-inch Ordnance Survey or its recent successor; it was along this track that the corpse would be brought to St Petrock's for interment. Another reminder of the importance of this area and its long-thriving industry is to be seen a few miles south of Lydford and close to the A386. This is the ruin of the engine-house and chimney curiously named Wheal Betsy, on the slope of Gibbet Hill. Such relics are perhaps more common in the mining areas of Cornwall, but this one is particularly impressive for its isolation among the moors. Gibbet Hill (1,158 feet) has of course gathered about itself a string of legends referring to felons who were left hanging there for the crows to pick at their bones through their fluttering rags. Drinkers at the Elephant's Nest, one-time miner's rendezvous, will assure you that Gibbet Hill and, for that matter, the engine-house itself is haunted to this day.

Yes Tor and High Willhays, Dartmoor's highest summits, stand practically on the boundary-line with the eighth and final segment. Here the dominant town is Okehampton, overlooked by the ruins of its thirteenth-century castle. Of greater interest, however, at least to the ever-growing band of enthusiasts for the various manifestations of industrial archaeology, is the hamlet of Sticklepath, a few short miles to the east. Here, for a century and a half from about the time of the Napoleonic Wars, the Finch family ran a major foundry powered wholly by water adapted to the driving of a number of different pieces of machinery, such as trip-hammers. They manufactured tools for the tin miners and workers in many trades throughout the district. The foundry is being rehabilitated (as at Ironbridge, Morwellham, and elsewhere), and you can see there the Museum of Rural Industry which has been developed and expanded over the past seven or eight years by enthusiasts working with and for the Museum Trust.

You might not expect to find anything of this sort even on the northern fringes of Dartmoor. But then Dartmoor is a granite treasure-house of history and prehistory, as well as of the purely dramatic-spectacular-topographical. This, then, is perhaps as good a note as any on which to bring to an end this all-too-cursory survey of a region that deserves (and indeed has received, from the present writer in his *Shell Book of Exploring Britain*) much ampler and more detailed treatment than has been possible in these pages.

Buckfast Abbey

Index

Page numbers in italics refer to illustrations.